The Love-Shy

Survival Guide

of related interest

Asperger Meets Girl
Happy Endings for Asperger Boys
Jonathan Griffiths
Foreword by Hugh Jones
ISBN 978 1 84310 630 2

Love, Sex and Long-Term Relationships
What People with Asperger Syndrome Really Really Want
Sarah Hendrickx
Foreword by Stephen M. Shore
ISBN 978 1 84310 605 0

Autistics' Guide to Dating
A Book by Autistics, for Autistics and Those Who Love Them or Who Are in Love with Them
Emilia Murry Ramey and Jody John Ramey
ISBN 978 1 84310 881 8

The Love-Shy

Survival Guide

Talmer Shockley

Jessica Kingsley Publishers
London and Philadelphia

First published in 2009
by Jessica Kingsley Publishers
116 Pentonville Road
London N1 9JB, UK
and
400 Market Street, Suite 400
Philadelphia, PA 19106, USA

www.jkp.com

Library of Congress Cataloging in Publication Data

Shockley, Talmer.
The love-shy survival guide / Talmer Shockley.
p. cm.
Includes bibliographical references.
ISBN 978-1-84310-897-9 (pb : alk. paper) 1. Man-woman relationships. 2. Bashfulness. 3. Dating (Social customs) I. Title.
HQ801.S528 2009

646.7'7--dc22

2008047870

British Library Cataloguing in Publication Data
A CIP catalogue record for this book is available from the British Library

ISBN 978 1 84310 897 9

Printed and bound in the United States by
Thomson-Shore, 7300 Joy Road, Dexter, MI 48130

Contents

Acknowledgments

I wish to acknowledge the following people who played critical roles in making this book a reality:

Beth, Nick, my female manuscript reviewers especially Jessica and Katie, Glenda, participants in the love-shy internet forums, the great staff at Jessica Kingsley Publishers who shaped this book into a winner, and special thanks to Dr. Brian G. Gilmartin for his seminal scientific study of love-shyness and his critique of my manuscript.

Thank you all so much.

A Note from the Author

There may be some of you who dislike the more spiritual and non-scientific aspects of this book. Although I peppered it with my personal beliefs, please do not dismiss everything else. At minimum, consider this book a case study, which is a form of scientific evidence.

I also issue a brief caveat to my female readers. Because the subject at hand deals with dating and sex primarily for a male audience, some of this book compares to men's locker room talk. Female readers may react negatively when I talk about women in terms of their looks. I do not mean to act in a sexist way, nor do I judge women only by their looks, but because love-shyness only flares up in men when they are in the presence of women to whom they are attracted, I need to make the distinction between women in general and those women in particular who turn love-shy males on. Try to see your infiltration of the men's locker room as an educational experience; if you can stand the smell, you could learn much.

Introduction

You see a happy couple with their arms around each other. They are obviously in love. Perhaps, they sit on their porch watching their beautiful children play in the yard. You think, *Why can't that be me? Why can I not have a romantic relationship like other people? I'm intelligent, reasonably good looking and a decent person, but I can't seem to have an intimate boyfriend or girlfriend. What is wrong with me, and how do I get out of this mess?* You pay the rent and mostly function fine in society yet are more than clueless regarding romance. Romance-wise you live outside of society. It is as if you are looking through lighted windows at satisfied couples and families, while you are alone, out in the cold; and you wonder, *How can I become one of those happy persons?*

You have always been somewhat shy, and even though you never dated in high school, you figured college would be different. But even then, if your friends set you up or you had opportunities to date, strangely nothing worked out.

Neither you nor any of your friends and family know what to do with you. Professional therapists are likely to say that you have social anxiety. You may have. Or perhaps you only become super-anxious in potentially romantic situations. Does it seem like it would be easier for you to find a cure for cancer, than to

walk over and start talking to that exceedingly attractive person and ask for a phone number?

If this description fits you, read on. Your condition is not unique. Although mental health professionals do not officially recognize it, your condition is *love-shyness.* Other related terms for it include involuntary celibacy or romantically challenged. Even if you don't match the exact definition of love-shyness, if you never or rarely date or have sex, this book is for you.

If you are reading this not because you may be love-shy, but because you believe this description applies to someone you care about, read Appendix B for advice on how to present this book to him or her. Do not just jot down this title or email him or her a website address. The love-shy person tends to not take action with many things. You must make the first move. After giving the person this book, feel satisfied that you have sufficiently answered the call of duty and it's up to the recipient to do the rest.

This book is a practical guide, written by someone who struggled for years and years trying to find a way out of the love-shy jungle and finally did. My observations come from living my life in this invisible jungle. I am not a mental health professional, and my love-shyness played a major role in preventing me from graduating college. Since people with love-shyness have so little support, they are my main audience and their recovery is my primary concern. I clearly mention books that can be of definite practical value to the distressed by including these recommended books' titles in the text and listing them in the Useful Resources. In contrast, I reference sources not deemed intrinsic to the personal quest of love-shy escape as chapter endnotes.

The general reader without personal or professional ties to a love-shy person or this subject can still find this book a great read. Almost everyone can use some relationship or dating advice, so a book dedicated to those with extreme dating problems should teach everyone something. By thoroughly investigating love-shyness and its possible treatments with an open mind, I uncovered significant and uncommon information.

Be forewarned. This book is for adults. I talk bluntly and to the point and may occasionally use coarse language. It is for your own good. Someone has to metaphorically kick you in the ass to get you into action. Love-shy people need direct instruction, which may sound condescending to non-love-shy readers coming from a barefoot guide with a ripped shirt. You are lost out here in the wild jungle where the meek and clueless get eaten alive. If I tell you to gather wood to build a fire, I don't want to hear you complaining, *Oh, these sticks are muddy, I may get dirty.* Yes, you have to get your hands dirty. You have spent your life on the sidelines not playing the game, and now is the time for action. Getting dirty is good and may include things like going into smoke-filled bars. It means you are playing. Maybe not winning yet, but playing.

As well, I understand your unique emotional needs and provide support for them. Although I title this book a survival guide, I intend for you to do more than simply survive. After years of crawling over rocks and roots, when you finally step out of the jungle imagine how fast you will walk on concrete sidewalks. By expending the same past effort to make your way through the jungle, you will experience life like running down the street.

As a boy growing up in a small village in Austria, Arnold Schwarzenegger was "scrawny"[1] (p. 6). After discovering weight lifting to bulk up, he set his goals on winning body building competitions, coming to America and being a movie star. After obtaining those lofty goals, he took his successes even further by becoming governor of California. If you have the vision, the drive and the tools, you too can accomplish almost anything. You too can have that beautiful young wife or handsome, awesome husband. Do not lose any more time. Let's get started!

Note

1. Learner, L. (2005) *Fantastic: The Life of Arnold Schwarzenegger.* New York: St. Martin's Press.

Chapter 1

The Important Basics

What is love-shyness?

Dr. Brian G. Gilmartin coined the term "love-shy" in his 1987 book *Shyness and Love: Causes, Consequences, and Treatment.* His is the definitive and basically only scientifically based book on the subject of people who, due to psychological reasons, cannot have romantic relationships whatsoever. Studying adult virgins he found, rather than a variety of reasons for their involuntary situation, a single identifiable syndrome with standard causes and symptoms. Based on shyness, love-shyness works specifically to keep romantic and sexual relationships from happening. In simplest terms, love-shyness is a phobia of romance and mating. Any romantic or prospective romantic situation induces such a high level of anxiety in the love-shy sufferer that almost any dating and sexual relationship proves impossible. The more attractive and available the romantic interest, the greater the phobia.

This anxiety so strongly dominates during the formative years that the love-shy child fails to learn and pick up on the human mating ritual. One cannot easily learn a subject one fears. The knowledge and social skills related to romance and sex that a typical young adult intuitively grasps are absent in a similarly aged love-shy person. Thus, in addition to general shyness, love-shyness doubly curses romantically. Not only is such a person extremely nervous in social situations involving someone to whom he or she is attracted, he or she is usually clueless about what to do in such situations. The immediate phobic reactions prevent a relationship from even starting. These factors tend to culminate in a person who never marries and ends up a life-long virgin. So, the working definition of a love-shy person is someone who cannot have romantic or sexually intimate relationships because of substantial anxiety surrounding sexuality along with a failure to comprehend proper courtship and mating rituals.

Do not confuse love-shyness with homosexuality. Unfortunately, because love-shys are not seen with romantic partners, casual observers can easily label them as homosexual. Theoretically, homosexual love-shys exist, but I have not found any nor know of anyone who has. This book is chiefly addressed to a heterosexual readership. Gay and lesbian love-shys will still find the information in the book quite relevant and will just need to alter the perspective to fit their situation.

Some people have labeled the love-shy condition "involuntary celibacy," or incel for short. However, the literal interpretation of involuntary celibacy includes prisoners and married people whose spouses have stopped having sex with them. In contrast, love-shyness is a psychological phenomenon where the problem exists solely in the head of the person. Although the outside world may have played a crucial role in the development of this condition during childhood, the outside world does not force one to be love-shy. Because the term involuntary celibacy relates to sexual activity, it would not include a person who wants an intimate romantic relationship but does not want sex due to religious reasons. Furthermore, a love-shy person could employ the services of a prostitute and would not be celibate but would most likely still be love-shy. Involuntary celibacy encompasses any chronic serious reasons why an adult cannot date successfully, of which love-shyness is a major subset.

People incapable of relationships usually gravitate to either a love-shy or incel label. Although shyness seems to separate love-shys from the rest of incels, many more women choose the incel category. Unlike most cases of love-shyness, many incels report obvious childhood abuse, which appears to manifest in adulthood as more gender-neutral psychological problems. Male love-shys may say, *I cannot go after women I'm attracted to,* while male incels more likely complain, *No woman finds me attractive.* While the parallels and differences between love-shyness and involuntary celibacy are hazy, no matter how they define themselves, incels should still find this book helpful.

People generally find it difficult to relate to love-shys and incels and wrongly assume we could obtain romance if we tried harder or lowered our standards. Because we look generally normal and attractive and usually have enough going for us, people cannot fathom why we have such problems when attempting romantic connections. Except in extreme cases, physical looks or abnormalities do not prevent love-shys and incels from romance. Also, people wrongly assume our problem revolves around a fear of commitment or a standard type of fear of intimacy. Love-shys may have these traits, but their relationships never get off the ground to the point when commitment or intimacy become issues. Moreover, people cannot relate to a phobia of love. People without a phobia of snakes and spiders can easily relate to those who do; many people are fearful or turned off by these creatures even though they do not have a phobia about them. But few can comprehend a phobia of an available sexually attractive person. Worse, a person with a spider or snake phobia can often adequately deal with an encounter with these animals even as he or she is gripped by fear, while a person's love-shy phobia will prevent him from performing sufficiently during romantic encounters where acting smoothly, subtly and confidently is critical.

A love-shy man in his late twenties from a New England town describes his problem:

> A good way of describing the intensity of my fear and anxiety with women is to simply explain that despite the fact that I know that women are often attracted to me and give me clear indications of this on a fairly regular basis, *I still don't approach them.* In fact, I often avoid good-looking women who I know for sure are attracted to me. There is no question that ugly dudes with normal confidence, and without the crippling anxiety that I am unfortunately saddled with, get lots more loving from the ladies than I do. I'm good looking, naturally in good shape, sensitive, smart, etc., and women are checking me out all the time. But it just doesn't matter, because this godforsaken fear and anxiety persists. It's hell.

While males are more likely to be love-shy, it is by no means solely a male phenomenon. Dr. Gilmartin chose to focus only on adult virginal males for his study, because in our society love-shyness causes more problems for the male. Human courtship generally expects the male to be the initiator, while passivity and shyness in females is more or less acceptable. Even though love-shyness may limit a woman's romantic possibilities, female love-shys are much more likely to date and marry. Because many female love-shys marry, some more than once, estimates of their numbers are probably low.

Even if the phobia and social skills naïveté is overcome and a lasting relationship happens, as any married person can tell you, marriage is no escape from one's problems. The married love-shy will continue bearing many of the characteristics of love-shyness. A husband may simply label his love-shy wife as somewhat frigid and vice versa. Worse, love-shy parents may be more likely to raise love-shy offspring. While at times I address women, I usually refer to the love-shy as male, but this is not to underestimate

the importance of dealing with female love-shys. Most of what I say applies to both genders.

Gilmartin (1987) estimated that 1.5 percent of heterosexual males are love-shy. However, his criteria for love-shyness were probably a bit restricting. For example, he only included virgins in his study. Any love-shy who visited a prostitute or happened to have any kind of sex would not have been included in his study. Some love-shys mistakenly assume that, since they don't completely match Gilmartin's description, they are not love-shy. Assuming that there are fewer female than male love-shys, I would say that at least 1 percent of the whole population is love-shy, which makes a minimum of three million sufferers in the United States alone. Gilmartin does not disclose how he arrived at his figure, but 2 percent, or 1 in 50, is probably the more accurate estimate of people afflicted with some level of love-shyness. One needs only to look around at one's whole collection of friends and acquaintances, particularly at work, to pick out those few people who, though pleasant and attractive enough, never seem to have a romantic partner.

Strictly speaking, one's virginal or marriage status is not a true indication of love-shyness. Not every person who goes through life without ever marrying fits the definition of love-shy. Some people choose to not marry or choose to remain celibate. Some people are naturally loners or asexual. Society should not judge these people as necessarily having psychological problems. Perhaps, the freest people are those who do not feel the need to have romance relationships. They need not worry about the impression they make on others and have plenty of undisrupted time to pursue their own interests. Yet, I suspect a fair number of these people lack the inclination for romantic relationships in part due to love-shyness.

Some love-shy men may have a sexually intimate girlfriend or encounter, thus they and those around them may conclude nothing is seriously wrong. Most likely, these men were only able to obtain women to whom they were not much attracted, making their love-shy anxiety flare up only slightly. They may conclude that the problem with the relationship was a lack of attraction rather than love-shyness. Lack of relationship experience may also doom such pairings and further mask the love-shy issue.

Both the sufferer and those around him have a hard time detecting the love-shyness, because many people have problems with shyness and anxiety when it comes to the opposite sex. On a conscious, rational level love-shys are generally not sex averse. Like all phobias love-shyness operates in the subconscious realm. Anyone trying to make an accurate diagnosis must dig through all the extraneous problems and go by the many common love-shy symptoms. When I discovered Gilmartin's book, I was surprised and relieved to learn not only that my psychological condition was not unique, but also that love-shys have many of my physical and personality characteristics in common. Eyeglass wearing, profuse sweating, blockage of the nasal passageways when not sick, and fine, thin width hair are all characteristics I share with many love-shys. Other common love-shy physical characteristics include allergies, dry mouth and halitosis, skin sensitivities such as problems wearing wool, ambient temperature sensitivities and bright sunlight sensitivity. Of course, most of these are negative characteristics when it comes to dating and further stack the deck against love-shys. Luckily, love-shyness does not directly affect one's sexuality physically as no one reports problems producing or maintaining an erection.

General shyness is usually a given with love-shys, and most love-shys have few if any friends. Many love-shys could be diagnosed as having social anxiety or, perhaps, avoidant personality disorder. However, love-shyness is a specific condition of social anxiety. For example, I worked hard to overcome my shyness. Eventually, I had little problem with tasks like job interviews and giving oral reports at department meetings, and I could even be the life of the party, but I was still love-shy. While functioning great throughout most days, I utterly failed when interacting

romantically or sexually with a woman I desired. People say, *Just be yourself around women.* What about when being myself makes me run away from women to whom I'm attracted?

Psychology professionals have a difficult time believing in love-shyness, because they think that it is a different name for something that already fits in one of their neat categories. Love-shyness is certainly not gynophobia, a fear of women in general, nor is it caligynephobia, a fear of beautiful women. How could modern science have missed such a major psychological disorder? One problem may be that shyness itself is not considered a psychological disorder. Also, other conditions mask love-shyness. In the subtle realm of romance, the phobic reaction is interpreted as lack of interest and non-attraction. Love-shyness is invisible, because its sufferers are invisible. Sex therapists miss it because they focus on couples' sexual issues and offer no help for the single person whose biggest problem is obtaining a sexual partner. The sex therapist Teresa L. Crenshaw reported in 1985 about "sexual aversion syndrome,"[1] of which love-shyness seems to be a subset. While she mentions some similar characteristics with love-shyness, such as low self-esteem and depression, all four of her case studies were married.

Love-shyness is closely related to shyness because both have anxiety and fear as common symptoms. Where is the line between shy people who have a problem dating and love-shys for whom relationships are near impossible? I say that full-blown love-shyness causes or programs one to bury his or her sexuality and subconsciously "turns one against" romantic relationships. Simply shy people have their mating instinct and social knowledge intact and only have general shyness problems. Even for a shy person, the anxiety during dating can ratchet up significantly because it's a high-stakes situation. However, mere dating anxiety does not lead to a lifetime of romantic failures. In perhaps the best practical, up-to-date book dealing with shyness in general, *Shyness: A Bold New Approach* (1999), Bernardo J. Carducci devotes a chapter to love and shyness. Dr. Carducci reports from one of his shyness studies that less than 7 percent of generally shy people reported that shyness interferes with their intimate relationships. Who knows how many of those 7 percent are love-shy?

From a practical recovery aspect, this book should work for seriously shy people. However, its approach at times may seem heavy-handed and too basic for the merely shy. Any post-college age person who is still a virgin not by choice should read this book. Obviously, the mating instinct has not worked for this person, so he or she has some serious issues that probably have never been dealt with. Most likely this book can help you, even if it doesn't focus upon the original cause of your romantic issues. I wager that through using the techniques in this book, you will uncover the cause of your loneliness and get directed to the proper course of treatment and action.

The picture and understanding of love-shyness is incomplete. No matter. This book concerns itself not with exact definitions and diagnosis criteria but with results. Additionally, I strive to make this book a guide for academics and clinicians. Scientific study and funding has been virtually nonexistent even though love-shyness apparently affects at least as many people as does autism. While not directly related to anything dangerous, love-shyness wreaks havoc on the social and emotional well-being of those afflicted, as well as their life in general.

Although not a life-threatening predicament physically, the life of a love-shy is very lonely and depressing. All the positive aspects of relationships and marriage are foreign to love-shys. The condition saps one's ability to have a fulfilling life, not just romantically, but in other major areas of life. For example, love-shys tend to be chronically underemployed. Adding to this bleakness both the sufferer and the outside world are probably oblivious to the condition. The chronic stresses that build can lead to occasional crazy antics, and one might think there would be many love-shy suicides, but, luckily, love-shys are fairly resilient and, although may consider a drastic course of action, rarely follow through. If this book has one intention, it is to give a ray of hope to those with none.

Gilmartin (1987) compiled the ominous statistic that:

> 36 percent of the 300 love-shy men studied...had given serious consideration to taking their own lives. *Zero percent* (nobody) of the 200 non-shy men I interviewed had ever given any thought to suicide, and none had ever experienced frequent bouts of depression. (p. 63)

This is the dangerous jungle. Those most susceptible to suicidal thoughts are usually those who have no idea of the jungle they inhabit, no idea how to survive and no idea that escape is possible. Unfortunately, during the teenage years when people are most susceptible to suicide, love-shyness and other severe problems are difficult to discern from normal teenage issues.

I doubt people can fully appreciate the severe isolation us love-shys endure, especially when seen as functioning normally out in the world. While some of us may prefer a little more time alone than the average person, going days at a time without talking to anyone and going decades without comprehending why it is impossible to have a romantic relationship induces significant emotional trauma. The stresses build up and never go away. Because of my severe loneliness, I dreaded weekends, and vacations only made me feel more alone. With never a woman and barely any friends and without much of a career, I went to my family for some kind of sympathetic sustenance. But they provided me with little emotional support and acted as if nothing was wrong. Thus, with no proper diagnosis, no way to defuse massive amounts of tension and stress, no one to understand them and no visible way out of their predicament, love-shys may act out. Some love-shys get accused of stalking or displaying other forms of demented attention towards women and find themselves in legal trouble, making their problems worse.

Dr. Carducci, one of the few academics to acknowledge Gilmartin's research, provides a quote from a shy man who has troubles with love that seems to indicate how and why love-shyness happens. "'I found that by avoiding potentially disastrous situations and the tests of 'manhood' I could survive—by being invisible'" (1999, p. 287). Although future researchers have much to discover about love-shyness, this documented syndrome devastates many.

What causes love-shyness?

Both genetics and environment contribute to love-shyness, and Dr. Gilmartin performs an excellent job analyzing these causes. He concludes that a combination of inborn temperament, upbringing and social environment work together to create love-shyness. While understanding the contributing factors leading to love-shyness may not help much when developing treatments, this knowledge is critical for preventing love-shyness.

Everyone including animals has an inborn temperament. According to Carducci, "Scientists have been studying shy cattle as well as shy cats, shy fish, and shy dogs" (p. 3). One only has to experience a litter of newborn puppies to see that even ones of the same sex have different temperaments. Some puppies will be more adventurous, and some will stick close to mommy.

Gilmartin references the work of Dr. Hans Eysenck, who created the Eysenck Cross of Inborn Temperament. On one axis of the cross is plotted the inborn trait of introversion versus extroversion, and the other axis is labeled emotionality. Emotionality is better described as anxiety threshold and is generally known as inhibited versus uninhibited. An anxiety threshold is the likeliness that something will cause anxiety. People with high anxiety thresholds act uninhibited and adventurously, while low anxiety threshold people can easily have their anxieties triggered and thus act more reserved. Gilmartin concludes that the people in the quadrant of introversion with low anxiety threshold have the greatest tendency to become love-shy. Love-shys analyzing themselves with the Myers-Briggs Type Indicator claim they are overwhelmingly INxx. The I stands for introverted and the N means they trust their intuition rather than their senses for gathering and interpreting information. Love-shys appear scattered throughout the IN quadrant.

Many love-shys need only look a short distance on their family tree for a history of the condition. This condition was almost inevitable for me, because I see examples of it in both my parents and some of their relatives. On my father's side, something was somehow passed down only through the males. The sons of my father's brother had problems getting married. Yet, the son of my father's sister and the daughter of my father's brother were OK and married at a normal age to good people. A few of my father's male cousins who carry the family name also had the problem.

On the other side of my family tree, both of my mother's brothers married well, and I see no indication that either is love-shy. I consider this fact strange, since I believe my mother, her father and probably my grandmother were love-shy, even though they married well. I remember my grandfather in his late eighties who, after his loving wife of over six decades had passed, became obsessed with a woman in his old folks' home. Although barely able to walk and see, just like a schoolboy he would talk to his family visitors about his obsession with her but could never seem to deal with her properly. Although one can easily attribute his mental state to senility and a history of mental illness, I see him acting in a typical love-shy manner. His abnormal childhood experience may have played a significant role in fostering his love-shyness. When he was a child, his mother forbade him from doing farm chores with his father and brother. Instead, with a large picture of Hell hung in the home, she raised him herself with the goal of my grandfather becoming a minister. Having only a female for role model and teacher and a strong fire-and-brimstone Christian upbringing I consider extremely telling. His

actions when elderly show that even if love-shys marry and raise children, they never get over the condition and may end up passing it on to their children and grandchildren.

A mother's condition during pregnancy can affect her unborn child. A recent study shows that a stressed pregnant mother can transfer the stress hormone cortisol to her fetus.2 While much more research is required, I believe a connection exists between elevated fetal cortisol levels and fetal testosterone functioning, since generally cortisol tends to decrease testosterone levels. Testosterone washes through the male fetus's brain at a few certain key times during pregnancy and causes many changes. If not every area of the brain changes appropriately, it may develop effeminately in a few areas. This lack of brain masculinization may contribute to heterosexual love-shyness or perhaps homosexuality. Former Harvard Medical School neurobiology professor Simon LeVay notes, "[I]n most species courtship behavior is influenced by the circulating levels of gonadal steroids, both in fetal life and in adulthood. It seems probable that these hormones influence courtship behavior in humans"[3] (p. 61).

Gilmartin (1987) uses the confusing term male lesbian to describe what he believes is the resulting condition if levels of testosterone have been low. He writes:

> [A]ll [the love-shys he studied] wanted to remain as males. However, all deeply envied the prerogatives of the female gender and truly believed that these prerogatives fitted their own inborn temperaments far more harmoniously than the pattern of behavioral expectations to which males are required to adhere. (p. 125)

I use the term passive male to describe my condition of taking the female mating ritual role of passivity and expecting to be chased by female suitors. For example, some years ago a woman invited me over for dinner on a Friday night. I recall as I bought a

bottle of wine on the way over to her place how I so hoped to get lucky that night with this special lady. After dinner she dropped plenty of sexual references, and I waited in vain for her to kiss me. I lost her forever. Remaining passive is a completely unacceptable way for men to act romantically and sexually. How much of this passivity was due to brain development in the womb and how much was due to an environmentally induced psychological abnormality is unknown. While the mother's pregnancy situation doesn't explain causes of love-shy women, it supplies a clue as to the greater numbers of male than female love-shys, homosexuals and transsexuals.

After birth one is molded by one's environment and by how one reacts to situations in that environment. Love-shyness may partially result from the child feeling overwhelmed and confused by his life situation. By being both introverted and inhibited, one tends to become shy. However, as Gilmartin documents, the standard love-shy is more than just shy. Usually as boys they tend to be more sensitive and have no interest in playing rough-and-tumble sports like football. So, by both being shy and not fitting in with their peer group, they tend to become socially isolated. They don't develop normally socially, which makes them even more socially isolated. A terrible downward social development spiral results with the child always playing catch-up, which usually includes things like being severely teased and bullied.

Interestingly, Gilmartin (1987) notes that love-shy boys often develop romantic interests at an earlier age than their peers:

> The paradox is that love-shy men become romantically interested in the opposite sex significantly earlier in life than do non-shy men. And the more severely love-shy a man is, the earlier in life he is likely to have become deeply interested in the other gender from a romantic/esthetic standpoint. (p. 266)

This seems strange, but while discussing Gilmartin's book with my mother, she said, "When your brother was in first or second grade, he tried kissing some girls." My brother, more love-shy than me, has never been on a date in his life. But at that time, at six or seven years old, he was more concerned about which girls rather than which boys were coming to his birthday party. Gilmartin reports many instances of early elementary school infatuations. Society does not know how to deal with such children, who, although severely shy and perhaps somewhat socially retarded, are early bloomers when it comes to love. Yet this situation provides the clearest signal that a child is or will become love-shy. Read Appendix A for advice on dealing with shy and possibly love-shy children.

Not interacting with girls seems to be a factor in male love-shyness as many male love-shys grew up without sisters. Many of Gilmartin's love-shy male subjects report as young boys being quite upset that they had to play with the boys and couldn't play with the girls. I believe Gilmartin is correct when he states that segregating children by sex and having them do different activities is unhealthy. Luckily, as our society becomes less homophobic and girls fight for their right to play football with the boys, the situation appears to improve. Gilmartin also warns that being raised primarily by opposite-sex adults without good same-sex role models contributes to the creation of love-shyness. Divorce exacerbates this problem.

Aspects of each parent's personality play a role in causing their children's love-shyness. While the most obvious causes of phobias are specific traumatic childhood incidents, others phobias develop by children "learning" them through observing their parents' phobic responses. Social insecurities possessed by parents often rub off directly on their children. Parents' sexual issues can have a more complex influence on their children. Noticeably relevant is having a "sex anxious" father, who is uncomfortable discussing sexual topics and tends not to demonstrate romantic feelings in front of his children. I assume my father's lack of touching his wife and not expressing himself affectionately affected my siblings and me. My sister now seems subconsciously to want a similar man, which translates into an inability to have boyfriends. I recall when I was about four, my mother tried to get affectionate with my father, but he pushed her away seemingly saying, *Not in front of the children.* At least, that's how I remember it and how this significant event seemed to program me. I've been running away, many times literally, from women to whom I have been attracted for decades since.

Lack of positive ego development and poor self-esteem help foster love-shyness. Many male love-shys report having mothers who were unusually anxious or prone to fits of anger or rage. While physical abuse is obvious, subtle constant condescension may inflict similar amounts of emotional damage. Gilmartin (1987) determines that "throughout their formative years the basic keynote of the psychoemotional abuse the love-shys had received from parents was persistent belittlement and ego deflation" (p. 221). "[A] central part of the problem was that the love-shys' parents could not accept their sons as they were" (p. 222). This abuse often came from the mother. Gilmartin keenly observes that:

> women who are tense, high strung, poison-tongued vis-à-vis their sons, etc., are usually quite conservative and conventional. In essence, they tend to be highly defensive about their own shortcomings as these are reflected in the inadequate social behavior of their sons. (p. 158)

Some mothers of love-shys may not necessarily put down their sons directly, but may criticize the male gender generally, for example by saying, *All men are pigs.* This kind of statement may confuse and stymie the young boy who now doesn't want or know how to be a man and associates normal male sexuality with perversion. I believe a serious lack of self-esteem combined with confusion or misdirection regarding sexuality are the biggest factors inducing love-shyness in a shy child.

Gilmartin's study found over a quarter of love-shy males were the parents' only child, compared to just 7 percent of his non-shy, confident male control group. While typically only children are better adjusted and have higher self-esteem than their peers, love-shy children become the opposite. Shy only children may not develop proper social skills and assertive behaviors to compete for toys, food and parents' attention. Gilmartin blames inadequate parenting combining with inborn inhibition. Also, there are no siblings to provide camaraderie against their parents' capricious and abrasive behavior. Gilmartin claims:

> Even now as adults, virtually none of these only children seemed to like their mothers to any extent. The love-shys' mothers seemed to have conveyed an extremely frightening and obnoxious image of womanhood—an image that is anything but attractive or alluring. (p. 167)

Freudian psychoanalysts call the age between about three and six the Oedipal phase, and love-shyness seems to develop during this time. During this childhood period critical events need to happen to create sexual programming. This programming happens subconsciously, so most people don't recall it. Freud astutely observed young boys developing romantic attractions to their mothers. Rather than competing with his father, a boy learns to emulate his father's romantic actions. As some male love-shys report that their fathers were "manly men," the main issue may revolve around the boy's inability to receive his mother's validation. The power of romance during this Oedipal stage cannot easily be stifled. Thus, boys treated coldly by their mothers may act romantic with female kindergarten classmates.

The late Johns Hopkins University professor John Money coined the term "lovemap" to help explain how people develop their sexual proclivities.[4] Money conjectured that the type of person to whom one is attracted and one's sexual fetishes seem to get programmed around the ages of five to eight years old and stored in one's lovemap. Money claims that boys are more vulnerable to developing lovemap disabilities. Love-shyness appears to vandalize the lovemap, making love-shyness more intractable than a simple phobia. Love-shyness short-circuits the brain by directly connecting normal sexual/romantic arousal to an avoidance/fear response. Since love-shy males have an overwhelming desire for women of exceptional natural beauty, love-shyness seems to influence lovemaps in a consistent manner. Sexually assaulted children develop serious issues, but love-shys overwhelmingly have not experienced such trauma.

There are a few cases of a child having fairly normal parents and early elementary school socialization and a severely embarrassing situation apparently triggering love-shyness. A child who wets him or herself in front of class, say in the third or fourth grade, may become emotionally scarred for life, especially if the teacher and the parents do not take appropriate supportive action. Such an incident may require some form of counseling if the child is expected to socially recover from it. Likewise, an obvious physical deformity or handicap, such as scoliosis or cerebral palsy, can trigger love-shyness if the person believes his or her physical condition to be a real turn-off to the opposite sex. Even being short during elementary school can induce serious self-esteem problems. When one is an outcast on the playground, taunting due to a perceived difference can traumatize. A few men and women claim childhood bullying produced their love-shyness, but it is possible that they already had some detrimental, love-shy-related traits that caused them to get bullied in the first place.

Gilmartin (1987) explains why abnormal environments can easily contribute to the formation of love-shyness:

> People with the inhibition and low anxiety threshold genes condition (learn) much faster and more thoroughly than extroverts, ambiverts, and high anxiety threshold people do. And it is especially for this reason that an adverse

> family background would be expected to do far greater damage to the "thin-skinned," pre-love-shy male than it would to the vast majority of the rest of us. (p. 224)

A significant causal factor not mentioned in *Shyness and Love* is Asperger's syndrome. In a personal correspondence Gilmartin estimated that 40 percent of his love-shy subjects have Asperger's syndrome, a condition which also affects males more than females. Asperger's syndrome is related to autism. One can look at a severely autistic child, struggling to relate to the world around him, and quickly conclude that as an adult this child will never have romantic relationships. Dustin Hoffman superbly portrayed an autistic man in the 1988 movie *Rain Man.* Mentally dial down the severity of his autism and think about at what point this person would end up functioning mostly normally in the world but would likely have great difficulty with the intuitiveness of socializing and romance. I estimate around 20 to 25 percent of those on the autism spectrum are love-shy, and more than that percentage have significant hurdles to romance and are incel. This quarter fraction is roughly the same as the number who are born on the introverted-inhibited quadrant of the Eysenck Cross of Inborn Temperament, assuming shyness develops in people with Asperger's at a similar rate as with the general population. Though foggy estimates, these percentages seem to suggest the deck is stacked towards environmental factors turning shy autistics into love-shys.

Some of the major symptoms of Asperger's syndrome include impairment in social interaction, repetitive behaviors or rituals and problems with nonverbal communication. The Wikipedia article on Asperger's states:

> People with AS lack the natural ability to see the subtexts of social interaction, and may lack the ability to communicate their own emotional state, resulting in well-meaning remarks that may offend, or finding it hard to know what

> is "acceptable." The unwritten rules of social behavior that mystify so many with AS have been termed the "hidden curriculum." People with AS must learn these social skills intellectually...rather than intuitively through normal interaction.[5]

One observant writer compared having Asperger's to having color blindness of social situations and communications. Although the black and white communication is picked up, the subtle coloring of the message is lost. Additional characteristics of people with Asperger's include making literal interpretations, being too honest, unable to read body language and facial expressions and unable to imitate others. Obviously, these things would have negative effects for one trying to perform courtship rituals. These traits would also make an already shy child even more withdrawn. No wonder the address of one Asperger's support website is www.wrongplanet.net! Because Asperger's and autism are brain development disorders, no cure exists.

I have Asperger's and always sensed I was different. For most of my life I've sensed that a small piece of my brain related to socialization was missing. I compare myself to a car whose radio was ripped out. Like most adults living undiagnosed with Asperger's, I never thought to seek a diagnosis or treatment and never considered that others may share my affliction. Even after watching *Rain Man*, I didn't make the connection to myself because, like most adults with Asperger's, I'd trained myself to piece together whatever was missing in my head and control the strange behaviors so that I can get along well enough in the world. Except when it comes to love. One easy, but not totally accurate, way to spot Asperger's in a family tree is to look for relatives who have never married, especially males. I consider my father to have borderline Asperger's, which I believe makes it difficult for him to bond emotionally with his family. His love-shyness exacerbates this issue.

Even though my brain lacks something, Asperger's is not necessarily a negative condition. Many people with Asperger's and autism feel nothing is wrong with them; their brains just got wired differently. Some cite speculative studies suggesting that super-scientists such as Isaac Newton and Albert Einstein had Asperger's, which gave them increased intelligence and creativity and allowed them to intensely focus on a single problem.[6] I doubt my brother would have been the second-best math student in the state if his brain was not "Asperger's wired." I attribute some of my intelligence, creativity, exceptional memory and ability to focus on a single interest or task (such as writing this book) to Asperger's. Also, by not being socially wired, I didn't fall for most of the societal brainwashing that normally affects people. Thus, I became more open-minded and have a rare and valuable perspective to offer the world. Like many people with Asperger's, and even some with autism, I would not want to be cured if someone discovered a cure. Instead, we on the autism spectrum want respect and accommodation for our ways of thinking and being.

Characteristics of Asperger's suggest that it may be some type of more spiritual state or, at least, a quite positive and admirable way of being. Not concerned about jewelry, fashion and materialism; living in the moment; compelled to tell and seek out the truth; authentic; possessing no hidden agenda; economical and not wasteful; nonjudgmental; non-competitive; fiercely dependable and loyal with friends and employers; having a strong need for justice; not affected by mob mentality and possessing greater intelligence and creativity are attributes many with Asperger's share that are indicative of high spiritual states. However, Carducci (1999) claims the common Asperger's trait of perfectionism results in low self-esteem as "shy individuals set impossibly high standards for themselves" (p. 44). The Aspergian trait of relishing aloneness tends to help on many spiritual paths, because silence and aloneness allow one to communicate with one's inner and higher self without outside distraction. While many of these

traits are quite desirable in a romantic partner, ironically, most of them hinder navigating the dating world.

To make matters worse romantically, Asperger's and autism can affect one's sexuality. Some autistics are asexual and not interested in any romantic relationships. Strangely with such cases of asexuality, their low libido and their lack of desire for a life partner seem intertwined. But such issues are very personal and hard to fully express to researchers, and these asexuals may merely ignore or bury mating desires. More generally and more importantly, autism and Asperger's decrease the connection between the person and his or her sexuality. This same poor brain connection issue also relates to how those on the autism spectrum often have poor motor skills and have poor contact with their emotions. It is difficult to describe this effect, but it often causes confusion about one's sexuality or gender identity. Unfortunately, relevant researchers seem mostly blind to the sexual problems autism spectrum disorders cause, as the lack of social intuition and related problems mask underlying sexuality issues. Isabelle Hénault probably comes the closest to understanding the sexuality of Asperger's.[7] Also, the range of sexualities of those with Asperger's further confounds researchers, since many males on the autism spectrum have a normal or above average amount of testosterone and have a healthy need for sexual intercourse. Asperger's seems to delay sexual psychological development and awareness, but this delay may relate to love-shyness. Furthermore, many with Asperger's and autism have idiosyncratic routines and cannot handle the disorder and intrusion intimate relationships bring.

Interestingly, many similarities exist between Asperger's and love-shyness, including the following:

- Both require intellectually acquiring missing social skills that are normally acquired intuitively.
- Both cause the child to act like an adult and not be interested in standard childhood activities like sports.

- Both cause the person to have few if any friends.
- Both cause the afflicted to act and/or be perceived as asexual or homosexual.
- Both affect males more than females both in numbers and in severity of social isolation. The innately more socially wired female brain helps most females better mask and deal with both conditions.
- People afflicted with either have difficulty displaying emotion and feelings.
- People afflicted with either often have skin and other sensitivities.
- Both cause underemployment.
- People afflicted with either have difficulty in informal situations. They don't know what to do when there is no "script."

Could one account for these similarities by saying that vastly more love-shys than Gilmartin estimated have a very mild form of Asperger's? No. Plenty of love-shys demonstrate Gilmartin's stated characteristics but do not have Asperger's. More suspect is the attribution of symptoms of Asperger's as characteristics of love-shyness. No doubt future researchers will identify a few Asperger's characteristics wrongly identified as love-shy attributes. Since Gilmartin studied love-shyness before Asperger's became known, Asperger's slightly tinged his results. Yet, these similarities lead one to wonder if a thorough understanding of love-shyness and its causes will lead to a breakthrough in the understanding and treatment of autism. Autism affects the "hardware" of the brain, and love-shyness affects, or at least is caused by, "software" running in the brain. Yet both produce similar symptoms.

An early strongly held theory of autism was that it is produced in a similar way to the theories about the causes of love-shyness, with "cold" mothers as the cause. If one does not look at the genetics or physical symptoms of autism, it is understandable why they would believe this theory. Scientists already knew that if babies are severely deprived of touch, social stimulation and mothering they become permanently scarred. These children end up responding negatively to social stimulation and develop repetitive, self-stimulating behavior. Dr. Rhawn Joseph mentions that:

> of those who survived an infancy spent in institutions where mothering and contact comfort was minimized, signs of low intelligence, extreme passivity, apathy, as well as severe attentional deficits are often characteristics. Such individuals have difficulty forming attachments or maintaining social interactions later in life. Indeed, this can even affect their ability to feel love and affection, even when they have grown up and had children.[8] (p. 85)

A person whose brain is somewhat disconnected from his or her body would mimic these symptoms. Autism is certainly complex, and a spectrum is a good way to describe it. Unfortunately, I predict the parallels between love-shyness and Asperger's will make it harder and take longer for love-shyness to become an officially recognized psychological disorder.

You may have three conditions to deal with: shyness, love-shyness and Asperger's. All three are related, and, unfortunately, tend to reinforce one another. For example, the negative characteristics of Asperger's tend to flare up in stressful situations like those caused by love-shyness. During periods of stress, people often automatically resort to their more fundamental and basic programming, their knee-jerk reactions. Thus, it is important to work to overcome and control each condition separately. Dealing with your general shyness will help your love-shyness, just as developing social skills not picked up due to Asperger's will also help your love-shyness. Luckily, the full task is not Herculean,

because, I hope, as an adult you have already overcome enough of both your shyness and your Asperger's syndrome to function sufficiently in most situations, your workplace, for example. Additionally, you may have passive male syndrome, which also intertwines with the other three conditions. Since love-shys in general are passive, the passively wired male just needs to work on overcoming all of these other serious obstacles to a romantic life.

The combination of autism spectrum disorders and shyness has not been investigated as far as I know. Even Dr. Tony Attwood in his excellent *The Complete Guide to Asperger's Syndrome* (2006) ignores shyness. A lack of social skills makes people with Asperger's socially cautious for good reason. The shy person with Asperger's is continually in doubt about whether he is holding back socially because he doesn't know what is going on or whether his shyness is compelling him to withdraw. My Asperger's combined with embarrassment caused by public love-shy mistakes compelled me to make a complete and total break from whole social groups. Also, the stresses induced by love-shyness often triggers one's Asperger's to flare up and cause a meltdown.

Even if you don't have a condition like Asperger's, if one of your parents or an older sibling had a similar disorder that tended him or her towards asexuality, his or her personality may rub off onto you. This "imprinting" is more likely to happen if the person with the condition shares the same sex as you. Asperger's syndrome itself is only a stumbling block to romance as many people with Asperger's get married even without diagnosis or treatment. Love-shyness, on the other hand, can completely block the road to romance. I believe I would have been married long ago if I only had Asperger's and not love-shyness. Any brain development disorder or any physical handicap on its own does not seem to be enough to cause love-shyness without corresponding inborn traits and environmental factors. Catching and dealing with both severe shyness and autism-related conditions early enough may prevent a child from becoming love-shy. But those Aspies, as

people with Asperger's sometimes call themselves, who already developed love-shyness will not eliminate it with standard autism-related social skills training and counseling.

Even though you may have failed to internalize the mating ritual and other aspects of socialization properly, all is not lost. Just as it's easier for a child to learn a language while young, adults can still learn new languages. I hope that, as you recognize and understand the causes of why you became what you are, you will come down much less hard on yourself. You may see that even the most intelligent and aware child has almost no chance to overcome his or her situation if the deck is stacked strongly against normal childhood development. So, now that you know what and why you are, let's start overcoming these issues.

The first steps

The good news is that one can overcome love-shyness. The bad news is no simple, easy treatment or drug exists to do so. Do not expect a quick fix. It is not a simple walk out of this jungle. Do not think, *If I could just get a girlfriend, or if I could get married, everything would be OK*. Getting a boyfriend or getting a wife is not the solution; it is the result. No single therapy will do it all. You need to pursue as many helpful paths as possible for a decent chance of success. I group these paths into four general, overlapping categories: knowledge, therapies, real-world experience and personal improvement. Knowledge includes an understanding of both love-shyness and the dating world. This multi-pronged approach means that it is solely up to you to overcome your love-shyness. Do not expect anyone else to do it for you, and this includes financing. Start a personal love-shy recovery fund that includes each of the above categories, and allocate a certain portion of your weekly or monthly income to each category. While many resources and people are available to help you, you alone bear responsibility for dealing with your condition. Repeat out

loud three times, *I alone am responsible for my life.* This includes your responsibility for your own happiness.

The corollary of this mantra is to not blame anyone else for your situation. Everybody has issues with their parents. Do not hold them responsible for anything negative in your life. Forgive your parents. They did the best they could, and they were products of their own parents and of an even less enlightened society. However, if they abused you as a child, complete forgiveness may be premature. If so, at least give up the need for revenge without necessarily absolving them of responsibility. This one little paragraph won't undo years of hurt and resentment, but it's a start. Nobody's getting any younger. Say what you need to say to them before they're no longer on this planet.

As the saying goes, "*To err is human, to forgive divine.*" Now forgive yourself. Although we humans have free will, we are a product of our genes and our environment. Do not live in the past. Do not keep dwelling on the past with thoughts like, *If I had only gone over and talked to that woman the other week.* Learn from your mistakes but do not keep focusing on them. Forgive yourself for all your mistakes with the opposite sex which I hope you can see were due to the love-shyness. Perhaps my Asperger's causes me to be a perfectionist and beat myself up for any little mistake. Live, learn and move on. Obviously, these things are not easy to do, so don't beat yourself up because they are too hard. I hope that you can at least open your mouth and repeat three times, *I forgive myself for all the mistakes I have done and will do.*

If the above spoken statements didn't sink in, or it seems like you said them without really believing them, repeat them every day until you truly believe them. Take a few deep breaths. At least you can do that. Now you are ready for some help. I know a few of you out there believe you can do everything on your own and to receive help signifies weakness or a flaw in your character. Learn to accept assistance in whatever form the universe presents it to you. Since you are reading this book and have made it this far, I assume you are ready.

For this first phase of action, seek help from three different resources: books, online support groups and one-on-one talk therapy. If you are male, the most important book you need to purchase now is Michael Pilinski's *Without Embarrassment: The Social Coward's Totally Fearless Seduction System* (2003). Pilinski totally nails it when it comes to explaining exactly what you need to do to play the human mating game successfully. Although he never uses the term, it appears he was love-shy:

> I had somehow grown extremely fearful of approaching a woman in any kind of a social setting, and the strange part was that I was otherwise a very outgoing and humorous kind of guy... But I had developed some kind of *phobia*... (p. 232)

He overcame this and wrote his book seemingly specifically for the love-shy male. He inspired me to write this book. As a love-shy you did not intuitively assimilate the human mating ritual. His book will explain it to you. In addition to addressing love-shys specifically, what separates his book from other pick-up/seduction books is that other such books focus on how many notches you can add to your bedpost, rather than how to form the basis for a long-term relationship. As at the time of writing this you won't find his book at your local or online bookstores. My website www.loveshyproject.com has a list of all books I reference with links to obtain them. Or use www.worldcat.org to locate your nearest library providing a particular book and request a free interlibrary loan through your local library.

His book is for men, but I will cover any of his relevant points that apply to women. Leil Lowndes wrote the closest equivalent volume for women with *How to Make Anyone Fall in Love With You* (1996). Although not as precise and thorough as Pilinski's primer and not written specifically for love-shys, it is still a great book. Its target audience includes both sexes, so I highly recommend it for all of you. It also covers much more about relationships than

Pilinski's book, which is much more of the nuts and bolts of the mating ritual. As a former shy herself, Lowndes writes directly to the shy person and also authored *How to Talk to Anyone*[9] and *Goodbye to Shy*.[10] While good books, they are ancillary to the love quest and not requirements.

The third book I highly recommend is *Healing the Shame That Binds You* by John Bradshaw (2005). Bradshaw hosted PBS television shows related to his books, and this book sold millions. The subject is toxic shame, which is mainly brought on by our parents. I won't attempt to sum up this complex subject which Bradshaw tackles superbly. Suffice it to say that reading this book will really make you see how each of us is a product of our parents. According to Bradshaw, every personality flaw and psychological condition of our parents and every "family secret" gets handed down in some form to us. Since this book goes a long way towards healing people who were physically or sexually abused as children, it will certainly help the love-shy, many of whom had less than perfect home lives. Shame most likely prominently contributes to your negative attitudes about sex and romance.

Buy these books, all of which are available in paperback and possibly inexpensively obtainable used from online resellers. Chances are you already have some self-help books like *Dating for Idiots* or *How to Pick Up Hot Chicks*. Since these types of books are not geared to the love-shy, you likely found them mostly useless. Like many things produced without the understanding of the love-shy's unique problems, these more mainstream publications probably generated more frustration than hope and success. Go after material specifically tailored towards you. Once the love-shy focused books have brought you up to speed, then employ your general audience dating books. Any book is just a book by a human author with finite knowledge, so don't put your complete faith in any one book when your life loudly tells you differently.

Next, check out internet resources for love-shys. Arguably the most important website is www.love-shy.com. It makes available a free downloadable copy of Gilmartin's *Shyness and Love.* Since I summarize and quote the book's relevant material here, it is not necessarily required reading, but when I found it I intensely read all 641 pages. It seemed that with every chapter, he described me almost exactly. A condensed version was produced a few years later (1989) as *The Shy Man Syndrome*,[11] but it presents nothing new. A website with a group discussion of involuntary celibacy topics can be found at incel.myonlineplace.org/forum. If you think you have Asperger's syndrome or autism, an internet search will yield many support websites. However, a professional diagnosis is highly recommended. The internet constantly gets updated, and love-shyness continues to gain acknowledgment, so never stop investigating and learning.

Since I try to include all pertinent love-shy information available on the internet in this book, what is most important about each of the aforementioned websites is their links to online support forums. Become a member of at least one online support community. Even if you never post anything and only lurk, being a part of such a community is important. A women-only group can be found at health.groups.yahoo.com/group/loveshy_women. Being able to ask questions and discuss issues that only other love-shys can understand is almost cathartic. Express your exasperations in the proper place, so you don't end up venting in the wrong place like at work or at the club. Unlike Asperger's and autism where support groups exist in most major cities, love-shyness is so unknown that no in-person support group exists. Bear in mind the minor paradox of internet support groups; they consist of people giving advice who have not completely overcome their love-shyness. The ones who have overcome it now have busier lives and don't have the time or need for such groups.

If you do have an autism spectrum disorder, attending a support group is recommended. Luckily, more adult-orientated support groups are arising out of the greater numbers of those diagnosed with Asperger's and autism, but a relevant group may be hard to find. Focusing on the characteristics of autism and

noticing your fellow group members behaving the same way you do can help you develop control over these socially detrimental features of the condition. Yet I have found such groups have limited benefits when dealing with love-shyness. Even though I get together outside of the group with some of these men with Asperger's and develop basic friendships, due to the nature of our condition they are unable to offer me emotional support. Worse, the therapists running these groups are neither familiar with love-shyness nor equipped to deal with it.

Which brings us to your next required action: obtaining a therapist. Even though I figured something was wrong with me, during those many lonely years I never went to a therapist unless forced to go. Why didn't those who really cared about me get me into proper treatment? I guess they were like me in that I intuitively knew that a therapist would not know what was wrong with me and, thus, could not help me. When I finally found Gilmartin's book and discovered my proper diagnosis, my intuition was proven somewhat correct. I saw six different psychiatrists, psychologists and therapists and none knew what love-shyness is, although one had heard of the term.

If a psychological condition is not listed in the American Psychiatric Association's *Diagnostic and Statistical Manual of Mental Disorders,*[12] or *DSM,* then it might as well not exist as far as the mental health field is concerned. One would think that 20 years after Gilmartin published his thorough love-shy study, it would be better known. Even sex therapist, researcher and author Dr. Helen Singer Kaplan complained in 1987 that "sexual phobias have been specifically excluded from the category of phobic disorders in the DSM-III (1980), and these syndromes have received no mention at all in the section on psychosexual disorders"[13] (p. 3). Consider that Asperger's syndrome only first appeared in the *DSM* in 1994, while Dr. Hans Asperger published his findings in the 1940s, albeit in German during the war.

That does not mean a therapist is useless. Quite the contrary. Although I found a few not helpful, most were absolutely

worthwhile. The important consideration when looking for a therapist is to find one you like and who you believe can help you. Shop around. Do not feel obligated to go to one you dislike or don't respect. I strongly recommend choosing a therapist of the opposite sex to you. A major reason for seeing a therapist is to have someone to talk to about things you can't discuss in person with anyone else. One problem with overcoming love-shyness is that you can't comfortably discuss many issues related to it with friends, family or any potential love interest. By having a therapist of the opposite gender, it can be like talking to all those women or men to whom you really wanted to explain your problem, but couldn't. It also gives you experience of talking to that gender, especially about intimate subjects. Since you don't have a significant other to talk to about your most intimate feelings, and since it is likely you have few close friends to confide in, your therapist will fill this much-needed role.

Some believe that everybody, not just love-shys and others with severe emotional problems, could benefit from some form of therapy. Since nobody's parents were perfect, everybody has issues from their childhood that created psychological problems. Whether people acknowledge their own problems and want to change is the real question. Some of the craziest people are those who don't think they need any help. Do not feel embarrassed to go to therapy. Instead, be concerned for the people who don't think they need it. Strange how some people run to the doctor's office over any little sniffle but do nothing when faced with major anxiety or depression problems. Men, in particular, tend to be raised to be self-sufficient and not to seek help until close to death. Break from this mindset, because seeking professional support is a sign of strength.

As far as recommending either a psychologist or psychiatrist or whatnot, I will not go there. Since you will likely find no mental health professional knowledgeable about love-shyness or involuntary celibacy, it may not matter much. You are looking for the professional who can work well with you. I suggest finding one who is understanding and personable, yet acts like a sports coach who inspires you and makes sure you do what you need to do. Any such therapist worth her salt won't let you get away with anything. That's what you want. If your love-shyness caused or exacerbated a drug or other type of addiction, now is the perfect time to deal with that, since you will, I hope, soon be ending your loneliness and will be flowering into a new life. I would recommend against a therapist who delves too much into your childhood to try to find the cause of your love-shyness. Like any phobia, coming to grips with the childhood incident that caused the phobia does remarkably little to ease it.

Make sure your therapist is open to the idea of love-shyness. Show her Gilmartin's book to back you up. The love-shy concept can help her understand that problems like your depression are due to the love-shyness rather than you having a predisposition to depression or it being a symptom of another mental health disorder. Without your therapist knowing about your love-shyness, she will likely have a hard time figuring out what is causing what. Years ago when I first visited a therapist, I complained about depression and aimlessness. I didn't last too long with this therapist. Now I see that it would have taken a long time and much digging to uncover my problem with women. Love-shys can be quite hesitant about talking about love-shyness with a therapist. Don't beat around the bush.

Understand that you will have issues other than pure love-shyness. Mental health professionals use the term comorbidity to refer to other conditions which exist and are related to the main condition. These other conditions are usually not full blown but *shadow syndromes:* see John J. Ratey and Catherine Johnson's refreshing book of that title (1997). Their book highlights the need to look for symptoms associated with mild forms of obsessive-compulsive disorder, attention deficit disorder, brain development disorders and other mental conditions. Autism disorders cause social and communication skills deficits and can lead to mood and anxiety disorders. Realize that the number one trigger of behavior problems with children (and adults too, I assume) with an autism spectrum disorder is stress. Discuss traumatic experiences related to your love-shyness and come to terms with them. Use your pent-up emotions to fuel your therapy sessions. You need to deal with your unexpressed anger constructively or you will eventually unleash it on those you care about the most. You need a therapist to help you stabilize your life so you can constructively deal with your love-shyness and not get bounced helplessly from one stressful situation to another.

Depression of various degrees seems universal among loveshys. Ratey and Johnson's *Shadow Syndromes* (1997) states:

> Depression—even partial depression—even in someone with normally normal social functioning will cause a decrease in social functioning. A big danger with mild depression is that it will not get treated. These people may assume that most people normally live stressed and burned out lives. (p. 89)

> The mildly depressed person reacts to his pain by battening the hatches, by drawing inside himself and shutting out the world and its stresses. (p. 100)

> [T]he mildly depressed person is in no position to seek out more stress, he is…chronically stressed (p. 102)

> [W]e must alleviate depression by whatever means we have at hand: depression is antilife. That depression has been implicated in women's infertility is poetic symmetry; depression brings with it a closing down of possibility, a dimming of the light. Depression, even the mildest of depressions, silences the soul. (p. 103)

I see now how my Asperger's and my love-shyness kept me in a state of some form of depression almost my whole life. This continuous, low-level deficiency of mood and energy is standard for the depression most love-shys endure. This type of depression is called dysthymia and contrasts with full-blown clinical depression, which is episodic. Dysthymia symptoms can include fatigue, poor self-image, poor concentration, indecisiveness, problems with appetite, problems sleeping and feelings of hopelessness. Since these issues are usually not acute and deemed to be caused by a depressing life situation, professional help for mild or continuous depression is not usually sought. However, depression works directly against treating love-shyness, so confront your depression head on.

I see depression as a symptom of love-shyness, particularly because feelings of helplessness and hopelessness promote depression. As you overcome your love-shyness and gain control of your life, your depression subsides and a positive spiral results. Since your mood is much more susceptible to the winds of your emotions and your environment than the average, stable person, do not get depressed about getting depressed about every little stumbling. This turns each little mental rut into a sinkhole. Don't leave it all up to your therapist to cure your depression. Go someplace where people aren't depressed so their positive mood rubs off on you. Try staying depressed in an Irish pub on St. Patrick's Day or while riding a jet ski.

Male depression often camouflages itself. When sad some women may cry, but men often get angry which masks the sadness. Men may also often express their depression through substance abuse, unnecessary risk taking and other self-destructive behavior. Male emotional problems leak out and express themselves as physical ailments and crazy antics. Isolation makes these symptoms worse. Society and upbringing teach men to avoid their emotions. When a boy hurts himself playing sports, he is told not to cry and to suck it up. Men are not supposed to talk about emotions in any deep way with other men, and men learn that certain topics are not appropriate in the locker room. Thus, men become distanced and removed from their emotions. Even when directly asked about their feelings, many men will often express their thoughts instead of their feelings. They express their sadness, frustration and disappointment through anger or tantrums, which turns off those closest to them and further exacerbates the problems. Autism researcher Simon Baron-Cohen characterizes autism as extreme maleness,[14] and the fact that autistics are even less in touch with their feelings and more emotionally immature than average men supports this view. Men usually only express their significant emotions with their girlfriends or wives, thus love-shy men are most at risk for depression.

To defend themselves from their feelings of inadequacy, love-shys can lash out at women. Downloading these emotions onto a therapist becomes of paramount importance. Don't wait until you get fired or break down from stress before seeking assistance. The wise man notices the warning signs and goes for help to avert disaster instead of waiting and seeking professional help to recover from it. Learn to open up to your therapist. This is not the time only to make idle chitchat or discuss surface issues. Love-shys seem to have a difficult time discussing the hard issues. One, probably bipolar, love-shy who came extremely close to committing suicide did not bring it up at his therapy session the following week because he feared they would lock him up. Opening up about your problem reduces the likelihood of institutionalization as your problems can be dealt with at an earlier stage, as well as the chance that you will end up six feet underground. I'd like to think it was this suicidal man's active participation in an internet love-shy forum that played as much of a role in saving him as his inability to find a long enough rope.

How often and how long you see a therapist is mainly up to you. With all your various love-shy issues, a few months is the bare minimum. Many love-shys end up using a therapist for well over one year. Stay in charge of your own life. If you feel things are really going well, start seeing your therapist less frequently.

Or increase the frequency of the visits if you feel inundated by your world. Act assertively if you continue to find the sessions not worth your while. Bear in mind, though, that the sessions you feel the least motivated to go to usually produce the biggest results. My belief about therapy in general, which my therapist shared, is that seeing a therapist is like seeing a physician. You seek treatment for a specific condition or traumatic event, and once the condition clears or the professional can do nothing more for you, then you have no reason to continue using her services. Strange how people go to therapists every week for years on end without noticeable changes. I think some people get addicted to therapy instead of developing the necessary friendships and intimate relationships for which much therapy substitutes.

If progress is slow, it may not necessarily be the fault of the therapist. Talk therapy is only one part of what you need to do. Visiting a therapist is like communicating with your coach and does not substitute for actually playing the game. Spend more time in the social arena than the therapist's office.

Find a therapist who does more than just listen. Since she will end up knowing you fairly well, as a professional her suggestions for you are significant. If you only want someone to open your mouth to, talk to your pillow; it's much cheaper. A good therapist will provide both the intuitive and practical perspectives you are missing. Don't hold back expressing your feelings with your therapist, within reason of course. Those pent-up emotions have to be let out somehow. Likely, these emotions are related to something significant. The more you express, the more your therapist has to go on. Remember, you are not there to be judged, you are there to be helped.

Many of you will complain that you don't have the money for it. Check to see whether your insurance will cover it. Many companies these days offer an employee assistance program with six completely free, completely confidential sessions with a counselor unattached to your employer. I received my Asperger's diagnosis through such a program. An employee assistance program is only

a first step, and the therapist will guide you towards proper long-term treatment. Usually some type of campus counseling service is easily available for those in college. Although these college services may be limited, at least they are used to dealing with dating and relationship issues. Do internet searches with terms like "sliding scale counseling" and "low cost therapy" along with your city. I know therapy isn't cheap, but your health, which includes your mental health, is one of your most valuable possessions. Take care of it now and know that an immediate outlay of effort and cash will pay out big time in the future.

Notes

1. Crenshaw, T. (1985) "The sexual aversion syndrome." *Journal of Sex and Marital Therapy 11*, 4, 285–292.
2. Guardian, The (2007) 'Mother's stress harms foetus, research shows.' May 31. Accessed March 26, 2008 at www.guardian.co.uk/science/2007/may/31/childrensservices.medicineandhealth
3. LeVay, S. (1993). *The Sexual Brain.* Cambridge, MA: MIT Press.
4. Money, J. (1986) *Lovemaps.* New York: Irvington Publishers.
5. Wikipedia. *Asperger syndrome.* Accessed on July 20, 2007 at http://en.wikipedia.org/wiki/Asperger_syndrome
6. Wikipedia. *People speculated to have been autistic.* Accessed on April 30, 2008 at http://en.wikipedia.org/wiki/People_speculated_to_have_been_autistic
7. Hénault, I. (2006) *Asperger's Syndrome and Sexuality.* London: Jessica Kingsley Publishers.
8. Joseph, R. (1993) *The Naked Neuron: Evolution and the Languages of the Body and Brain.* New York: Plenum Press.
9. Lowndes, L. (2003) *How to Talk to Anyone.* New York: McGraw-Hill.
10. Lowndes, L. (2006) *Goodbye to Shy.* New York: McGraw-Hill.
11. Gilmartin, B. G. (1989) *The Shy Man Syndrome.* New York: Madison Books.
12. American Psychiatric Association (2000) *Diagnostic and Statistical Manual of Mental Disorders DSM-IV-TR.* Washington, DC: American Psychiatric Publishers, Inc.
13. Kaplan, H. S. (1987) *Sexual Aversion, Sexual Phobias, and Panic Disorders.* New York: Brunner/Mazel.
14. Baron-Cohen, S. (2003) *The Essential Difference: Male and Female Brains and the Truth About Autism.* New York: Basic Books.

Chapter 2

The Big Picture

Don't panic

"DON'T PANIC!" Douglas Adams' succinct command plastered in bright, bold letters on the back of his (fictional) guide book[1] are words to live by at *all* times. If I were to print a similar command on the back cover of this book, it would say, *RELAX*. Of course, when a novel social situation makes your anxiety flare up and shuts your mind completely down, such trite expressions will be of little use. However, I am talking about your fears of the big picture of your life. *How can I ever get a decent spouse when I am this old and inexperienced? I so much wanted a young, beautiful girlfriend, and now I'm old. How do I make up for all those wasted years? It's so depressing seeing all my high school and college friends and my cousins getting married, while I don't even date.*

Just because you are way behind with your romantic skills development does not mean getting the romance you've always dreamed about is impossible. I used to picture myself in a wheelchair in the retirement home still never being able to talk to an

attractive woman my age. Whether you are 18, 21, 27, 35, 45, 57 or even older, your only fear should be that you will never overcome your love-shyness. Writing this in my late thirties, I have a hard time not chuckling when I hear some 21-year-old complaining about all those wasted years.

Someone always exists who lost his or her virginity at a younger age than someone else. There is no such thing as sexually normal, and comparing ourselves to others or to some hypothetical ideal is not healthy. We each have our own unique life path to journey on with its own pitfalls and challenges. Life includes many other facets than romantic success. Never compare yourself with another. You may compare yourself with someone younger who seems more successful and wish, *If I could just go back in time and do it over.* Of course, you would wish that you had your knowledge that you have now, especially regarding your love-shyness. But how did you obtain all your knowledge? By living. Do you really want to go back and do it all again? I certainly don't. Just give thanks you've made it this far as well as you did. The past is the past. Dwell in the present and plan for the future.

Romance is just one part of your life. All those years without a girlfriend or boyfriend were not wasted; they were just short by one or another aspect. By focusing on what we don't have, we fail to appreciate all that we have and all that we have accomplished, especially with our love-shy handicap. Who is the more impressive climber? The climber who quickly makes it to the top of the mountain or the blind climber who takes much longer but eventually reaches the summit? For the blind climber the success is all the more delicious. Everyone has hardships in his or her life. Even though the world seems to tell you otherwise, you are so much more than your romantic relationships. Making a list of all the blessings in your life can be quite therapeutic when you feel that your life is completely empty. If gripped by self-loathing, write down all the positive and wonderful qualities about yourself.

Like most love-shys you are romantic, but do not let your daydreams cloud your thinking. Do not place such an emphasis on losing your virginity, especially to that perfect person in that perfect setting. Making up some fantasy scenario just increases the stress of everything surrounding your first time. Almost nothing you do for the first time happens perfectly. Lose any hard and fast rules regarding sex and relationships except when it comes to safety, hygiene and birth control. Chances are your rules came from misguided thinking. Just go for it. Love-shyness aside, in a relationship sex will happen when it happens.

For you older men, do not let age stop you from approaching a younger woman, even the beautiful woman of your dreams. Not all 25-year-old women will want to date a 40-year-old man, but if you present yourself properly many will. I've found that when that little voice in my head said, *She's too young for you,* it is my love-shyness misguiding me. In fact, as a man in his late thirties, I tend to relate better with younger women than with ones my own age or older. Women my own age want a man with more experience, especially familiarity with children. Older women are much pickier and usually know exactly what they want in a man, while younger women are still figuring it out. While it seems like a working single mother with no free time would complement a single guy with all the time in the world, solidifying this type of connection proves hard. I used to think that an older woman would react positively to my advances, and welcome a younger stud like me. However, I found the opposite to be the case. Most likely having been married at least once, such a woman rarely goes for casual encounters and cannot relate to an inexperienced love-shy guy. All things considered and within reason, the woman will often choose the older man.

A younger woman may relate better to you, a love-shy man, because both of you have approximately similar dating experience and relationship expectations. For dating someone more than a couple years younger, though, you need to do and be a few things. You should be physically fit. You need to have at least some of the same interests as the younger crowd, such as being into hip new music and going out to clubs. Luckily, younger people have less stringent criteria for potential mates and feel freer to experience a variety of romantic partners.

Just hanging around places with younger people is great for meeting them, and it helps keep you feeling younger, *if* you feel that you fit in. Fitting in is a state of mind and action. If you are doing and enjoying what everyone around you is doing and enjoying, then you fit in, even if most of the people there don't find you sexually attractive. It's not the year printed on your driver's license that matters, but how you act and how you are. If a woman asks, don't hide or be embarrassed by your age, because women like truthful, confident men. Having old school manners, I never ask a woman her age or weight, but they will usually state the former after they ask my age. If not, I tend to say, *I don't ask a woman her age,* perhaps with a wink in hopes she will offer it.

A thorny question older love-shys are asked, usually by older people, is, *Why aren't you married?* This is a legitimate question, so if someone asks you it very soon after meeting, do not take it as an insult. Instead, act like it's a compliment reworded from something like, *You seem like such a cool and attractive person, it's amazing you are not married.* And it's true. It is amazing that such a decent person like yourself has never married. Respond to the marriage question with something like, *The right person hasn't come around yet.* If you look the person in the eyes and say it right, you imply to the person that she might be the one. Because years ago at least one right woman did come along for me and I hate to lie, I say something like, *The right situation hasn't happened yet.* I may include, *I had the chance, but I thought I was too young and immature at the time.* These statements may still be white lies but come across far better than the truth. Act like it's OK you're still single and that you're confident the right person will come along soon, even if it tears you up inside.

As far as your inexperience when it comes to relationships is concerned, love-shys inordinately fear this problem. Even with little relationship background, if you act natural, truthful and loving and you experience actual mutual attraction, the other person will usually overlook an innocent faux pas and forgive your mistakes as long as you learn from them. As Franklin D. Roosevelt once said, "The only thing we have to fear is fear itself." Nervousness itself may be the biggest issue. Since fears regarding inexperience mainly focus around sex, let's set the record straight. By acknowledging right before you are about to have sex that you are a virgin, you remove performance pressure. One non-love-shy woman claims that plenty of women entertain fantasies about sleeping with a virginal man. Women, you have little to worry about as far as knowing what to do. Because many men will want to take sex as far as they can, most concerns boil down to how comfortable you feel. The man should take the lead and you follow as far as you want to go.

The first time two people have sexual intercourse with each other usually will not be that great as far as the sex goes because of both people's nervousness and not knowing each other well. A sexual encounter is about intimacy, not just intercourse. The movies and over-exaggerating peers create unrealistic expectations of how both men and women are expected to perform sexually. Any woman who rejects you due to initial sexual problems is not worth your time. I made the mistake once of being so embarrassed about my initial performance that I ran away from the relationship, even though she called me later and still seemed interested. Good sex requires good communication, so not telling and asking what each of you want and need, rather than poor performance itself, may cause a potential relationship failure.

Older people get concerned that their bodies aren't as supple and toned as they were at 22. Looks matter, of course, but never think that this precludes everything else. Don't worry yourself over how you look naked. No one has a perfect body. By the time you first see each other naked, unless you have something seriously and uniquely wrong that someone can't tell with your clothes on, in the heat of the encounter your partner will overlook any of your flaws, as you will theirs. Once you have consummated the relationship, your feelings for each other will likely blind both of you to any imperfections, at least for a while. The media and popular culture shove sexual images of really attractive people in our face, because sex sells. Since everyone likes watching sexy people, advertising, movies and television do not accurately portray reality.

Never worry about a lack of available possible mates. A recent *New York Times* article states that half of all women in the United States right now are single.[2] The article also confirms the continuation of the decades-old trend of women marrying later in life. This planet currently holds well over six billion people. In our heavily populated, internet connected world with relative ease of transportation, the availability of romantic partners has never been greater. The world does not lack single women and men, it is what's in your head that's lacking. The universe has always provided me with plenty of possible girlfriends. There is no reason to assume that this trend will not continue, although the time period between possibilities seems to increase as we get older. I hope you realize that plenty of awesome mates are waiting for you to get yourself together.

Your environment is you

Inhabiting a cheerful environment can improve one's mood remarkably. Everyone is a product of his or her environment, so do what you can to improve yours. This is your life, so take charge of elements that need changing. You don't have to paint your apartment bright orange to sharpen your outlook on life, but you do need to take a good, objective look at everything in your life including your home, your clothes and your car and identify what needs replacing. These things define us and make us play the role our things suggest.

The best way for an actor to get into character is by putting on his costume and going on the set. Are your clothes, crib and car the costume and set of a lonely guy who sits around all day playing video games? Are they the costume of a frumpy girl who sits home alone on weekend nights without a date? Put on a sports coat and tie, walk down the street and notice how different you feel and act compared to your life in T-shirts and ripped jeans.

For you guys, your apartment, clothes and car make very strong statements about you to prospective women. Does your place look like home to a dungeon master or to a suave, sophisticated lady's man? You need not buy a brand new car, just have one with no rust, looks normal and is not a station wagon or minivan. Don't go out and buy big gold chain necklaces if that's not your style, but get a style. Just as you have a suit for job interviews and special occasions, buy clothes for going out clubbing and for dates. You eventually need more than one such outfit, but until you develop taste and style, you might not want go wild on your clothes purchases, since fashions continuously change. Place special emphasis on your shoes, because arguably women judge a man by his shoes more than any other single article of clothing. Buy and use shoe polish. Get comfortable wearing dressy clothes. Find smart clothes that don't itch.

Getting a new hairstyle is worthwhile, as change in and of itself is positive. Seek out a good hairdresser who can advise you and cut your hair consistently well. Don't make a game out of how long you can go between haircuts. If you wear glasses, invest in a pair of designer frames. Or ditch the glasses for contacts. Alternatively, laser eye surgery now competes with the price of a couple of pairs of expensive glasses. For older people, bifocals are sexier than wearing granny glasses down on your nose and looking over and not through them. I recommend against hair transplants, boob jobs or other such types of surgery. However, a visit to your dentist for teeth whitening treatment pays off as white, straight teeth seem to be one of those things to which people really pay attention. Nice choppers give you a reason to smile.

Are you and your clothes, car and apartment clean inside and out? Shirts ironed and tucked in? A comedienne once joked that guys are bears with furniture. If you have lived in your place for a few years, and especially if you own a house or a condominium, think seriously about hiring a maid service for a spring cleaning. Even if you keep your place basically sanitary, we never seem to get around to cleaning certain places. At least once a year move large furniture like your bed and vacuum underneath.

Having a girlfriend requires a clean household and a clean body. Basic hygiene is a must. Bad body odor and foul-smelling apartments are showstoppers. It doesn't matter how perfect your game is if your smell or breath repulses women. Shower and change clothes often, more than once a day if necessary, rather than trying to mask your odor with heavy cologne or aftershave. Ask trusted friends for their opinion and assume they are biting their tongue. Combat bad breath by drinking more water, chewing gum, brushing your teeth often and avoiding certain foods and drinks like garlic and coffee. Another joke goes, *How does a guy clean his apartment? He moves.* Move to a new apartment with a clean smell and preferably with amenities like an exercise room and pool. Some apartment complexes that cater to singles may even have free social events like barbecues. These things will get you out of your apartment and around people. The hardest part of moving is finding friends to help lug your stuff.

If you live with your parents, likely in a basement room, YOU MUST MOVE OUT OF THE HOUSE. *But, my parent is sick and she will lose the house if I don't help out with her and the mortgage payment.* That may be the case, but figure something out. In the mean time, spend as little time at home as possible. Make moving out of the house a prime goal and work towards that goal, even if you don't know exactly how to accomplish it yet. Ideally, your parents will understand that your health and well-being is at least as important as theirs is. Get a second job for a while if you must.

By continuing living with them, they persist in exerting subtle and not so subtle influence on you. Since your parents may have love-shy characteristics, these characteristics that you now work to eliminate continue to reinforce themselves. How you act with your parents tends to revert to your old childhood way of being. Being around familiar people tends to reinforce familiar habits, as people always treat you in the same way once they get to know you. Mothers cannot help but act motherly and treat you like a six-year-old. Even if you are a successful businessman, mom will still tell you to *Put a jacket on, it's cold out.*

Women can find adult guys living at home a real turn-off. How could you ever bring a woman back to your place after a date? Even if your parents are open-minded to such possibilities, your date will have serious reservations. Your parents may have difficulty with such an arrangement, especially if they continue harboring their own sexual anxieties that influenced your love-shyness. Women still living at home may also raise a big red flag with male suitors. Even if you explain how you provide urgent care for your sick parent, sympathy rarely trumps the reality of the situation for either sex. A potential mate does not want to compete with your mother for your affections, and living at home indicates where your true sympathies lie. You need to grow out from under your parents' wings. You need the independence and responsibility that your own residence provides and requires. You need to choose how to furnish, organize and decorate your own place. You need to bear responsibility for the bills and keeping the place clean.

Even if you have to move into a one-room efficiency in the seedy part of town, better to reside there than in your childhood bedroom. Keep your nice and expensive stuff stashed at your parent's if necessary. Move to a college town or a diverse metropolitan area with a constant turnover of new people and a vibrant nightlife. A love-shy living in a small town has a much harder time reinventing himself and may stagnate and regress without a supply of new opportunities and people. This is not to say you should disown your parents or move to another part of the country or even to another country all together. Initially, it is best if you don't move too far away from your family, friends and familiar areas. Communicate with and visit your parents regularly. Use these visits to show how you are improving, even if you don't yet bring a date home for the holidays.

This advice goes for college students as well. Do not live at home while going to school no matter what your financial or geographical situation. One of my favorite lines from the television show *South Park* goes, "There is a time and a place for everything; it's called college." College is a time to branch out and discover who you are, and for all the reasons just listed, living at home will majorly curtail such growth. On the opposite end, don't make the mistake my sister did by going to a university on the other side of the country, which turned out to be too isolated and removed from her family and high school friends. If you attend college, instead of moving back home for the summer, try to arrange an out of town internship, some field study program, a trip around Europe or any kind of traveling anywhere, even if only for part of the summer.

Speaking of college, if any love-shys out there are reading this book before going on to an institution of higher learning, remember that love-shyness is a serious condition that interferes with many aspects of your life. Taking stressful course loads is not what you need right now. Don't think like I did, *I'll worry about women after I get my college education and a good job.* It won't work. Do not put off facing your love-shyness. Make it known to your parents that you have a serious condition. You should probably go to a school closer to home, even if a prestigious university far away accepts you. What does it matter how good the professors and the facilities rate when your depression will prevent you from showing up for class and graduating? The cream always rises to the top, so no matter what school you start at you can eventually transfer to a better one later. For landing a decent job outside of

academia, it's usually a matter of what kind of person you are rather than which school you attended.

The teaming up of my Asperger's and love-shyness along with basic shyness prevented me from completing my college education, thus squandering a precious opportunity, and I don't want that to happen to you. I was too shy to make friends in class and to ask for help with exceedingly difficult subjects. I became too socially frustrated to focus on classes and homework. To top it off, as my adult "special interest," the term used for the intense esoteric obsessions common in people on the autism spectrum, took root during my college years, it veered me further away from my academic career. Furthermore, I had to understand about myself, and at that time neither Asperger's nor love-shyness could be discovered through any school's curriculum. However, many shys "escape into reality" by delving into book learning and becoming academically successful. Gilmartin (1987) warns about pursuing advanced degrees that, although quite interesting, may not provide a realistic foundation for a career outside of academia. He recommends, rather than seeking a liberal arts education, obtaining a degree in a technical field, which allows for occupations with lower social skills requirements. When choosing an academic path to launch a career, he emphatically states, "The choice of a major is of infinitely greater importance than grade point average" (p. 452).

Even if you are out of ma and pa's house, objectively evaluate your current living situation. Love-shys tend to find themselves in "safe" environments where they feel comfortable but are not conducive to dating. These environments usually allow them to hide their love-shyness where being single is the norm, or at least not openly dwelt on by others. Perhaps you squat in a party house where everyone does drugs. Or you may live in an isolated religious community that frowns upon dating. On the surface, living as a member of a tight community may seem good for overthrowing your love-shyness. Yet the exclusion of outsiders and the lack of available romantic partners place you in an

isolated, lonely cocoon. While your current living situation may be excellent for you financially, spiritually or otherwise, at some time you must break out of the cocoon in order to become the beautiful butterfly. You can always go back to the community once you obtain a mate.

Since your friends are a part of your environment, objectively look at each of the friends you hang around with much of the time, because your current friends tend to reinforce your old ways of being. Did your friends choose you, or did you choose each of your friends? Are they real friends who are respectful of you, or are they false friends who are often possessive and intimidating? Even if your close friends truly care for you, they may not be open to changing themselves as you change. If so, you may need to re-evaluate your friendships with them. As you move onward and upward, you don't need to feel trapped with people who refuse to take charge of their own life and who may work to keep you down at their level. Hanging out with people resigned to not having romantic relationships rubs off on you. The newly created openings in your life will make room for more positive friendships.

For our purposes here, consider the contents of your refrigerator and everything else you put in your body part of your environment. What foods you eat definitely affects your moods. Too many refined carbohydrates and unhealthy fats play havoc with your brain chemistry as well as with your weight and well-being. Anxiety and depression can cause undue stress on the brain and body, so eat healthily to counteract these conditions. Put down that soda pop, even if it's only one calorie, and get to the grocery store. Healthy eating is part of that positive spiral. You start eating better, which gives you more energy. Then, you work out more, which makes you feel better about yourself, eliminating cravings for unhealthy comfort foods. Eat healthily for the majority of the time, so you don't have to create unnecessary stress on yourself worrying about every little bite. Replacing fast food with home cooked or raw vegetables can also improve body odor.

Likely, you spend much of your waking hours in an environment you seem to have little control over: your job. Due to shyness, lack of social skills, low self-esteem, non-competitiveness, high anxiety and lack of assertiveness, most love-shys are chronically underemployed. The lack of drive for money and a career may partially be due to giving up on life. Not only do love-shys have problems obtaining and keeping a job, but the jobs they do have usually fall beneath their skills and abilities. Do you consider your current job menial and well below your potential? Are you doing what you spent years in school training for? At the end of the workday how do you feel? Complete this sentence: *If I was assertive and not shy, I would like to earn my living by—*. Those on the autism spectrum find life most rewarding when they have a job involving one of their special interests.

Our occupation defines us and gives us much of our social status ranking. Therefore, do not underestimate the importance your job plays in obtaining a mate. Many of your same traits hindering romance hold you back at work. Strive to move up the occupational ladder. Try to acquire the experience and skills necessary for a higher position. If you want that promotion, look the part. Most days, come into work dressed for the job you want, not the job you have. Then act the part. But don't overstep your bounds, such as bossing around your coworkers before you receive that promotion to management. Take extra responsibility when you can, especially on your own initiative.

If you have a dead-end job or have no desire to move up at your present company, strongly consider looking elsewhere. Good employers value enterprising, hard-working employees with initiative. Keep abreast of the local job market in your field. You may even need to go back to school, which provides an excellent opportunity to meet single people. Perhaps, find a job where you can meet cool people and have fun. Since your environment defines you, work to create the environment of the person you want to be. When you can look in the mirror dressed to kill while standing in your home that is just the way you want it and is acceptable to women, your pride will help you to make a move on a woman and bring her back to your place.

The map of the jungle

The mind is completely malleable. The brain takes a bit more work. When I was in any way sexually stimulated by an actual woman, even if just talking with her, my mind would shut down. This response requires a serious reprogramming, a retraining, of the brain. Yet, so much of clearing love-shyness depends on eliminating the negative. As Gilmartin (1987) states, the love-shy are unable to "let go and let God" (p. 411). The human mating instinct has been honed for eons. What to do and how to do it are all instinctual. The universe wants it to happen. You want it to happen. And she (or he) wants it to happen. So why doesn't it happen?

It's a matter of eliminating the anxiety. It's a matter of doing the right thing at the right time. It's a matter of not saying the wrong thing. It's a matter of living and focusing in the real world and not fantasizing. It's a matter of eliminating negative thinking and maintaining a positive attitude. It's a matter of exploiting information and tricks that work in this unforgiving jungle. Not until you conquer all aspects of love-shyness can you enjoy a truly healthy relationship. Needing help with basic relationship skills or being unable to fulfill your mating role correctly is not healthy for either person in a relationship.

The anxiety is so strong, so automatic. When you first see her dressed up, when you have a chance with her right now, the anxiety instantly controls you and makes you recoil. So much for first impressions. Then, you spend the rest of the time trying to recover in your mind and with her. Not only is the reaction from the anxiety so immediate as to preclude any hint of conscious control, but the thoughts that come into your mind don't seem like they come from the anxiety, at least as you experience them.

Therefore, this anxiety needs to be dealt with on various levels. Even though you observe and learn about your anxiety and try to take conscious control over it, it takes repeated direct experience with what induces the anxiety to overcome it.

Repetition causes the brain to learn and to program or re-program itself, hence the necessity of repeating something three times before it sinks in. The immediate repetition sets the short-term memory. You need then to access that new memory or stored action in the next few days or weeks to make it a long-term memory. Reading this book, analyzing yourself and working to change your thought processes alone in your room are all well and good. However, you must actually deal with the opposite sex on a potentially romantic stage for the anxiety to lose its voice and control. Actions must follow reading. Knowing what to do does not mean you can do it.

To avoid letting the thoughts spawned from love-shy anxiety control you, be aware of and ignore the negative thoughts. Learn to identify any negative thought or emotion that comes into your head. I do mean ANY. For example, you drive to the store, get there and see the parking lot is empty and the lights are off. You think, *The store is closed.* This is a fact. But then you probably think, *That stupid store. This kind of bad luck always happens to me.* These sentences are not actual facts but negative thoughts. Throughout your whole day, observe all your thoughts and figure out which ones are the negative ones. You will find whole patterns of such thoughts. In the love-shy jungle you need to be continuously on guard. This alertness is as much or more about the happenings in your own head than the affairs of the outside world.

Notice the words you use to describe yourself negatively. Are they all-or-nothing words such as "always" where you label everything as black or white or as an absolute, even though life happens in color? Are they extremist words that greatly exaggerate your mistake or the situation? Are they judging or labeling words such as "should" that cause you to beat yourself up for weeks afterwards? Are they victim words such as "can't" and

"impossible" that make you impotent and unable to change yourself or the situation? It's bad enough that you lived your life on the receiving end of continuous reproach. Don't perpetuate these lies by continuing them yourself.

Facts are not negative or positive, they just are. Things just happen. It is up to you to choose how to react to them. Now that you can recognize your negative thoughts, transform them into positive ones. When that SUV cuts you off on the highway, instead of swearing at the driver, transform your negative thought into something like, *That driver must really need to get somewhere fast. I'm glad I'm not that stressed.* Stress is a big cause of creating mountains out of molehills. When you beat yourself up for not talking to a woman, rephrase the thought as, *I'm proud of myself for making prolonged eye contact with such an attractive woman.* This simple technique is a very powerful tool for your whole life. When your boss yells at you, think, *He is just doing his job making sure everything around here runs well.* You will be amazed how much less stressed you become as other people's negativities roll off you like water off a duck's back. As you consciously train your mind, eventually your negative thoughts become fewer and fewer and positive thoughts replace them quicker and quicker.

Once you really get into this, you will find that not just thoughts but negative emotions as well can be transformed into positive ones. Every negative emotion, such as anger, is generated from a part of you that is not your true, or "higher," self. Not only will this understanding save you from suicide, but by becoming a more mature and positive person, your social status increases. By not reacting negatively to unfavorable situations, people will respect and admire you. As Pilinski (2003) constantly hits home, to get the girl you men need to be, or at least appear to be high-status males. Expressing or harboring rage and other negative emotions reeks of low status. Acting mature, calm and positive in the face of unforeseen, unfortunate circumstances is the way of the confident, successful individual.

Watch out for any negative attitudes you have towards the opposite sex. Chances are you harbor grievances towards a particular woman or all women in general. The most obvious of these attitudes produce blanket statements like, *All women are manipulative, cold-hearted bitches.* A woman may think, *Men don't care about me, they just want to get in my pants.* These are erroneous and detrimental thoughts. I've had a problem with my attitude towards female authority figures, which was likely due to subconscious resentment towards my mother and other women who I feel treated me poorly. If you were romantically rejected, don't act like it's the other person's fault that you're not together as a couple. No, most likely the cause was in some way your failings. Just remember to forgive yourself for it.

Be vigilant for all your negative thoughts about sex and romance. Such thoughts need to be transformed into positive ones. What happens when you see an attractive person walking down the street? Do you just sneak a quick peek, because you know it's not nice to stare? Can you behold someone's ass or her breasts or his package and not get embarrassed? Can you look at the person the whole time they are in view and "drink them up" with your eyes? If you have a problem with these things, then practice looking as long as possible at people you find sexually attractive. If you can't even look at an attractive person, how will you be able to interact intimately with him or her? Do you subscribe to the false ideas that women don't have a sex drive or dislike sex?

Don't let society's negativity towards sex validate these thoughts. While youth culture appears sex saturated, general society is still averse to things sexual. Notice in the United States how much easier broadcast television can show a murder, the worst thing one could do to another human, than to show sex, arguably one of the best acts you can do with another. Read John Ince's *The Politics of Lust* (2005) to understand society's problem with accepting sex. He insightfully argues that society has an unacknowledged phobia of sex and things sexual. Almost everyone has varying degrees of this erotophobia. Since the time we were little children, family and society has always told us, or implied to us through their actions and reactions, that our genitals are a source of shame and should be covered up. Notice how people often feel embarrassed about buying tampons or birth control but not toilet paper. We all have this general feeling that children shouldn't be exposed to nude bodies and sex, but no scientific study has ever backed this up. I highly recommend this book to love-shys as it points out various aspects and examples of their aversions to sex. Erotophobia easily justifies one's love-shyness and one's aversion to things sexual.

Gilmartin claims in a personal correspondence that erotophobia does not directly cause love-shyness. Nonetheless, erotophobia blocks the treatment of love-shyness. In order to improve the love-shy can not harbor any negative attitudes towards sex. As Ince (2005) puts it, "That people avoid thinking about things that provoke anxiety is well documented. This is one reason highly erotophobic people are very ignorant about sex" (p. 24). Just as people don't want to deal with or even acknowledge their own erotophobia, they don't want to do anything for others with acute forms of it. Erotophobia hinders people from thinking rationally about sex, sexuality and sexual public policy. Unfortunately, much of our society's erotophobia is institutionalized through laws and religion. Just as racism and homophobia create violence and unhealthy negativity, so does erotophobia.

Your religious upbringing may have caused such negativity towards sex, or at minimum your religion may reinforce your love-shy attitudes. Sex is a natural bodily function like eating and defecating and should not cause shame and fear. Yet a common theme running through many religions is that sex is "bad." While most people accept that some religions' attitudes towards sexuality are outdated, many love-shys fail to pick up on the subtle nature of current sexual conduct and instead internalize the historic concrete teachings of their religions' doctrines. Sex links to romance. You cannot get around it. And romance links to love. Theoretically, two people can be romantically intimate without being sexual, and it does happen. Realistically, denying sex and the pleasures of the body denies romance. As one love-shy observed:

> I think my Catholic upbringing has something to do with my current problems when dealing with the opposite sex. For example, in my early teens, I used to think that anything remotely related to sex was terribly wrong and had to be avoided at all costs.

David D. Burns, in his fabulous 1985 book *Intimate Connections,* blames his "very conservative religious family" upbringing for undermining his ability to be in romantic relationships (p. xv).

Like many love-shys, the Catholic Church seems to place sex on some high pedestal. The Catholic Church's position that sex should only be for procreation is a different "pedestal" than the love-shys', but both attitudes make sex almost taboo. I believe there is no sin in pleasure itself. I'm not suggesting that one should focus solely on the pleasures of the flesh and ignore spirituality and God. However, times have changed with modern science producing effective and safe birth control, so why not use it? Just as the Catholic Church had to release its hold on the belief that the sun revolves around the earth, the time has come for religions to relinquish their hold on sexual mores.

Usually the act is called making love, and since God is love, one would assume God would be pro sex. Where is the sin in giving other people physical and emotional pleasure as long as it is not physically or emotionally harmful? Except for the commandment *Thou shall not commit adultery,* everything the Church preaches about sexuality appears wrong to me. Note how sexist the Catholic Church is by allowing only male priests. Religions trap people by declaring that masturbation, sex and "impure thoughts" are sinful. By denying an outlet for one's natural sexuality, the Church contributes to the mental and sexual disorders of millions of people. Renowned sex researchers and therapists

Masters and Johnson documented this fact in 1970. "[T]he factor of religious orthodoxy still remains of major import in primary orgasmic dysfunction as in almost every form of human sexual inadequacy"[3] (pp. 229–230). Masters and Johnson recorded Catholic, Jewish and fundamentalist Protestant backgrounds all creating significant sexual problems in marriages. While these religions overtly support healthy marriages, sexual inadequacy is a leading cause of marital problems. While being celibate may make a monk more pious and closer to God, for the general population these arcane rules tend to have the opposite effect by creating obsessive-compulsive type disorders or driving people away from church altogether.

A recent article in *Playboy* magazine reports that male fetuses can have erections in the womb as early as 16 weeks![4] Humans truly are sexual animals, and celibacy is contrary to the human animal. Some homosexuals and some love-shys become priests to avoid dealing with their sexuality, but their sexuality cannot be stifled. Just because Jesus Christ and other founders of the Christian Church practiced celibacy does not mean everyone needs to. The Protestant Church realizes that ministers can lead both a sexual and pious life. Society needs to corral immoral behavior, but sex is just sex after all. The Adam and Eve mythology with its negativity towards sex has caused Earthlings much confusion over the centuries.

Having a healthy sex drive and being secure in one's sexuality does not necessarily lead to promiscuity. While some may worry about the consequences of completely unbridled sexuality, note the social standard where even non-religious women do not want to be seen as easy. Even after the sexual revolution, the double standard of a man having multiple sex partners being a stud while a woman exhibiting the same behavior is labeled a slut is still strong. While it may seem as if this convention is losing power, one recent non-scientific survey found that over half of atheist and non-religious men of high school and college age want to marry a virgin. While the topics involving the intersection of

religion, sexuality and society are complex and part of public debate and personal faith, the relevant bottom line for love-shys is that religions' views of sexuality often create psychological problems. Do not take this denouncement of religions' sexuality beliefs as a critique on any other aspects of religion.

As you correct and eliminate your various negative thoughts, the natural flow of you and your world can happen. And then, seemingly by magic, opportunities abound. However, your previously quashed mating ritual learning still requires you to understand the process and practice it until it is automatic. You must put yourself in situations where the opposite sex abides and act accordingly. You must take action. Regardless of your gender, as a love-shy consider it a requirement for you to make the first move. Both sexes must be active in the process, and first impressions are very important. Everything must be done to make sure such situations progress as smoothly as possible. It's a full life change for sure. And fully possible, if you put in the required effort. But it's fun. The human animal is a social and sexual animal, and being with people and displaying your sexuality is the natural and healthy state of affairs. You should have fun. *Do not take it so seriously.* There will always be other women (or men).

Make every encounter a learning experience. Look back on each situation and figure out what you did right and what went wrong. Remember, the other person isn't perfect either, and so often the chemistry just isn't there. You may be able to get someone else's opinion. Unfortunately, love-shys usually have few close friends and don't ask for help. If you don't talk with anyone about your situation regarding a potential romantic partner, a good chance exists that you live in a fantasy. Your inexperience and desire may make your interpretation of the situation more a dream than reality. Of course, you have to have some dreams to keep you going while you're in this love-shy prison. But you aren't really in prison, because you interact with and inhabit the real world. Don't let your imagination misguide your actions.

Love-shys tend to obsess about love interests relentlessly. Often the object of a love-shy's obsession is someone, such as a movie star, with whom he has no possibility of succeeding romantically. Even if he has contact with the person, if he obsesses, it usually means he has no chance. If you've been fantasizing all semester about someone in your class, chances are you only had a couple of weeks at the beginning of the semester to act. Some love-shys even fall in love with a cousin. Usually their obsession and ignorance combine to produce a state of unreality that further stresses the situation. Try to observe and figure out which beliefs of yours about the world are false. Think of a test, such as actually asking him or her out, to verify your beliefs, and then act out your test.

Don't let your observations of your internal dialog stop you from making positive affirmations about yourself. There is a big difference between saying, *I am a smart, attractive person who deserves a great boyfriend/girlfriend*, and *So and So will go out with me if I can just—*. To really get revved up and better understand the incredible power of positive affirmations, similar to the power of prayer, watch Rhonda Byrne's 2006 movie *The Secret.* The movie explains that we attract into our lives what we concentrate on, which is another reason for transforming negative thoughts and emotions into positive ones. When our mind fixates on an unobtainable love interest, other possibilities are prevented from happening. Related to this, you must be able to envision what you are going to do before you do it. If you can't picture yourself going up and talking to that attractive woman, you will never do it. You need to identify and eliminate these mental blocks.

As the movie demonstrates, even though we may attract incredible opportunities, we need to act on them right away. Do not let having no idea what you are going to say or do stop you. Once you see your big break, make the decision that you are going to act now. Making the decision to act forces you to ignore any little voices inside your head telling you to stay in your shell. Woody Allen says, "Ninety percent of success is showing up." For

the love-shy this means showing up where that person is standing and opening your mouth. Something will come out.

Do not preoccupy yourself with your shortcomings when you pass up a super moment that seemed like a gift from the gods. *But the universe put this great opportunity in my lap, and I blew it. Aren't I thumbing my nose at the universe and God?* Sure, everyone would have been a lot happier if you had hooked up, but it's not the end of the world. God is a kind and patient God who created this world for us to have a place to learn and make mistakes. Likewise, the impersonal universe just did what it was commanded; produce romantic situations for you. It will continue doing so. The river always flows whether you drink from it or not.

An Australian describes what love-shy anxiety does:

> Last year after months of her giving me hints, a girl from one of my classes took me to a quiet place. She took my hand and said, "my hand and my heart." I did nothing. I was speechless. A million things went through my head. My heart was beating rapidly, and I turned red. Seconds turned to minutes. Eventually she let go of my hand and walked away.

I label some instances of this inaction "non-existence." The inability to think and act characterizes moments of non-existence. In similar situations I would completely black out mentally and not realize I was supposed to make a move right then. This state of mind is one in which you expect other people to live your life for you, such as setting up social situations for you. Notice whenever you fall into living vicariously through other people. When you talk with a woman are you looking at the ground or at her eyes? Some attribute this problem to a lack of valuation of oneself. Whatever it is, once it happens you're a goner. When the woman of my dreams in so many words extended her hand in marriage to me and all I could do was just sit there because my mind was blank, it shows the insidiousness of this problem. Talk

about a single misstep having life-altering consequences! Even being in love with a woman who wants me could not overcome the perfect storm of my love-shyness. And nobody, especially me, could understand it.

For many of you shys out there, you are too nice. You suffer from Nice Guy Syndrome. When you tell a date she is the most beautiful girl in the place, and she responds with, *You are the nicest guy in the place,* you have been shot down. With both barrels. A women telling you that you're nice is like saying that an obese person has a great personality. Of course, acting nice is an admirable trait, but don't let it interfere with your understanding of and action with the mating ritual. When it comes to taking physical romantic action, such as kissing her, do not ask, just do. Your self-confidence will prove more attractive than your sending a tentative message of low self-esteem.

While women's liberation is well and good, the movement can easily confuse a love-shy and lead him deeper into Nice Guy Swamp. When women protest against date rape and sexual assault, their message is for the overly aggressive guys on the complete opposite end of the spectrum to you passive males. But love-shys take the message to heart as it confirms that their seduction beliefs are correct in that men are too aggressive. *See, the women say so.* Do not fall for it. As a male, assertiveness is a requirement for romance. Acting assertively means not asking cravenly for permission. A woman gives off signs either showing her interest or lack thereof. Clouded by their own desires, men may misread the negative signs, so men need to know when *No means no.*

To combat sexual assaults a few colleges in the United States have explicit rules requiring men to ask permission before kissing or having sex with a female student. Unfortunately, these rare extreme measures serve to confuse love-shys instead of empowering them. Rather than college, the workplace has become the microcosm for society where what is acceptable for male–female interaction is spelt out exactly, but there is no need to take this to the extreme. Although women have a right to protection from

harassment, this does not mean you cannot flirt with coworkers. Flirting is not harassment. If it is, then what you are doing or your definition of it is wrong. Continued persistence is not proper either if your actions have been continuously and solidly rebuffed. Unless a workplace obsession makes you crazy and out of touch with reality, you should be sexing it up at work. Make it a goal to reprogram your coworkers to see you as a sexual person, even if you're not attracted to anyone at work.

Dr. Robert Glover wrote an excellent book in 2000 dealing with Nice Guy Syndrome called *No More Mr. Nice Guy.* This book resonated strongly with many in my love-shy support circle. Since most of you men fall into this category, you will appreciate this book. Perhaps one can think of love-shyness as an extreme form of Nice Guy Syndrome. Dr. Glover observes the following characteristics of nice guys. They are conditioned to seek the approval of others. They avoid conflict and upsetting others. They strive to do everything "right" and hide their perceived flaws and mistakes. They do not feel safe being masculine or acting like a man, and they disassociate themselves from other men and their own masculine energy. If you wonder why misogynistic jerks get plenty of women while a nice guy like you is forever lonely, you need to read this book. Women want an assertive male. Of course, you should still be polite, respectful and kind. I conclude that powerlessness due to love-shyness causes passive-aggressiveness. Possibly, your perceived lack of self-worth causes you problems, because you seek the approval of women before acting. Your judgment of your worth is what matters. So you better believe you are truly worth it, whether or not that woman at the bar the other night seemed to think so.

Love-shys should practice becoming more assertive in all areas of their lives. Do not let your feelings that you are acting rudely stop you. In fact, do something minor that is assertive (not necessarily a good idea at work) that may even cause people to think of you as abrasive. Such exercises can help desensitize you from worrying about being overly polite, just as doing something

intentionally embarrassing in public can lessen your fears of embarrassment by showing that the sky isn't going to fall when you make a social mistake. Almost anything you do is going to upset somebody somewhere. However, rudeness is not a requirement of assertiveness and is something one should try to avoid. Read Pilinski (2003) to affirm the difference between a frustrated, callous loser and a confident, high-status man. If on the road to recovery you pass through an "asshole stage," then so be it. Once you have broken through the barrier of not worrying what other people may think, then you can work on the proper balance of politeness and assertiveness. Act assertive for assertiveness' sake, not out of stress or desperation.

Many of you, especially those with Asperger's, need to analyze your "loneness mentality." While spending some time alone has healthy benefits for everyone, obviously, love-shys take it to the extreme. Most of the time you probably don't want to be alone, but you are. Making yourself uncomfortable being alone, at least in certain respects, can force you to get out of the house. At least observe your actions and thought processes that make you alone and antisocial. For example, a defeatist attitude ends up sinking you and keeps you by yourself. *Oh, it's OK if I'm by myself the whole day.* Or, *I don't really need to talk to that woman at the bar over there, I'll just go home and masturbate.* Go over and talk to her, and then when she shoots you down go home and… Even if you just stand quietly in a corner, being in the presence of people is still better than being alone.

Ultimately, you need to make peace with your aloneness. In the *Osho Zen Tarot* (Sarito 1994) Zen Master Osho writes:

> When there is no "significant other" in our lives we can either be lonely, or enjoy the freedom that solitude brings… [B]e aware of how you are choosing to view your "aloneness" and take responsibility for the choice you have made… [T]here is a tremendous difference between lone-

> liness and aloneness… Loneliness is the absence of the other. Aloneness is the presence of oneself. (pp. 20–21)

The *Osho Zen Tarot* book also states:

> [A]ll of us at one time or another might feel that the only way to survive is to close off our feelings and emotions so we can't be hurt again. If the pain is particularly deep, we might even try to hide it from ourselves. (p. 122)

You must be constantly on guard so that your thoughts and feelings do not lead you astray and back down the path of isolation.

Intimate Connections (Burns 1995) superbly deals with shyness and loneliness. My big epiphany while reading this book was that it's OK to be alone. You have to be able to love yourself totally before you can love others and expect others to love you. From the book:

> The belief that you need a loving partner before you can feel happy and secure is one of the major causes of loneliness… Learning to like and love yourself is the key to intimacy… The more needy and desperate you are, the more likely you are to get rejected. (p. 29)

When it finally didn't matter anymore whether I was alone or not, that's when I obtained nirvana. This is not to say that you should have no need for a significant other. Studies prove that married people enjoy better health and well-being than singles. Just don't make having an intimate relationship a requirement for your happiness.

To conclude this chapter, consider that love-shys tend to look too far in the future. Some women give a guy their phone number and already he is thinking about marriage. Play it one step at a time. It helps to put yourself in the other person's shoes. What are they expecting from the relationship right now? What is the

normal course of events at this stage in the relationship? On a related note, I used to think about every word I was going to say for a future conversation. By the time the actual conversation happened, since I had already gone over it in my head I had lost much of the enthusiasm. Plan ahead and act realistically, but don't live in the future. Enjoy the voyage, appreciate the scenery and don't focus solely on the destination. Overcoming love-shyness requires opening up a variety of battlefronts, so don't become overwhelmed by the size of the task. Each journey starts with a single step. By constantly making forward steps, no matter how small, you get to that incredible destination.

Notes

1. Adams, D. (1979) *The Hitchhiker's Guide to the Galaxy.* New York: Harmony Books.
2. *New York Times* (2007) "51% of women are now living without spouse." June 16, pp. A1, A18.
3. Masters, W. H. and Johnson, V. E. (1970) *Human Sexual Inadequacy.* New York: Little, Brown and Company.
4. Rowe, C. (2007) "The sexual male, part two: Are we not boys?" *Playboy*, June. p. 100.

Chapter 3

Get Out There

The eyes have it

When it comes to interacting with a potential romantic partner, the importance of every little nuance of movement and body language is amplified. *Is she moving her tongue around her lips because she had some food there, or is she flirting with me?* Probably both. On a date each person looks for clues indicating that the other is truly, naturally, significantly interested in and compatible with him or her. Each looks for positive signals based on the actions of the other person. Anything ranging from conscious thoughts to completely subconscious processes produces these actions, so love-shys must make sure all levels of their being function properly.

Shy people compete at a distinct disadvantage during courtship, because their shy-based actions signal non-interest in the other person. Even for love-shys not generally very shy, during a date their shyness can reemerge and affect mundane actions they usually perform quite normally. Yet for most love-shys their non-

romantic life displays aspects of shyness, some quite subtle. One of the most identifiable indications of shy people is their lack of eye contact as shy people commonly look away from those to whom they talk. Do not underestimate the importance of eye contact regarding human mating.

The eyes have been known as the windows to the soul. Even though objectively, shifting eyes and looking away may not mean much, the other person tends to perceive these actions as indications that the person is lying. Looking away when talking to a potential romantic partner is deadly. Not focusing your gaze on the person indicates that you are not interested in the person. It shows that not only are you are not interested in the person herself, but you aren't even interested in her body, especially if your eyes keep wandering around to others in the room. When your other typical love-shy reactions piggyback onto your lack of focus, you have no chance.

People on the autism spectrum, even if not shy, are noticeable for having a hard time looking at the person with whom they are talking. This looking away is usually attributed to information overload, as the person with autism or Asperger's cannot simultaneously formulate their thoughts and process incoming complex facial information. Next time you have a chance to look someone in the eyes for more than a second, notice all the information and impressions you take in. If you have problems with eye contact, start by continuously looking at the head of the person with whom you are speaking, and it will put both of you in a better light.

If you just look down at her legs or feet, this is bad. Looking away from someone, and especially looking down, signifies submissive behavior. For a woman, if a guy is already talking to you, averting your eyes may be acceptable behavior for a while if you are holding up your part of the conversation. For a man, however, it is toxic. Men should appear as dominant and, therefore, unafraid to make eye contact. Pilinski stresses the importance of eye contact and mentions the shy salesman trick of focusing on the bridge of nose of the other person, so the person doesn't notice the lack of actual eye contact. While using this trick in a pinch is OK, it becomes a useless crutch as you learn to walk properly. There is no substitute. You must make real eye contact.

Luckily, making eye contact is simple with no hidden techniques to learn. You can easily practice anywhere there are people, and you can pat yourself on the back for any little improvements. Maintaining eye contact while talking with someone can be both distracting and stressful. Your assignment is to make as much eye contact for as long as possible with as many people as you can. This activity is necessary practice so that when that important situation happens, it will be second nature as you dreamily fall into the eyes of your lover. Make eye contact with every person you talk to directly. Talking to a group of people? Switch around and maintain eye contact for some seconds with each person who listens to you.

Making long eye contact may be one of the most important simple steps for overcoming shyness in general. Not getting nervous when people "see into your soul" strikes at the heart of shyness. This takes time and effort. Work at it until you're usually the one maintaining eye contact longer than the other person. Self-esteem and self-acceptance and other important personal issues come into play in this action. If you can't confidently inhabit your own skin and clothes, you aren't going anywhere. After doing this action with acquaintances, you may be surprised when they stop thinking of you as shy—*they ain't seen nothing yet*—and respect you both as a good speaker and a good listener. When people have positive assumptions about you, they expect you to succeed and will treat and help you accordingly.

Walk down the street and make eye contact with everyone you can. When you make eye contact you make a type of deep interpersonal connection not normally present. You build this kind of connection during courtship. *Yes, I sensed a deep connection with him. I don't really know why.* Consider almost all eye contact a positive thing. Of course, if you glare at someone like you want to kill

him or her, that's not positive. Also, people become uncomfortable when you continuously stare at them. Making positive eye contact forces you to be in a good mood. Be happy and confident. How much eye contact a person makes says a lot about him or her. How much eye contact strangers make with each other walking down the street says much about society.

Walk around in public and make eye contact with everybody while at the same time smiling at them. Notice how smiles are contagious as even some people in bad moods or those not wanting anything to do with you will still crack a brief smile. This reaction is more than politeness. Try both an open mouth and a closed mouth smile with different people. Notice how most people copy your exact type of smile. Humans are mimicking creatures. We can't help but copy what we see others doing. If you want people to smile and look at you, do the same to them. Some people take this exercise to the next level by saying, *Hi* to everyone on the street or at least the ones they find attractive. I recommend only verbally greeting the ones who actually make eye contact with you. The more this exercise seems out of your comfort zone, the more urgently you need to do it. Smiling is important, because it sets the other person at ease. When someone looks at you repeatedly, if he or she smiles it signifies that he or she is sincerely interested in you at some level and doesn't think you look goofy or weird.

If your eye contact, smiling and saying, *Hi* has people looking at you funny, think about the strangeness of the situation that a love-shy has to show the world how to interact with people in a positive way. You will begin to notice how so many people won't make eye contact with you, because they stay in their own little world. They walk like it's raining and only concern themselves with getting to their destination. Instead of acting this way, observe your surroundings at all times, which opens you up to more possibilities.

Normally there is no such thing as too much eye contact as long as you do not stare. If the person doesn't like it, all he or

she has to do is look away. For you women, though, if you make prolonged eye contact with a man, it means you like him and want him to come over and talk to you. Don't make extended eye contact with a man you don't want to talk to. If he does start talking to you, you can always brush him off.

All initial interaction with someone you're attracted to starts with the eyes. Pilinski (2003) explains this well and even diagrams ideal contact and look-away times (pp. 117–120). As a basic rule, hold your gaze longer than you instinctively would but not continuously. Lowndes (1996) also discusses eye contact as the important first step of the mating ritual. Although the male is most likely to be the initiator, the woman usually first chooses the man with her eyes. For you women, it's simple. You find a guy attractive, so you look at him. For most women instincts take over, and I think they can't help but look at the guy they find most interesting. This eye contact turns a guy on.

Knowing and using this basic concept of eye contact can keep you from making any cold sales pitches. By only going over and talking to someone with whom you have made positive eye contact, your chance of rejection decreases markedly. Positive eye contact means more than just a brief look at you as you walk into the room. Depending on the situation, at least two or three glances likely mean the person finds you interesting. This positive eye contact should arm you with the confidence to approach her. Even if she is already with some guy, if she is giving you long and multiple looks, she wants you to go over and talk to her. It could be that the guy she's with is some loser who just came over and started talking to her. When the guy leaves to go to the bathroom make your move. This action takes more balls than you have right now, but you need to understand the power of eye contact. Women understand it requires courage to approach them, so they give you the eye contact to go by. Ultimately, you will need to have the ability to start up conversations with women who haven't noticed you, but for now you have plenty to work with.

After prolonged eye contact, and, I hope, smiling and flirting at the same time, you must either go over and talk to her or stop staring. Of course, the biggest problem love-shy men have is that they don't take action at the proper time—or any action at all. Guys, your window of opportunity for responding to a woman's overtures is quite narrow. All it takes to stop you is for your anxiety to start putting distracting and doubtful thoughts into your head. Ignore these negative thoughts. *Those who hesitate are lost.* Hesitation signifies weakness, indecision and lack of confidence. Think of eye contact as ringing a doorbell. If she answers the door by making positive eye contact and perhaps subtle flirting, then you must start talking to her right then. You can't just stand on her porch with her holding the door open with you thinking about what to say or even if you should say anything. Go over and start talking to her. It usually doesn't matter so much what you say at first, but that you actually move your feet that short distance and open your mouth and talk.

If you don't start talking to her in a reasonable amount of time, she will shut the door. FOREVER. Do not pause, because that increases the incertitude in your brain. The basic rules of going after someone are simple: 1. Make eye contact. 2. When serious positive eye contact is made, go over and talk to her. That's it. It's simple to state, but seemingly impossible for a love-shy to do.

Perhaps due to their inborn temperament, love-shys avoid risk. You will rarely see a love-shy in a casino, no matter how much innate card counting or odds computing ability they possess. Starting any relationship involves risk, and with romantic relationships all the more so. As any entrepreneur will tell you, making money involves taking risks. Likewise, starting a real relationship requires risk on your part. The size of the reward is proportional to the risk. Sure hitting on that drop-dead gorgeous model will most likely result in rejection, but what if you get a positive response from her? You might end up with her as a girlfriend! If you think that you could never have such a woman for a girlfriend, notice your absolutist negative thinking. I've heard that a surprising number of models and centerfolds complain about a lack of dates, because men are too certain of rejection to approach them. You must invest in the relationship. Eventually, you will invest time, money and emotions in the venture, but the first investment always involves the risk of rejection. There is no shortcut or sneaking around the back to avoid it. The entrepreneur and the gambler risk real money. You merely face rejection and most likely with a person whom you will never see again. So what's the big deal?

The anxiety is real. But is it related to the risk? If that beautiful model politely turns you down, so what? You will certainly not have been the only one to have been rejected by her. Unfortunately, when you find that person who appears to be your ideal mate, then your anxiety will totally shut you down. Those special few with whom the stakes are so high produce your killer anxiety. It's the difference between placing a $10 bet versus a $1000 bet. The game may be the same, but you are so much more nervous when the stakes are high.

Some people play high-stakes poker well, but most cannot. Yet all you risk when initiating a conversation is rejection and perhaps the price of a drink or two. You must learn not to take rejection personally. You are trying to find a compatible mate. Think of it like playing the children's card game of Go Fish. Take her rejection of you at near the same emotional level as her telling you to *Go fish; there was no match.* Ironically for me, the actual rejection, especially from a woman I barely know, often doesn't bother me much. It's the not going for it that can eat me up inside for weeks afterwards when I thought I was making tangible progress with my love-shyness. You must take the risk.

Why do women always sit in groups and rarely go anywhere, even the bathroom, alone? That makes it much harder to approach them. Women are social creatures and are concerned with their safety. It can seem like they intentionally increase the effort a man needs to expend to talk to them. They raise the bar. They circle the wagons. Instead of starting up a conversation with one strange

woman, you have to do it with many at once. This tack helps keep the riff-raff away. It also keeps the shy guys away.

Once you receive positive eye contact signals from a woman in a group, do not be daunted by the task. Break it down into steps. First, you must break into their conversation. Depending on the situation these women may be quite open to meeting men and could just be making small talk while waiting for men to approach them. They will usually give you some latitude. Although if they appear in serious conversation, you probably want to pause. Once you walk over there, you must start talking soon even if they don't initially acknowledge you. Raise your voice a bit without shouting and address the group as a whole. Start with some pleasantries such as asking what they've been up to this evening or how they all know each other. It's better if you talk with one of the more outgoing women first to ensure a decent conversation. Then, focus on the one you fancy, perhaps with a compliment, and work into a one-on-one conversation with her. If she is in a big group, it's usually easier to break away and converse with just her. By addressing the whole group first, you show good manners by not ignoring them. The opinions of her friends may make or break it for you, so treat them well, possibly by buying drinks for everybody, even if you can't remember all their names. If there are men in the group, do not let that stop you. The strategy remains the same and can be easier because you may have a better chance of connecting with a common group interest.

For women the risk is more about just being out and presenting yourself. As a woman, do what you can to make it easier for that shier guy to approach you. Occasionally distance yourself from the group and walk over to the jukebox or whatever so you are more by yourself. Or go to the bathroom alone, so a man will have an easier chance with your friend.

Nothing ventured, nothing gained. Recall all the stories about inventors and entrepreneurs who failed many, many times before achieving success. What's the worst that can happen? Realistically,

the only thing that works is actually approaching women and getting turned down. Repeatedly.

Now that you have an idea of how to approach a group of women, I hope that going up to a single one will seem easy. By using your eyeballs to check someone out first and waiting for a positive response from her peepers, you minimize the hazard of rejection.

Have a life

As a love-shy you may think the only requirement for overcoming your condition is having the ability to approach women whom you find seriously attractive. That only those few precious minutes when that opportunity arises with the woman of your dreams matter. Unfortunately, you can't focus on a single moment that may happen once a month or so. You must concentrate on all aspects of your life all the time. Otherwise, when you finally emerge from your cave, you will be out of sync with the world. When the time comes to go over and talk to that beautiful woman and you haven't spoken a word to anyone for a day or two, the shock will be too great to allow anything to flow smoothly out of your mouth. If you can actually make conversation with her that leads to a date, likely she will not be impressed with you if there is very little else going on in your life. Not having friends or ever doing much outside of your apartment are big-time turn offs. Besides, how are you going to meet people if you don't get out?

If you don't have any friends or hobbies that facilitate meeting single members of the opposite sex, you are left with going to bars and nightclubs to meet people. Nothing is wrong with bars and pubs per se, and I certainly recommend them as classrooms for learning social skills. However, it has been my experience that the chance of meeting in a bar a quality person with whom you can have a serious, long-term relationship is remote. Also, bars tend to be high-anxiety places for love-shys. Love-shys need to get to know someone more slowly and deeply rather than the way that's required in a loud, meat-market nightclub.

You need to get out and do things with people all the time. Well, not every waking moment, but certainly much more than you do now. Our modern world offers so many opportunities that it seems a shame to let them all slip by. Besides, getting out boosts your mood. It's hard to feel depressed and suicidal when you are out interacting with people. Maintain a typical sleep schedule to allow you more chances at interfacing with people and to make you appear normal.

You need to do more than take a community college class one day of the week, especially if you do not work full time. You need to set a goal to do something every day with social interaction. Look at your calendar and plan something for every day of the week. Ideally, these daily activities will include friends, or at least acquaintances who share common interests. Studying your calendar gets you planning for the days and weeks ahead and gets you thinking about what needs to be done to fill each day. The activities do not necessarily have to focus on meeting available people of the opposite sex. The point is to get out there. Then, the opportunities with women become much more likely to happen and are more natural and spontaneous. If you find you haven't done anything social by the end of a day, go to the corner bar and have one drink. Or call up your brother or an old friend on the phone. By setting this goal of daily interaction, you work towards it. If you work it, the process will snowball and will soon require much less effort. Those weekend nights should now start filling up with dates.

Start by filling in your day planner with some physical activities. If right now you don't do much in the way of physical fitness, this inactivity needs to change. Exercise rewards you in numerous ways. Besides the obvious benefits of getting in shape and looking better, physical exertion helps you emotionally and mentally. *Shadow Syndromes* (Ratey and Johnson 1997) states, "A growing body of evidence links aerobic exercise to sharpened memory,

faster response times, elevation of mood, increased self-esteem" (pp. 351–352). The authors believe that during exercise one feels in complete control of one's body, therefore anxiety, which relates to feelings of loss of control, decreases. My physician claims that a daily workout regime improves one's mood by the equivalent of one antidepressant drug.

Fitness options abound these days. Almost any type of sport you can imagine is available. And the gyms, or fitness centers as they are called these days, are amazing. Not only do the good ones have four different types of treadmills and three different types of machines to work your triceps, but these clubs offer various classes from yoga to hip hop dance. Talk about an excellent place to meet people of the opposite sex. But be warned: most women are sick of getting hit on at the gym.

Getting started with an exercise program is usually the hardest part. Once your body gets used to the exercise, your body will crave it. Start easy and build up to more intense workouts. I find it necessary to have a goal to work towards, even if only an appearance goal like losing fifteen pounds or having washboard abs. You have to figure out what motivates you. For some it's the scales, for others the mirror. For some it's passing mile markers or hitting a maximum bench press. For some it's the feeling. Search out a routine that you look forward to and can be proud of. If appropriate, include weight loss as part of this goal. Weight loss in and of itself offers numerous physical, emotional and social benefits.

For women who are too self-conscious to train in front of men, try starting with a membership at a smaller women-only club and then switching to a more popular health club once you feel more confident.

Yoga classes are a superb way to meet women who are into fitness and healthy living. I highly recommend martial arts training, which will help you on many levels. Besides the increased fitness and flexibility, knowing self-defense builds serious confidence. Plus, you learn an art handed down for centuries. Perhaps

most importantly for men, such training helps one move and act in a more masculine manner. Don't worry about your age or that you don't have the perfect body shape as most programs are for anyone, and they are great places to meet in-shape, focused men and women. It helps to be in decent shape before you begin martial arts, but you can always start on a less strenuous path like Tai chi. Tai chi and yoga work well to reduce stress. While not much of a cardio workout, the Feldenkrais Method focuses solely on body awareness, and those on the autism spectrum and others who don't seem to have complete control of their bodies may find it quite helpful.

Whatever physical activity you choose, do something enjoyable to make sure your behind gets off the couch and your eyes separate from the screen. If you don't have the money for health club dues, buy a pair of running shoes or a second-hand bicycle and go out and use them. Don't buy a treadmill or other equipment for your apartment, because a big reason for exercising is to get out. If you never played a team sport growing up, why not start now? With all the many possibilities of adult leagues for any fitness and ability level, I won't begin to list them. Earn double or triple points by organizing after-work soccer games with your coworkers. Being physically fit sends many positive messages to the opposite sex. It shows that you are active, take care of your body and do what it takes to make yourself look good.

On a related note, you must lose that pale, deathly skin tone. I don't mean going to a tanning salon. Instead, get outside and be active, even if you go for a walk or lie in the sun by yourself in the park. For those of you with sun sensitivities, go out later in the day and buy dark sunglasses. The ancient Egyptians knew the power of the sun, the energy source for all life on earth. Bright lighting, and sunlight particularly, improves one's mood, as those who suffer from seasonal affective disorder during dark winters can attest. Ultraviolet rays from the sun power our bodies' conversion of cholesterol into vitamin D, which has important health benefits. Be careful: put on sunscreen, avoid the midday sun and never stay out so long that you burn. A healthy tan shows that you do stuff outdoors, and a golden tan really improves your looks. Just start slowly and don't overdo it.

I don't wear headphones when out jogging or bike riding, because I like to fully experience my surroundings. While listening to music when exercising helps to motivate and maintain a rhythm, a Walkman or an iPod works to tune out the rest of the world, making it hard for someone to approach you. That said, do not let headphones discourage you from starting up a conversation with a person wearing them. Just make sure you get her attention first, perhaps both visually and verbally. Wait until she has removed her ear buds, paused her music and is looking at you before you start the actual conversation. Do not be surprised if she starts talking loudly if she was listening to loud music. During the conversation you can ask what she is listening to.

Some of you may have the mindset that you need to get over your love-shyness or at least lose your virginity before you can really start making friends and doing stuff. *I want to have a fresh start so that no one knows the old me. How can I have any friends that will respect me when I don't even respect myself? I'm too depressed and embarrassed to associate with other people.* The problem with this state of mind is that you will never start. Do not wait until you have achieved perfection before you start to have a life. You get that perfect life by building it one piece at a time. You become that complete person by having a life. Your shyness and love-shyness tell you not to embark on social endeavors. You must fight these tendencies by doing things and making friends. Even if you have no one to go with, do not let that stop you from doing things and having fun. Some loners don't like doing things alone in public that they perceive people do not do by themselves, such as eating out. Get over it. Almost all places will accept and accommodate you. Most restaurants have counters or bars where singles can eat. You don't necessarily have to drink alcohol while eating at the bar, and you might strike up an interesting conversation with a person sitting by you.

Most love-shys like myself have few if any friends. While we may not care too much about not having a large social circle, the reasons for our lack of friends may correlate to reasons for our lack of romantic partners. Analyze where everyone in your life, aside from family, fits on the basic levels of relationships:

1 *Acquaintances.* Casual contacts like neighbors and most work colleagues. You know each other but exchanges are only polite or superficial and often you have no control over who they are.

2 *Companions.* Someone who accompanies you on activities. The activity is more important than the person.

3 *Friends.* Being with the person is more important than the activity. You are emotionally invested in the person and are there for the person in good times and bad.

4 *Romantic intimates.* A friend plus romantic and sexual intimacy.

If you place everyone in your life only in the acquaintances and companions categories, making the jump to having romantically intimate relationships may prove difficult if you aren't used to having friends. Think about what stops you from taking some of your acquaintance and companion relationships to the next level. You want a boyfriend or girlfriend with whom to be close and intimate, so practice having a close friend or two. Try to bond emotionally with your friends. Since your friends are likely not to be the typical macho males, you should find that once you open up they start opening up too. This advice includes having opposite-sex friends. If you can get over your romantic and sexual frustration, a platonic friend of the opposite sex can help with your love-shyness. For a man, doing stuff with a woman gives you valuable practice interacting with women, and she can offer a woman's perspective (and vice versa).

Unless you live in some small, remote village, your town bristles with opportunities for you to get out of the house and meet people. Take a foreign language class at your local community college. Not only will you learn a valuable skill, you actually have to speak in class. In a beginning class everyone acts shy, because they're trying to grasp the new language, so you'll fit right in. There are plenty of other classes at a decent community college to satisfy most interests from drawing to small engine repair. Perhaps taking one class may begin a renewed educational career. Almost every book for lonely people recommends volunteering as an easy way to meet people and socialize while giving something back to the community. Since love-shys are so needy and don't have many good vibes to spare, I suggest volunteering at events like benefit concerts where a few hours of work can give you free admission to the whole show. Meeting people while volunteering can eliminate problems associated with dating coworkers since one can easily stop volunteering at a particular location if the romance doesn't work out. Try to become involved in group tasks rather than spending most of your time alone.

If you are religious, the place of your religious worship can be a great place to meet and be with people. You will already have something in common with everyone. Furthermore, deepening your spirituality gives you a more positive outlook on life and allows for greater hope. Most larger churches these days have singles events. Sharing a similar view of the world is important for a serious long-term relationship. If you are a pagan or an atheist, or if your beliefs fall quite a bit outside mainstream religion, don't fake it. At least be realistic. Find an association that shares your beliefs. Whatever groups you go to, don't worry about not fitting in. Groups continuously look for more members, and they do whatever it takes to make a new person feel comfortable and welcome.

Even while your calendar fills up and you're getting out there and being social, you must do one more thing. You must participate in the "game." For each week that you don't have a date, receive a woman's phone number (or for you gals, give your number to a guy who asks) or go to any social situation with a possibility

of meeting someone special, you need to show that you actually play the mating game. This means going out to a nightclub, bar or disco. While you may not yet want to go to a "singles" bar, neither do you want to go to some little bar with just a few guys sitting around watching the game on the television. Most areas have plenty of choices, or at least someplace lively. It doesn't have to have a long line to get in or an outrageous cover charge, but you are obliged to dress up. Even if you have no friends to accompany you, still go.

By dressing up and going to a place where it's normal for people to meet future romantic partners, you are in the game. You are a player. No more sitting in the stands acting invisible. If when you get to the club, you realize that your uniform is wrong, still go in and participate. Although it will mark you as a first timer, in the clubbing world this is a not necessarily a bad thing. As long as you don't look too geeky, fresh blood, especially female, is welcome, and it shows that you get out and try new and different things. As you walk around the place making eye contact with as many members of the opposite sex as possible, observe their reactions. Use people's general reactions to gage where you fit on the status scale. No matter how romantically minded you are and how strongly you yearn for a soulmate, remember the mating game is an open market. People size you up in seconds and place you on their scale of desirability. I don't mean to sound crass, and it's not really as bad as it may sound. Darwinism and natural selection are a part of all life. At least, you've gone from the sidelines to the playing field.

Although I bet beginner's luck will shine on you, you have just started. Don't beat yourself up if you do not encounter initial success. The goal is to play and have fun. Do not expect to score right away, especially competing with a bunch of experienced players. Going out to a club should be fun. The best opportunities for romance seem to happen, not when you act like the singly focused bloodhound on the trail, but when you actually partici-

pate in life and enjoy yourself naturally. You have to set yourself up for such opportunities by going out to places.

Life builds on itself. On Monday morning when your coworker asks what you did over the weekend, you can tell him about the new club you went to. Your coworker may now think of you as cool and invite you to go out with him and his friends. The more you're doing, the less time you have to feel depressed, lonely and sorry for yourself. While your love-shyness may not exactly melt away when you get a life, much of the accompanying baggage will at least stay hidden. Quash your love-shyness and depression by being too busy to introspect about them.

Don't dwell on your love-shyness when out socializing. *The first rule of love-shy; never talk about love-shy.* You've tried to hide your love-shyness your whole life, so obviously this is nothing new to you. The newness for you is having a name for your condition and focusing on it and actively getting out there working to form connections with the opposite sex. You should not mention your love-shyness with a potential romantic partner, at least not until the relationship is solidly under way. That's one reason you go to a therapist and hang out with internet support groups; so that you don't have to talk about your love-shyness with women you're interested in.

If a date persists in learning about your romantic past, say something like, *I've been so drained and busy from work that I haven't had much chance to get out.* Or just, *It's been a while.* Try to act so cool, or at least somewhat normal, that she would never suspect you never had a girlfriend. Try to steer the conversation away from the topic. Admitting that you have never had a girlfriend is about as detailed as you should get. Truth is very important in a relationship, but wait until at least the third date to discuss characteristics of your life with love-shyness if she has pried on a previous date or if your obvious quirks are beginning to add up. If this admission scares off some women, then they weren't right for you anyway.

Initial dates are sales pitches among other things, so minimize your negatives by avoiding mentioning your shyness and love-shyness and accentuate your plusses. It's not so much being superficial, but more like not jumping into the deep waters until you've gotten your feet wet in the shallows. You want to talk about yourself, so talk about the cool things in your life now that you have one. One big problem with love-shyness is that nobody else can really grasp it. Worse, the subject of love-shyness seems to turn most women off. On one first date I had with a woman whom I mistakenly told about my condition, she said she was shy briefly as a child but got over it. Everybody else wonders what is so wrong with you that you can't get over it. So, don't go there unless it's absolutely necessary. For Aspies who find it difficult to lie, think of it another way. Because you got a date, you are not cripplingly love-shy, at least temporarily.

However, mentioning your shyness may be good, because it will help your date understand you better. Some women may find your shyness charming and heartwarming, especially if they have previously witnessed you as loud and confident when you expound to a group on a topic you know well. Since women are generally shier and more passive, they may have a hard time recognizing even severe shyness in men. Perhaps my advice on not talking about love-shyness is more about how to appear normal to a date and may not be the best way to cope during the early stages along the recovery pathway. If your date is likely love-shy also, is it appropriate to diagnose her on a date? Probably not, since a date is not the place to deal with heavy topics such as a medical or psychological diagnosis, and you have no idea how she may take it. Just understand the large difference between briefly mentioning your shyness compared with dwelling on your love-shyness, explaining how it ruined your life and so forth. Mention your shyness, your Asperger's or your lack of experience, but stay clear of the love-shy topic if you can help it. Don't act like you are hiding something, or you will fail to build important trust.

Your date wants to know you and your conditions in order to understand what she is dealing with. But do not explain your love-shyness with the hope that your date will feel sympathetic and allow you to bypass required romantic actions. It doesn't matter how much the other person understands about your love-shyness. For a romantic relationship to happen, each must play certain roles naturally without explicit coaching from the other. Also, by stating to someone you are love-shy or even shy, you define yourself as such to that person, and both of you will act out roles in the relationship based on that definition.

If you really feel the need to talk about your love-shyness, do so with family, relatives and close friends. Not only does talking about it help these people, who may have known you your whole life, to understand you, but it helps you come to terms with it. By discussing it openly, you come to fully accept it in yourself and lose the embarrassment that comes with the condition. Your confidantes may even help you in ways you can't currently imagine. It's possible some of your siblings, parents or relatives have a touch of love-shyness too, so talking about yourself can open their eyes to themselves. If it's obvious to you that a certain family member is love-shy, you can mention it to that person and offer to give him or her this book when you are done with it. Be ready to accept that most people live in denial and will not readily accept your amateur diagnosis. Just keep talking to them about yourself and the ways that love-shyness forced your past actions and what you are doing to overcome it.

Monitor your social health to watch out for falling off the wagon and back into social isolation. Especially after you've been sick, work to climb back on. Just because you have initial failures and your new companions don't call you, don't give up. Friendship is a two-way street. Take the initiative and call them. People have busy lives, and their new friends and companions may fall by the wayside if you do not take action and contact them. If you finally get a date and it goes poorly, remember that it's only the first of many.

By having a life, you are not needy. Appearing and acting needy turns people, even your closest friends, off you. By having a life your social status increases significantly and things seem to fall into place. The hardest part is getting started and sticking with it. *Life is short. Play hard.* Confidence is knowing you're out there playing the game.

Be a life

Now that you're satisfying the bare requirements for having a life, let's move on to more advanced stuff. Although you may be getting out and hanging out with different people and having good times, the real question becomes *Where are good places to meet eligible women (or men)?* The answer is everywhere. No matter where you go, keep your eyes open. People are all around and who knows what opportunities may arise. This means that every time you walk out the door, you should be looking good. Not necessarily dressed to the nines, but at least clean-shaven and appropriately, or slightly better, dressed for your destination.

Think beyond the bar. Many people go to the bar because they're lonely. Thus, these people may be desperate. *Sounds familiar?* Going out to the bar is a time to escape the grind of normal life. Usually this means consuming alcohol, which affects both your judgment and the judgment of the person whom you come on to. These things tend to start the relationship off on the wrong foot. Your background of relatedness becomes one of partying, which is a weak basis for a relationship. For example, if one of you has a serious drug problem, the other is more likely to find it acceptable. Such problems only lead to other problems. Therefore, work to meet people in more "normal" environments.

The good news is that women have their guard down much more during the course of their regular day compared to when they are in a nightclub full of men. The bad news is that it takes more effort on your part to overcome your anxieties when approaching women in everyday places, especially if you haven't first drained a couple glasses of "liquid courage." Thinking that women are not expecting to be approached will make you more nervous. If they are single, most are looking for, or at least open to, meeting someone. Of course, unlike while in a bar, many people are busy and hurried, but don't let this discourage you. Go places where people are more relaxed.

With the popularity these days of coffeehouses and cafes, start there. Bring a laptop, newspaper or book (*not this one, you idiot*) and relax with your favorite beverage. Do not become dismayed if the person you are attracted to seems deep into what she is doing. She may be doing exactly what you are; keeping busy while hoping to meet someone special. After all, she could be doing what she is doing at home, but no, she wanted to get out somewhere with people. So, after some eye contact go over and make conversation. The tack is to be friendly. Sometimes it's her reactions to seemingly mundane questions that help you tell how interested she is in you. Once you start up a conversation, she will normally soon drop hints about her availability status. If she is younger without kids assume she is available. If she is older, find out if she is a single by flat-out asking. If she is married or in a serious relationship, keep talking to her for a bit anyway. You're just being friendly, making casual conversation, so don't appear as someone who came there to get laid. Cafes are decent, inexpensive places to escape your house and hang out.

Other places such as the grocery store can seem like impossibly difficult places to meet people. If you see that her shopping cart is mostly empty like yours, then at least you can figure she is single and living alone. Perhaps start a conversation around a particular food item. Going to more specialty or unique stores gives you something to relate to with her. Where you meet says a lot about the other person and what kind of relationship you're going to have. Where we shop and hang around constitute parts of our environment and say much about who we are. Therefore, employ your taste in a positive way.

Approaching a woman in a store is not easy, even for many non-love-shys. I think one factor preventing me from pursuing women in stores is my Asperger's controlling me to follow the typical script for what to do in those places. Counteract this undesirable programming by routinely talking to women. You can start by practicing starting up conversations with anyone in the store just for the sake of talking. You have to use some judgment. Does the woman feel safe? Is it an inappropriate time or situation? Some women will not respond at all to men while riding crowded public transportation, in the doctor's waiting room or when they are working with the boss possibly watching.

Many of you shys may find such initial face-to-face interaction too distressing and want to retreat to the faceless internet. Likely, you've already tried at least one dating site and didn't have any luck. Reading this book and perhaps hearing about a hot, new dating site, you think your chances will improve. However, I am not a fan of internet dating sites and view them like bars: places to practice certain dating skills. For a male, the male/female ratio is much poorer than a typical bar. Worse, you can't get much of a read on someone from his or her profile. Of course, everyone likes *getting the most out of life* and *long walks on the beach*, even if they live nowhere near water. And who can trust the photos? By contrast, experiencing someone in person for 30 seconds or less is usually enough to determine how much of a relationship you want with him or her. Love-shys need the involvement with actual people to gain experience with things like body language. Using chat rooms to meet and carry on typed conversations is a step in the right direction, but they are limited. At least in a bar you know the gender of the person you are conversing with and his or her approximate age. Non-dating websites like www.meetup.com are great for finding local gatherings geared for particular interests, and in some cities there are meetups specifically for singles in their 20s or 30s.

Nevertheless, internet dating cannot be ignored. Many adults, especially women, tire of the bar scene, and some women prefer getting to know a man through email first. Email provides a good way for a shy man to express himself without the stress and anxiety of face-to-face interaction. Given these modern times and regardless of my age, perhaps I should be embarrassed for not having an account at Facebook, MySpace or whatever the popular social networking site is these days. However, important things like flirting and touching are absent over the internet, and love-shys can have problems figuring out how sexual to portray themselves in an email. Without the voice and facial expressions to accompany them, texted sexual innuendo can come across badly. Or love-shys can have the opposite problem and have their correspondence come across like job interview questions. Yet putting yourself out there and having a woman initiate contact or just interacting with women through email can give a lonely man a boost of confidence. Don't expect things to happen fast. Women are much more careful with people they meet online and take longer to set up an actual date than when meeting in person.

One older, experienced love-shy known as P.B. claims success with internet dating, at least as practice dating. He advises on an internet love-shy forum:

> Online dating success takes skill. Have a decent picture but don't write too much or be deep and grave. Keep it fun, light and just a few lines. If you go into your personal problems you will not get responses. Avoiding the herd is important. The best women I met had no picture on their profiles and were not inundated with responses as a result. They were not at all ugly and were less desperate than those with pictures, and I had hands down some of the best dates with these women. Some sites work much better than others. Matchmaker.com always got me good results. Cruising Yahoo clubs and similar boards that are not singles' sites give even better results. Do not reject women because they are ugly, older, have kids or live far

away. This is only practice, and I don't consider the web the place to meet The One.

Another love-shy male in his mid-20s claimed that he had his first romantic kiss and later, with a different woman, lost his virginity, both thanks to eHarmony.com. Though more expensive than other dating websites, eHarmony (www.eharmony.com) advertises a high female to male ratio and its contact process is more "love-shy friendly" than regular dating sites. Free dating sites exist, www.PlentyofFish.com being the best known. Keep a cautious eye out when using any dating site. Many male users suspect that up to half of female profiles on some sites are not real members and were put up to entice users to the site or to lure lonely men to give their email address to spammers.

Adult themed internet dating sites exist with the purpose of finding casual sex rather than romance. These sites usually have members who advertise themselves in semi-nude or nude poses. While these sites may entice love-shys with their seemingly easy way to use casual sex to bypass the pitfalls of romance, love-shys don't have the aptitude to beat out the nine or nineteen other guys for each woman. However, you earn love-shy experience points for subscribing to such a service and posting a profile with photo. The only way I see love-shys finding success with these sites is to act more truthfully by advertising their virginal nature. Since that type of approach is a rarity on these sites, you may have a reasonable chance. You might open yourself up to predators, or you might hook up with a woman who loves to teach ignorant men about sex. Stay alert for prostitutes who use adult sites to advertise subtly. Normally most love-shys won't go for them anyway, because they write things like, *Looking for discreet man to shower me with expensive gifts.* Casual sex internet dating is a long shot for love-shys, and they may do better searching for "shy dating sites" or "geek dating sites."

Speed dating may be a way to go. In about every large city these days, some type of speed dating exists, often occurring during lunch. With this set-up a number of single men and women get together and pair up briefly for a few minutes at a time. Then they record their attraction to each other and switch to other people. The facilitator tallies the participants' scores, and if two people both liked each other, they are given each other's contact information. While a good way for meeting a bunch of prospective dates easily and quickly, speed dating may overwhelm shys who take much longer than the average person to warm to someone. My experience shows that love-shys do poorly when placed in direct competition and do best in unique situations that Cupid seems to set up. At minimum, speed dating is good practice.

Combine your need to meet people with your need for any kind of help by enrolling in a self-help seminar. Dale Carnegie (www.dalecarnegie.com) is the classic and gives the average person tools to help with tasks hindered by shyness such as remembering names and speaking in front of groups. However, I much prefer Landmark Education (www.landmarkeducation.com). Both are decent places to meet people striving to improve themselves, and both have seminars in every major city. Landmark's main seminar, called the Forum, gives you technology that can really help your life. In it you will do exercises where, among other things, you will identify childhood incidents that programmed you to act in certain ways. However, simply recognizing such incidents does not prevent the incident's programmed consequences from affecting you today. You must work their techniques in order to gain power over your programming. Landmark gets a reputation for being cultish by using its participants as its advertising, but it works. The program even tells you the meaning of life. Just don't expect either seminar to cure your love-shyness.

Branch out and expand your horizons. As a love-shy, you lived a confining life. Now is the time to grow and blossom out of that narrow box. Dance lessons, whether ballroom, salsa or hip hop, are excellent for getting out and interacting with women. Plus, you learn a skill that women find quite attractive. Chances are you have done little in the way of stage performance.

Expressing yourself through a role can take your mind away from your problems and limitations as it becomes your character, not you, talking and doing. Some people with Asperger's find that acting lessons help them learn about body language. Joining an improv class takes acting a step further by requiring you to think on your feet. While joining a local amateur theatre troupe may seem like a huge leap, start small. Do you sing in the shower? Take it a step further and sing karaoke. Practice one song thoroughly alone and then go to karaoke night at the bar. Women love expressive men and will usually give you the benefit of the doubt if you sing off-key or flub a few words. Not into singing? Buy a used electric guitar. Being fully expressed is part of living life to its fullest.

Even without taking a class, you should still learn to dance. Dancing is an important form of self-expression. At home, learn to move to the music so you will feel comfortable on the dance floor. Your moves don't have to be fancy, just as long as you get out there. Don't miss out. These days what passes for dancing in the clubs often is more "dirty" dancing and can resemble a lap dance. No matter what your age, merely being on the floor and feeling suave will have sexy women dancing real close to you. If you sweat easily, pace yourself and only dance to a song or two at a time. Don't get carried away. As Romy Miller states in her small yet informative *Understanding Women: The Definitive Guide to Meeting, Dating, and Dumping, if Necessary* (2004), if you're a typical guy "you can't dance," so have the woman come to you (p. 131). Instead of trying to emulate the latest music video, Miller advises men to keep their moves minimal and "let her groove around you and keep your eyes on her" (p. 131). The one place with more women than men is on the dance floor, so take advantage of it. Even women not dancing will notice you. Are you going to be the guy who refuses to get off his butt even though a woman is pulling you to the dance floor?

You may be reluctant to approach a woman for fear of her boyfriend. While you might logically hold off for a minute or two to see if a boyfriend returns to the woman whom you fancy, do not let this terror shut you down. Your anxiety is doing the talking. Think, *What would a normal, well-adjusted man do in this situation?* If you go over and talk to a woman and her boyfriend comes over and you walk away, nothing will happen to you. You will have done a positive thing by acting like a normally assertive male. Deep down the boyfriend may even see it as positive because you confirmed that his woman is prized and sought after and he fended off competition with only his presence.

Don't be resigned to failure before you even start. As my father used to say, "Can't never did anything." Are you making assumptions of failure, which come from your shyness or love-shyness without any basis in reality? As Burns (1985) says in *Intimate Connections*:

> You may tell yourself, "I can't" or "I just *couldn't* do that." But this isn't true. What you really mean is "I don't *feel* like it" or "I don't *want* to because I'm not used to doing something like that and it seems scary." The problem with saying "I can't" is that you may begin to take this language seriously and believe that you really are paralyzed and hopeless when in fact you really aren't. (p. 87)

You have to alter reality. The world happens in a mechanical way, but your will and consciousness can change the outcome. The world may present an opportunity for you by having a stunning and compatible woman walk by you, but unless you generate an alternative reality and make a move, she will keep walking. You need to envision going after a woman like being an entrepreneur; you have to create the business from nothing. Just as you can't walk into a store and order up a long-term romance, an entrepreneur can't walk into some hypothetical store and tell them to create his business. Both of you have to start with only the dream and the willingness to take a risk. Both of you have to open your mouths to market something the world has little idea exists. As the advertiser you have to do most of the initial talking. *Never expect the other person to make the first move.* Do you act or do you react? *You* must take the initiative. A recent fortune cookie of mine sums it up: "Life is about making some things happen, not waiting for something to happen."

Get her phone number. Guys, never expect a woman to call you first. Giving her your phone number without getting hers is useless. Either you get her phone number or she isn't interested. On the rare chance that a woman does call a love-shy guy, the man may have no idea what to do when she calls. *Answer the phone* is the first proper action. Love-shys are notoriously phone averse. Just hearing the phone ringing or thinking the phone is ringing can unnerve me. It should go without saying that you should go out and buy a mobile phone if you do not yet own one, even if you don't really think you need one. Owning a mobile phone shows you are a person on the go with the need for immediate communication. Just remember to turn off the ringer during a date or while attending a performance. Since you probably won't be using it much, check out economical plans for limited use offered by many service providers.

Love-shys may also wait a long time before calling her. It's a constant debate regarding dating rules as to how many days to wait after you got her number before you call. Men may say that calling her too soon signals your desperation. For love-shys it is usually better to err on the side of appearing too eager. As a general rule, I suggest one or two days, or the first day after the weekend. For one thing, it eliminates the possibility that she has forgotten about you or that she waited for days for you to call and since you failed to, she crossed you off her list. The one or two day rule also shortens the period where you are all anxious anticipating making the phone call. Once you happen to get lucky, call her the day after you kissed or had sex for the first time or the day after a great first date. Even call the woman the day after a one-night stand where neither of you plan ever to see each other again. *Just making sure you got home OK.* These are important basic manners, folks. If she says she is going on a trip for two weeks, wait until she is back before calling. While she might be brushing you off, at least you showed that you listened to her and understood her schedule. By asking about her trip, you will have plenty to talk about.

As text messaging on phones becomes common, it may seem like an easy way to communicate with women. Even though many love-shys and autistics would rather type than talk, do not delude yourself. Initial romance-building conversations must be done verbally. Once the relationship is well grounded, she still wants to hear your voice. Save the texting for your buddies. When calling a woman for the first time, have a general idea of what you are going to say and have a specific plan for a date including when, where and how. Women are much more apt to respond to an exact request rather than something nebulous. For example, *How about meeting at Spago's for dinner at 6pm on Saturday?* is much better than, *How about you and I going out sometime?* An exact plan gives her something to work with and shows that you are a man of action and planning who knows exactly what he wants. Your plans should give her an understanding of what she should wear. Never try to set up a date at the last minute.

As with any phone call, be prepared to leave a message if the person does not answer. Even when calling a woman for the first time, leave a message so you don't act like some weirdo. With most people having caller ID these days, a bunch of calls without any message appears strange. Leaving a message places the ball in her court and leaves you off the hook from worrying when to try her next. The message can be fairly brief. Enunciate your number slowly, so her not hearing it properly does not stop her from calling you. Unless you already discussed a plan of going out, do not say in your message that you want to go out with her. Relationship escalation occurs in steps. By mentioning going out in the message, you have escalated it too early. You ask her on a date after you have talked on the phone with her. It does not have to be a long, intimate conversation, but it must be some conversation. If after leaving two messages a couple of days apart, she still hasn't returned your call, toss her number away and move on to the next one. She might eventually call you back once the family emergency or whatever is over, but don't count on it. If it feels like you are pulling teeth to obtain the slightest positive reaction from her, she is not into you, so move on.

Shadow Syndromes (Ratey and Johnson 1997) mentions that "all animals possess wired-in responses of submission to any animal strong enough to kill them" (p. 304). In the same vein, a socially ignorant male, who knows instinctively that most women can have their way with him, will naturally act submissive around women. Therefore, you need to work consciously to act dominant and confident. However, act as an alpha male, rather than as a "macho" man. An alpha male knows he is dominant and has nothing to prove, while the macho man feels the need to prove his worth by picking fights and insulting others. Yes, there are double standards, and you may think that a woman should like you as you are. But if you want to succeed at the game, you need to play by the rules. There are millions of people in this culture, so do not expect to change long-standing social-sexual rules.

Romance is a game. Women may tell small lies. They are just playing a role. Even though your goal is for a serious relationship, each of you still must play certain roles. Ideally, it should all come naturally, but for us, of course, it doesn't. Do not make the mistake of looking at it logically or trying to analyze it intellectually. Unlike chess, superior logic and strategy do not make you win the love game. How a woman feels emotionally about a male suitor is all that matters. This is where romance comes in.

One nuance of romance that many love-shys have trouble grasping is romantic tension. Romantic tension in the movies is obvious. Boy and girl meet by chance and hit it off. Will they eventually hook up? It makes you want to keep watching to find out what will happen. In romantic comedy movies, the romantic tension is the main force propelling the movie along. In real-world situations, it's much subtler yet is a necessary part of

developing a romantic relationship. Unfortunately, love-shys tend to short-circuit it. Never say to a date, *I'm not really good with this romance stuff.* No doubt romantic tension is elusive and hard to put a finger on. It's closely related to sexual tension, so think of it as such. It's the reason you don't ask to kiss her, you just do it at the right time, such as when she is looking at your mouth and not listening to you. (And no tongue until you have plenty of kissing experience with her.) Women often like spontaneity and surprises such as small gifts. You need to build up their emotions positively instead of diffusing them by asking questions about what to do romantically. Love-shys tend to be quite romantic at heart but clueless in the head.

Don't fall for the theme of all romantic movies that fate will bring your true love to you. Although fate may play a role, you must do work. On the subject of movies, note the three common occurrences in movies that never happen in real life: all phone numbers start with 555, when a guy walks into a bar he orders "a beer" rather than a specific brand and the leading lady kisses the guy. Once a relationship is underway the woman may initiate kissing (and more). But for the first kiss, the man generally initiates.

You must start the sexual tension as soon as possible, because most women like having male friends who are just friends. If you don't show her that you are sexually attracted to her from the start, you will fall into the dreaded "just friends" pit and will only confuse her and delay the inevitable rejection. Many women don't realise that some men can't express their true desires and want it all from women, not just platonic friendships. Although a slight over-generalization, a woman's male platonic friend is either love-shy, married, gay or not sexually interested in her, or else he would have been coming on to her early in the relationship. The romantic-sexual tension would either drive them apart or into the bedroom. Making a move is always risky, but there is no reward without risk. Realize that the friendship is at stake when the male makes the move. Love-shy men erroneously think that they can be friends first and then slowly ease into a romance. Of course, you have to be friends and friendly with the woman, but you have to keep up the romantic tension from the beginning. Love-shyness produces its own sexual tension, but it's the wrong and unattractive kind.

You need some kind of tension between the two of you. There is no romantic spark without friction. If you agree with everything she says and does, then you are heading for the dreaded friends zone. Don't be so eager to appear exactly the same as her. Men and women are different, so accentuate that difference. The romantic movies show us what needs to happen. Man and woman have some conflict but are also attracted to each other. The pair's mutual attraction triumphs over their differences. Don't be the nice guy where you completely avoid conflict and confrontation. Playfulness helps. Teasing and tickling provide the necessary tension in a lighthearted way, but only get physical if you feel comfortable. Playing a competitive game can work as long as you are not completely focused on winning. Disagreeing on some esoteric intellectual point may work, but it isn't the sexiest.

Something about that which is not readily obtainable seems to make it more erotic. There is something about having resistance and obstacles that adds to the sexual charge. This is not necessarily totally healthy, but it seems to be how many, if not all, humans are sexually wired. Love-shys never seem to tackle that hump and instead go for the smoothest route with no obstacles. Love is never tidy. I'm not saying don't go for someone who is available, instead notice how the smallest roadblock can stop you dead.

Think of your life as a movie where you are the writer, director and star. This concept gives you much creative power in your life, so use this bold potential. The same things that would make an audience interested in watching your movie also make people want to participate as your costars and onscreen romantic partner. Your life movie needs things like excitement, roller coaster rides and resolution. Warning: the displayed tension must not be due

to your frustration or any other of your negative emotions, or you will end up playing the role of the despised evil villain. No matter how interesting you or your movie is, people gravitate to the hero, not the villain.

Part of the game of romance is that women play hard to get. Though this may be somewhat outdated and sometimes just due to cautiousness, you should understand it. I see at least three reasons for their action. First is to separate the wheat from the chaff. There are plenty of men out there. If you aren't going to take the effort to pursue her now, how much effort are you going to put into the relationship once it's off the ground? Second, she wants you to play the game of romance correctly by taking the initiative. Third, women never want to be seen as easy. Additionally, delayed or interrupted fulfillment tends to intensify both romantic and sexual desire. Since women usually will not be completely receptive to your advances, you have to control your reactions to any negativity you sense. If you get one little negative indication from her, do you immediately write her off completely? Requiring immediate approval from a woman may affect your success at the mating game. If your physical advances are rebuffed, show concern for her viewpoint rather than putting additional pressure on her.

Don't expect a kiss, much less sex, on the first date. Consider that as a love-shy, the physical part of the relationship will generally move slower than for more experienced people. Even if you have gone on a couple of seemingly good dates with her, don't fret if she still won't kiss you. It could be a bad omen, but every woman has her own timetable for intimacy. While some women may kiss an acquaintance on the lips as a form of greeting, others will only kiss a guy on the lips once they are ready to have sex with him. Unless a date was obviously a complete disaster, kiss her at the end of it, at least on the cheek.

Getting out there doing things and experiencing positive social interactions builds confidence. In the mating game, confidence is what it's all about. It's about using and maximizing what you have got and not worrying about what you don't have. I have a theory that women find a confident man who has some obviously less than ideal characteristics to be extra attractive or at least more interesting. Women may think this man must have some super qualities that give him his above average confidence to counteract his shortcomings. Confidence tends to be a major problem with love-shys, so at the very least have confidence in the fact that you know what women really look for: confidence. Believing in yourself about every aspect of your life, including those things you do especially well but are unrelated to dating, builds confidence.

As you become more aware and confident, you will find women actually talking to you first: not necessarily a conversation, but perhaps a casual, innocuous request. It is up to you immediately to recognize the situation as positive and turn her initial comment into a full-blown conversation. Even if there was no perceived attraction to you on her part, you shared some small moment together and she feels safe enough to talk to you. Go for it without delay. These situations to meet women will never happen unless you are out of your apartment. The more you are out doing stuff, the more you are likely to have the required confidence.

Chapter 4

Therapies

Practice dating

Most likely throughout your whole life, nobody ever correctly diagnosed your love-shyness. Chances are your parents, doctors and therapists accused you of being a lazy slacker or a drug addict, or they diagnosed you as suffering from depression or some other type of well-documented mental illness. Perhaps, they thought all you needed was a swift kick in the pants and maybe an antidepressant drug or two. Whatever the treatment, most likely it did nothing for your love-shyness and only ended up making you more depressed and frustrated that nobody can understand or help you. Often parents of love-shys see nothing abnormal in their children and trivialize their problem, because the parents have quite similar traits. *Just give it time.* Parents may focus on the acting out and fail to question and search for the underlying cause. *Mother, I'm 37 years old and never had a real girlfriend. Don't you think I'm severely stressed out?*

Even though in Chapter 1 I told you to go regularly to a talk therapist, she can only do so much for you. Gilmartin (1987) observes:

> Conventional psychotherapeutic approaches are simply inappropriate for love-shy men because each of these is premised upon the assumption that the love-shy client already possesses certain necessary "bootstraps" which all the best available data quite clearly indicate he does *not* possess. (p. 616)

It's like a therapist telling someone to climb a mountain, when the patient has never climbed mountains nor knows how to. Thus, these patients get frustrated they still can't do it when society and their therapists say they should. Love-shys are in the same boat as people with Asperger's. Asperger's expert Tony Attwood believes that "traditional psychoanalytical psychotherapy has very little to offer a child or adult with Asperger's syndrome" (2006, p. 316). Once all the extraneous conditions such as depression and obsessive-compulsive disorder are under control, standard psychotherapy can do little to help love-shys satisfactorily overcome their life-long affliction.

So now that you have discovered your correct diagnosis, what treatment options do you have? Although Freud is known as the father of psychoanalysis and discovered the importance of early childhood sexuality, his theories provide little for love-shys to use. Gilmartin claims traditional (and rare) shyness clinics are of little use to love-shys. Support groups not specifically focused on love-shyness may do little for the condition. He mentions:

> For example, it has long been known that alcoholics cannot be helped through participating in therapy groups that are composed of people suffering from a wide variety of different sorts of psychoemotional problems. On the other hand, as soon as they are introduced to Alcoholics

> Anonymous groups most alcoholics begin deriving significant benefits almost immediately. I believe that the love-shy are similar to alcoholics in this regard. They need and require therapy groups that are focused specifically and exclusively upon heterosexual love-shyness. (p. 26)

However, any support group where the love-shy feels he belongs and does not feel threatened or inferior is almost always worthwhile.

Gilmartin recognized the need for teaching love-shys social skills and dating logistics along with providing them direct experience with dating and romantic situations. Gilmartin's overwhelming focus on treating love-shys consists of practice dating therapy. With his ideal scenario, six love-shy males and six love-shy females meet as a whole therapeutic group facilitated by a clinical psychologist and support staff. The group sessions include lessons, advice and perhaps role-playing. Near the end of the group session, the facilitator pairs off the men and women and assigns them to go on practice dates. The male is expected to phone the female and arrange the date, which should not be something with little chance for conversation like going to the movies. At the next group session, the participants discuss the details of how the dates went, and the facilitator rearranges the pairs so eventually all possible pairings happen. This practice dating therapy provides the love-shys, most of whom have never dated at all, with a chance to experience interacting with the opposite sex in a semi-controlled environment.

Gilmartin claims that practice dating is the single most important therapy to cure a love-shy and references nearly a 95 percent success rate. Not only do the clients receive practice in going on dates so the actual experience of a date is not new, but they actually get to know the opposite sex as people. This getting to know the other gender helps bring them down to earth and not see the opposite sex as some lofty dream. Gilmartin claims this therapy will help the love-shy male get over his fascination

with women of high natural beauty, as the male will, one hopes, experience average or less than average-looking women as great companions. Without actually interacting in positive ways with women, love-shy men have little else besides looks with which to evaluate women. A participant may be involved with the program for six months or even a year and may be involved in multiple groups with different members. Gilmartin emphatically states the additional therapeutic benefits of practice dating therapy: "In sum, meaningful female companionship very effectively brings love-shy men out of their shells. Female companionship constitutes a very powerful therapeutic cause; it is not merely a therapeutic effect!" (p. 565).

Sounds Great! Where do I sign up? Not so fast. Practice dating therapy has some problems, the greatest of which is it doesn't currently exist. Although Gilmartin claims psychologists developed practice dating therapy in the early 1970s with many scholarly papers written about it, the therapy has not taken off. Why does a seemingly successful and necessary therapy not exist? First, love-shyness is not an official mental health condition. Even though Gilmartin performed an excellent job researching and documenting love-shyness, it seems that the psychological community mirrors the general public in their inability to see and acknowledge this serious condition and lack of inclination to do anything about it.

Gilmartin may have shot himself in the foot by including the unnecessary topics of astrology and reincarnation in his book. Because of his inclusion of a small amount of nonscientific material, perhaps scientists threw out the whole book. Was he trying to influence science with his spiritual beliefs by including them in an otherwise scientifically solid and important book? Was he trying to appeal to a love-shy audience who, according to his research, tend to have religious views outside the mainstream? No matter the reason, the fact remains that the mental health community failed to pick up and run with his book. Perhaps this severe lack of interest is due to the need to actually create a new type of therapy, rather than using already existing methods.

Practice dating therapy also suffers from logistical complications. A practice dating clinic is difficult to set up and maintain and involves many volunteers and staff. Also, since more men than women are love-shy, maintaining an even gender ratio is hard, especially since women tend to stay in the program a shorter time. Furthermore, the timetable for treatment can be long, a stubborn case taking over a year to overcome. Lawyers may question the clinic's legal liability regarding the extremely minute probability of one client date-raping or stalking another. Since practice dating is an ongoing, long-term treatment, these clinics must be community based, and an out-of-town love-shy would basically need to move to the city of the clinic. While these drawbacks are not insurmountable, it remains much easier for clinical psychologists to focus on traditional disorders and treatments.

Sadly, perhaps the closest readily available option to help one date, while not exactly therapy, is using a dating coach. The number of older divorcees who have been out of the dating scene for perhaps decades along with the large number of increasingly frustrated non-love-shy singles create a demand for dating coaches. A popular dating coach named David Wygant claims to have "literally helped thousands—from everyday people to celebrities and millionaires—become more comfortable with the dating process" (p. xv). He wrote *Always Talk to Strangers* (2005) to publicize his advice. Obviously, he and other dating coaches would help love-shys with the surface issues and perhaps even point out deeper psychological issues. But without any therapy specifically addressing love-shyness, such coaching puts the cart before the horse. This goes for dating services as well. While such services may have a good male/female ratio and can provide structure for asking women out, these companies do not provide therapy.

To Gilmartin's credit, he tried to start a Shys Anonymous based on the theory and practice of Alcoholics Anonymous.

Unfortunately, it never took off. Because love-shys are so prone to avoiding taking the initiative and joining groups, keeping such a group going requires tremendous effort. Also, many more people suffer from alcoholism than love-shyness, and alcoholics are a much more visible group with a more obvious problem. Even though a true alcoholic must cease drinking for good to be cured, alcoholics can be helped to a vastly greater extent than love-shys. Love-shys wish there were only 12 steps to recovery! Although some may label any sexual perversion as addiction, love-shyness is not an addiction. It is a phobia, which requires the opposite treatment. Love-shys need exposure to the very thing that induces the anxiety while in a controlled setting. As Gilmartin (1987) says, "And like any phobia, the *emotional* (NOT the intellectual) components of the person must be effectively reached and affected if therapeutic advances are to be made" (p. 453).

From my vantage point, practice dating may offer little serious therapeutic value to me now. I have been on actual dates, but even the few successful ones did not cure my love-shyness. Obviously, my past dates were not part of a therapy regime. Eventually, I seemed to do well enough in that I grasped the basics, which may be all that anyone can expect practice dating therapy to do for them. Although, if I had been involved in practice dating therapy in college, who knows how much better my future dates would have been and how much further along I would be now? Because of having very few dates, the pressure increased to succeed on the ones I had, which may have made things worse. I still could not ask out appropriate women, because of my phobic reactions and not my lack of social skills. Male love-shys nearly universally complain that they can talk to and perhaps even approach women in general, but when it comes to that desirable woman who rings their bell, actions prove impossible. A practice dating set-up may not include such a woman, although Gilmartin claims some practice dates turn into full-fledged romances and give love-shys valuable intimacy experience.

Conceivably, overcoming this specific phobia may not require a dating situation per se. A practical love-shy therapy should structure itself on the basic therapy for overcoming any phobia. Most clinicians use exposure therapy for overcoming typical phobias and anxieties, and it works quite well for simple phobias. Therapists can generally treat most anxiety disorders in a relatively short period of time if they deal directly with the exact anxiety. If you have a phobia of spiders, you need to be slowly and gradually introduced to them in a controlled setting. You learn to handle each level of exposure until your anxiety and fear subsides. You may start with imaginal exposure, which involves imagining the object of your phobia. Later, you view a small photograph of a spider and may work your way up to petting a tarantula. Exposure therapy works best when it provides rewarding experiences rather than merely neutral situations involving the phobia-simulating object, so the person reconditions him- or herself to connect positive emotions with the object.

The exposure therapy breaks down into steps with usually only one or perhaps two steps occurring at each therapeutic session. The patient should have the goal of completing all the steps and understand the process. At the beginning of each step the patient must start out relaxed yet alert. During the exposure some anxiety must be felt for the desensitization to be effective. It is best to start off slowly as too high a level of anxiety is ineffective and may actually make the problem worse. The patient should accept the anxiety and not necessarily try to fight it but go with it to show that it isn't the end of the world. Perhaps during the latter stages of exposure the patient tries to perform tasks, such as holding up unrelated conversations. It is best for the patient to relax back to a baseline stable state before starting the next level of exposure.

The love-shy has no such controlled therapy available to him. A therapist treating a love-shy does not have the object of the phobia at his disposal, nor is the therapist plausibly available to go out with the love-shy searching for such a person. And images fail to induce the negative reaction. Therefore, the only way for the love-shy to interact with the cause of his phobia is out in the wild. Normally without even a companion, the love-shy must overcome his phobia through repeated attempts to play the game. Such attempts rarely work out no matter how much friends and fate try to intervene. Love-shy therapies need to focus on gradual challenges rather than being immediately thrown into the lion's den.

Yet, some believe the most important action when dealing with a phobia is to face it head on. Such effort requires courage, an understanding of the problem and acceptance of yourself and the situation. Acceptance does not imply approval of your condition or that you should give up and not deal with it. Realize that your condition is not stupid and neither are you. Accept that you will be nervous when approaching women. Whatever you resist has power over you. Only by doing what you are most afraid of can you give yourself power. Don't worry what she or anyone else thinks of you. Don't worry if she can see that you're nervous. Watch out for avoidance behaviors that keep you from ever pushing yourself socially.

In a similar vein you could try a type of reverse psychology. The late Austrian neurologist and psychiatrist Viktor Frankl called his method paradoxical intention, where he encouraged his patients to wish for that of which they were most fearful.[1] Frankl would presumably tell love-shys to try to become as nervous as possible with a women. When consciously told to do so, the body seems unable to respond as, supposedly, the absurdity of the task breaks the vicious cycle. Frankl believed that many problems stem from an overemphasis on oneself. If you shift your attention away from yourself and onto your prospective romantic partner, your problems may disappear.

Without an actual woman to induce the anxiety, you might try imaginal exposure, which has been found to help deal with stressful or traumatic situations. Generally the brain reacts in about the same way whether directly exposed to something or

if the mind pictures the same situation. Write a script or create a scene that vividly reproduces a stressful situation with a woman. You may want to record yourself presenting the scene in detail in the present tense and loop the recording to repeat over and over. Then in a relaxed setting, close your eyes and play back the recording to imagine the scene and become fully immersed in it. Since you are not directly in the stressful situation, you are in a position to remain calm and reassured while mentally exposing yourself to the anxious situation. It is probably best to find a therapist initially to instruct and guide you before attempting this therapy alone.

Technology is taking imaginal exposure to the next level with virtual reality therapy (VRT). Various researchers use computer generated virtual realities to treat patients suffering from phobia and anxieties. Clinical studies have proven the effectiveness of VRT to treat fears of public speaking.[2] Researchers at the University of Washington School of Medicine use VRT to help burn victims focus away from their intense pain.[3] When these burn patients were immersed in a realistic virtual three-dimensional world used for dealing with a fear of spiders, the patients reported being aware of much less pain than if they were merely playing a two-dimensional abstract video game. In California the Virtual Reality Medical Center (www.vrphobia.com) has three locations that offer treatments for various phobias including social phobias. Other companies producing various virtual reality training packages are starting to offer similar phobia treatments. Setting up a VRT for dealing with anxieties around approaching women and going on dates appears doable and practical on a certain level. The idea that a potent love-shy therapy could come through goggles and a DVD is very alluring. However, I am apprehensive about this technology since it seems little removed from interactive pornography DVDs and computer games that simulate picking up women. I doubt any male love-shy therapy can work well unless interactions with actual women take place. The internet could perhaps video link love-shys to women trained to carry on VRT dating conversations.

I once thought if I could find, perhaps through a classified ad, an open-minded woman to whom I was really attracted, I could pay her to attend a session with my therapist and act as the object of my phobia. The irony is that if I could approach such a woman and convince her to take part in an unconventional therapy, then I should be able to ask her for a date. However, if the potential for her to be a love interest was removed, then talking with her may not be as difficult, since I can act like it is the therapist in me talking. If she would feel comfortable and agree to it, the therapist may not even be necessary and we could just meet at my place. Aside from basic conversations, I would repeatedly ask for her phone number and a date until it seemed second nature to me. Of course, while planning this situation my fantasies would take over with me trying to kiss her and one thing leading to another.

Actually, an accredited therapist may practically implement a similar scenario. An enterprising therapist could advertise for attractive women to be available. A love-shy male could choose from photographs or brief videos to find the person he was most attracted to and then arrange a therapy session with her. The therapist would first state that the hired woman is only playing a role to act interested in the man. If a woman actually becomes interested in a male client, she will tell the therapist who will relate it to the love-shy. Hence, unless receiving approval from the therapist, the love-shy must not make any contact. The session may include the love-shy holding hands with the woman or briefly touching her arm or shoulder. While having a therapist in the room may make the situation strange, I postulate that practicing in front of an audience makes the exercise more realistic and powerful. The women's honest opinions and critiques will have much credence with love-shys. The experience should end positively, so the love-shy does not leave thinking, *I pay her and she still turns me down.*

This type of therapy, while not nearly as inclusive as practice dating, overcomes practice dating's logistical problems. Since the beautiful women (or handsome men for female love-shys) are paid, the lopsided male–female ratio is not a problem. Also, this therapy focuses on short-term treatment with useful results from a limited number of sessions, which makes out-of-town love-shy participation possible. Because many non-love-shy men become awkward and shy in the presence of very desirable women, the therapy would not be limited to love-shys.

However, full dating experience is still important. A love-shy with no dating experience needs enough experience to progress to the point where dating becomes a normal thing like going to church, where you dress up, are in a social situation and need to do the right things at the right time. But unlike dating, you may have been going to church since you were a little kid. Also unlike dating, religious services follow a script orchestrated by someone else. Most people pick up the dating game, so once you eliminate the majority of your negative anxieties and thoughts about the opposite sex, dating should happen fairly naturally. With some exposure therapy and the knowledge and practice of approaching girls, you should wind up getting dates. While your failures on these dates may happen more often compared to other people, at least you gain valuable experience.

Good practice dating therapy may move you up to higher levels of dating experience, such as being able to flirt naturally and smoothly. Too bad such therapy has not been maintained, even though it has been shown to be possible to implement and treat love-shyness. Do not get depressed when you can't find a therapist to tackle your major love-shy issues specifically. Once love-shyness becomes commonly known and the extent of the problem recognized, I have no doubt that enterprising therapists and companies will offer effective treatments. Since we can't hold our breath until that time, we must gain any dating experience we can on our own. Luckily, alternative therapies exist.

Drugs

In this modern age we expect a drug to help us with almost any physical or mental ailment. If as a love-shy you suffer from both anxiety and depression, most likely your therapist will refer you to a psychiatrist to prescribe an anti-anxiety, antidepressant drug. As is typical, I was prescribed a daily dose of Lexapro, a selective serotonin reuptake inhibitor (SSRI). Why would I want my serotonin reuptake selectively inhibited? Will it help with my love-shyness? Are there better and safer alternatives? To answer these questions, to explain what serotonin is and how most antidepressant and anti-anxiety drugs work, we need to explore some of the basic mechanisms of the brain. For psychiatric drugs especially, it is important for users to understand how the drugs work in the brain and body and what side-effects they produce.

In 2004 the US Food and Drug Administration required drug manufacturers to print warning labels on packages of SSRI drugs like Prozac, which has been on the market since 1987 and is often prescribed to children, stating that the drugs may induce suicide. As so few of the millions of SSRI users exhibit suicidal and violent behaviors, I will focus on the more common side-effects and their biological basis.

The brain consists of billions of massively interconnected cells called neurons. Neurons, which can be very long as cells go, function both as the body's electrical wiring and as the switches for the miraculous computer that is the brain. Neurons conduct electricity along their bodies, which are covered by insulative sheathes. Every region of the body sends and receives electrical signals along neurons to and from the brain. The output "tentacles" of one or more neurons connect physically and electrically at a small input area of another neuron. In the simplest case, if the electrical signal emitted from one neuron is large enough, the neuron connected to that output will produce a similar electric signal to transmit to its own output connections. Each neuron performs logic functions that one can think of as similar to each of the millions of transistors running a computer. A neuron may need to receive sufficient signals from multiple neurons before producing its own signal. The rate of transmission, computation and retransmission is quite fast and can be completely automatic, as, when you quickly retract away when you touch something hot. Eventually, with effort, you can develop conscious control over your body's reaction so that with practice you will not automatically move away from a hot thing. As you learn and develop skills, neurons make new connections and strengthen other connections.

Along with the electrical connections between neurons, a more complex and slower, but still incredibly fast from a human perspective, electrochemical communication process happens between neurons. Instead of a physical connection, a small distance called a synapse separates one neuron's output area from another neuron's input area. To send a signal, a neuron releases a large number of identical molecules into the synapse. The receiving neuron has receptors build into its cell wall to receive these molecules. The receptor and molecule fit together like a lock and key. When a molecule connects with its proper receptor, a small electrical signal is generated. Once enough molecules connect with enough receptors, the threshold, or action potential, is surpassed and the receiving neuron generates an electrical signal.

The "key" molecule that transfers between neurons is called a neurotransmitter. Humans have about 20 different neurotransmitter molecules, and all have different functions in the brain and sometimes in the body. Better-known ones include dopamine, serotonin and acetylcholine. After a neurotransmitter molecule has coupled with a receptor, it needs to be recycled back into the first neuron so that the neuron can send another signal with it later. This returning process is called reuptake. If reuptake is hindered, neurotransmitters stay in the synapse area longer. Thus, each molecule has more chances to find a receptor and build up potential for the neuron to fire. Prozac and its SSRI cousins work by blocking the reuptake of the neurotransmitter serotonin. That, in a nutshell, is how the brain and today's common antidepressant drugs work.

But wait, how does neurons firing relate to what I perceive as thoughts and feelings? And why will having serotonin-related neurons fire more often decrease my anxiety? Well, science doesn't yet know the answers to these questions. Even though scientists continually fill in details of how the brain works, computers can simulate brain functions with neural networks and physicians routinely perform brain surgery, these big questions remain unanswered. Science does make progress. Today's antidepressant drugs are better than those of a few decades ago, because SSRIs *selectively* inhibit serotonin reuptake. This selectivity is a good thing, because serotonin, also known by its chemical name 5-hydroxytryptamine (5-HT), performs other functions in the body, particularly in the digestive system.

SSRIs replace the older class of drugs called monoamine oxidase inhibitors (MAOIs). Monoamine oxidase is the enzyme that breaks down serotonin for reuptake. An enzyme is a complex molecule that receives a specific molecule similar to a receptor. Unlike a receptor, an enzyme initiates a chemical change with its specific molecule by either breaking it down or building it up by combining it with a second molecule. Monoamine oxidase also breaks down molecules similar to 5-HT, namely the amino acids tyramine and tryptophan, of which the latter is the main building block for serotonin. When a person eats foods containing large amounts of tryptophan, such as turkey or warm milk, the increase in tryptophan causes the body to produce more serotonin and become sleepy. If one eats these foods after taking a dose of an MAOI, extreme pain results since the body is blocked from breaking down these substances that do not normally circulate freely in the body.

Although it is difficult to measure neurotransmitter levels in the brain, scientists have linked low serotonin levels to depression, particularly seasonal affective disorder (SAD). Exposure to artificial bright light helps treat people with this condition by raising serotonin levels. The SSRI Paxil was the first drug approved for treating SAD. There is little doubt SSRIs and related drugs improve one's mood, at least for a while. Gilmartin (1987) references work claiming that the potent MAOI drug Nardil can cure most people suffering from biologically based "anxiety disease" (p. 67). However, these drugs have definite side-effects for most users. Paxil, unlike other SSRIs, may affect judgment, thinking and motor skills in some people.

Since the digestive system uses serotonin, one common side-effect of SSRIs is weight gain. More unfortunate for many SSRI users, serotonin also relates to sexual functioning. Decrease or elimination of sex drive and, for male users, failure to obtain or maintain an erection are common side-effects experienced by SSRI users. Strangely, not only SSRI drugs but almost all psychiatric medications cause some decrease in sexual functioning. These side-effects cease when one stops taking the drug but can considerably distress a love-shy who has serious worries about his sexual abilities to begin with. Even non-love-shy men having no current sexual relations would often rather feel slightly depressed than take a drug that decreases their "manhood." Theoretically, SSRIs may benefit sexually inexperienced love-shys since these drugs can inhibit ejaculation. However, the optimal dosage for this effect is often much less than the prescribed dosage for psychological issues.

Another problem with SSRIs is that one cannot quickly stop and start using them. It usually takes a few weeks of daily dosing before the positive effects take hold. Then, one must not stop their usage abruptly as withdrawal symptoms can occur. Usually the withdrawal symptoms are similar to withdrawing from other drugs such as alcohol and coffee and can involve acute headaches and nausea. However, SSRI withdrawal can include atypical or crazy behavior and mood swings. Most likely, much of the violence associated with these drugs happens during this transition period. A user must taper off the drug slowly over a matter of weeks or months.

Luckily, I found an alternative to SSRIs. Instead of increasing the amount of serotonin available at the receptors by blocking its reuptake, why not increase the total amount of serotonin to begin with? One could eat foods containing high levels of tryptophan, which is two chemical steps away from serotonin. More effective is taking the supplement 5-hydroxytryptophan (5-HTP), which is only one chemical step away from 5-HT. Thus, significantly more of it converts into serotonin. Stores specializing in vitamins and supplements commonly sell 5-HTP. I took 5-HTP after reading *The Chemistry of Joy* (Emmons 2006) and internet recommendations, and noticed a positive effect. I believe I obtained about half the level of positive effects as I would have with an SSRI, but noticed minimal side-effects. I did experience some lethargy at the beginning of use, which is common for SSRIs too. One must follow the same rules with 5-HTP as with taking an SSRI and not stop abruptly, and be careful about taking other drugs that interact with the serotonin system. Always seek medical advice before using supplements, even if they are available without prescription. Your doctor will be able to advise you of an appropriate dosage.

While 5-HTP did put me in a slightly better mood, it didn't really do anything for my love-shyness. This is not surprising considering the psychiatric community generally agrees that exposure therapy, not drugs, is the best treatment for simple phobias. Since love-shyness only flares up during romantic or possibly romantic encounters, it is hard to see the compatibility of a drug that affects one continuously with our problem. For a situational problem that only occurs a small percentage of the time, a chemical imbalance in the brain seems an unlikely cause. Yet, Gilmartin stresses in a personal correspondence that drugs play an important part in love-shy therapy by enabling love-shys to perform the "homework" of getting out and socializing. Fortunately, there are other possible drug and chemical solutions.

Xanax is a relatively common prescription drug for single-use doses. A love-shy could take a Xanax before a social occasion to reduce social anxiety. Perhaps the most common side-effect with Xanax, which is sold under a variety of names, is drowsiness. Combining drugs is not normally recommended, and Xanax and alcohol is an especially bad combination. If Xanax is taken often, one might become heavily addicted and experience withdrawal symptoms, so I recommend only taking it occasionally. If you suffer from panic attacks rather than simple love-shy phobia, a psychiatrist can prescribe you more serious drugs. However, the more powerful the prescription drug, usually the greater its side-effects.

Do not believe that taking psychiatric drugs is a sign of weakness. However, drug-averse love-shys may want to investigate herbs and other supplements. St. John's Wort has found popularity as an antidepressant. Although herbs have various active ingredients, the main active ingredient of St. John's Wort is hypericin, which appears to act like an MAOI. In Europe, St. John's Wort is prescribed more often than Prozac. I found the amino acid supplement L-theanine at my local vitamin store, and the supplier claims it promotes "alert relaxation" with single doses. Another supplement is SAMe, S-adenosyl methionine, which some claim functions as an antidepressant by increasing levels of serotonin and dopamine. SAMe is actually more like an enzyme and helps with a variety of molecular bodily functions. *The Chemistry of Joy* (2006), discusses these and other natural and holistic antidepressant possibilities in depth.

There are a variety of drugs out there that affect all kinds of neurotransmitter and chemical pathways with new ones continuously coming to market. But love-shys overwhelmingly agree that no drug significantly helps with love-shyness. When presented with a case of depression and anxiety where the person has virtually no friends, the inability to have romantic or sexual relationships and no family to go to for support, psychiatrists often immediately write a prescription. It's as if you're an inmate telling the prison psychiatrist that you are depressed. So she prescribes you an antidepressant drug. *But, Doc, is it me or my situation that's the problem?* Prescribing drugs to "cheer a person up" when

they are in an obviously depressing situation may be quite unnatural. Treating the symptoms of love-shyness as a pathological state rather than one induced by extreme circumstances at best may serve to confuse and at worst lead the patient down a scary slope of strong and misguided antidepressant medication. More is not always better when it comes to drugs, and chemically treating something that is not a neurological problem can result in overmedication.

If you just need to feel better, then why not use the social drugs caffeine and alcohol? Coffee makes me more talkative and puts me in a good mood, so it can be good before a date or job interview. Too much coffee can make one jittery and anxious, so watch the dose and frequency. Alcohol functions quite well as a social lubricant by lowering both anxiety and inhibitions. However, it depresses the central nervous system, and excessive alcohol can prevent erections. Since the love-shy is often in a party atmosphere when he needs to make romantic moves, light to moderate alcohol consumption can be a logical choice. As drugs like caffeine or alcohol can be used occasionally, unlike prescription drugs which are taken continuously, the love-shy still has time to feel "normal" and confront his issues.

Another chemical avenue to explore for possible love-shy treatment is testosterone supplements. On casual observance, symptoms of love-shyness compare to characteristics of low testosterone. Being non-competitive and not pursuing women are signs of both conditions. One's testosterone level increases after winning a sports competition. Testosterone is a hormone which is a molecular messenger similar to a neurotransmitter except that instead of communicating over a short distance between neurons, hormones circulate in the blood stream and latch onto receptors in cells throughout the body. While one may think of testosterone as a male hormone and estrogen as a female hormone, both genders have and require both. Often it is not the amount of a particular hormone that matters, but its ratio to the amounts of other hormones. A variety of hormones run through our bodies including a number of male-types (androgens) and female-types (estrogens). Other commonly known hormones include insulin, which regulates sugar levels, and the stress-related hormones adrenaline and cortisol.

A love-shy with Asperger's discusses his chemical usage:

> I tried alcohol, which helped tremendously. I paid for it with 25 years of alcoholism, and it nearly cost me my life. By being drunk and being around drunken women I got laid and had relationships with alcoholics. But this only did a little for my love-shy disease. What helped most were the 12 step programs.

> I have a low but not abnormal testosterone level. I supplement with bio-identical 2 percent testosterone cream. It not only gives me more strength and energy but also makes me braver in approaching women. The main effect that I get from it is that I no longer have periods of depression. If I stop the testosterone the depression comes back. There does not seem to be any down sides to the natural human testosterone. I recommend it.

Testosterone is an antidepressant for both sexes. Estrogen, too, is an antidepressant and functions as a mild MAOI. Patches, gels or creams appear the best ways to take in testosterone. Eugene Shippen and William Fryer claim, "Testosterone has been shown to be an antagonist of the stress hormones: more testosterone, less stress hormone production. DHEA, another hormone that declines as we age, has also been shown to play an important part in controlling stress hormones"[4] (p. 91). Taking DHEA supplements are likely a smaller and safer step than taking testosterone for boosting androgen levels. Shippen and Fryer say this about dehydroepiandrosterone (DHEA):

> Nearly every cell in the body has receptor sites for this unique hormone, but its exact purpose is only dimly understood. [M]en and women who are middle-aged or older generally feel marked improvements in well-being when they take replacement doses of DHEA. [It] can be converted to many other hormones in the body, including testosterone and estrogen. (p. 33)

Another love-shy offers these recommendations of ways to increase your testosterone.

- Power weight lifting for at least 20 reps/set in a standing position.
- Taking androstenedione or "andro." This is a legal (but classified a dopant by many sports) testosterone precursor that helps your body produce more of the hormone.
- Taking part in aggressive, confrontational activity such as martial arts. (Note that career women have far more testosterone than stay-at-home housewives.)
- Eating yang foods. There is a reason the Chinese classify food items as ying (feminine) and yang (masculine). Meat, nuts, beans, fish, eggs and dairy increase testosterone, while pastry, bread, fruit and pasta lower it.

Cholesterol in meat and eggs is a building block for testosterone (and other hormones). Also, sexual thoughts and activities may increase this male hormone. By whatever means you increase your testosterone levels, I suggest weight lifting or, at minimum, strenuous exercise, to relieve your increased aggression especially if you are not having sex. Testosterone promotes low-fat muscle buildup, so take advantage of it by working out. Also, Shippen and Fryer claim that for both sexes obesity leads to higher estrogen levels and lower amounts of testosterone (p. 51).

Testosterone levels decrease as men age. There is a male version of menopause, except it happens more gradually and usually

without notice. Men and women of middle age or older should look into getting their testosterone and other hormone levels checked by a knowledgeable endocrinologist if considering replacement hormone prescriptions. Shippen and Fryer discuss testosterone and male menopause in depth and dispel much mistaken conventional wisdom about these topics, including the idea that properly administered hormone replacement therapy can increase one's risk of developing cancer and heart disease. They unequivocally state, "[Testosterone deficiency] is powerfully linked to nearly every major degenerative disease. Use of this remarkable healing hormone could reverse suffering and prevent early death" (p. vii). Even some older women require small amounts of testosterone supplementation.

Hormones have incredible control over our sex and love lives as Crenshaw thoroughly reports in *The Alchemy of Love and Lust* (1996). This book explains our sexuality from before birth to old age through the influence of hormones. It profiles a cornucopia of hormones and how they influence us, our romantic lives and each other. Many of our feelings control our body's hormones, and our hormones feed back and influence our moods. Loneliness actually changes how the body functions at the molecular level. Crenshaw documents how levels of the hormone oxytocin increase when someone is touched and suggests that we can end up craving the touch of our lover to release this chemical in us like a drug addict craves the next fix. Orgasm releases large amounts of oxytocin, thus promoting bonding after sex. People on the autism spectrum who dislike being touched may suffer from low levels of oxytocin. Researchers have begun testing the nasal ingestion of oxytocin for temporarily overcoming shyness and social anxieties.

Even chemicals outside our bodies effect us. Pheromones are hormones transmitted through the air allowing an animal to detect a mate miles away. Desperate love-shys may seek a quick fix by using colognes containing pheromones. The tack seems useless since humans' pheromone system seems to have fallen out of use after living in densely packed cities, and any kind of aphrodisiac or chemical attractor will not help when you still have phobic reactions to women.

These days one cannot help mentioning Viagra. I had assumed this drug only helps with achieving and maintaining erections and does not increase one's libido, but one 21-year-old love-shy claims that after he was prescribed Viagra for reduced erections due to Lexapro, he had assertive and aggressive behaviors typical of increased testostorone. He believes that Viagra, "brought out a sexual part of me that otherwise would have not been there." For love-shys not on medication and who do not have diabetes, erectile dysfunction is most likely to be psychological rather than physical in origin. You might want to ensure that stress and depression, both general and related to sexual performance, and drugs like nicotine and alcohol are not to blame before popping the blue pill. However, aside from known reactions with a couple of types of prescription medication, Viagra itself appears quite safe.

For those of you with Asperger's, do not ignore biomedical treatments. While autistics often go to Defeat Autism Now! doctors who are knowledgeable about various biomedical autism treatments, people with Asperger's rarely think that they can do anything physically for their condition. Yet particular treatments producing noticeable effects with autistic children can help adult Aspies. The supplements methyl-B12 and grapefruit seed extract had a positive effect on me. I can't claim any clear distinctions, yet I feel my brain is healthier. Perhaps a slight improvement in brain health improves the chance that an Aspie will not meltdown in a given situation.

While I cannot recommend a street drug since the legality, purity, actual molecular composition and proper setting to use it cannot be assured, the serotonin-related drug MDMA, commonly called ecstasy or E, shows promise for love-shys. Many users report diminished social inhibitions and feelings of true empathy and love for the first time and feel a oneness with everything. One

love-shy credits MDMA use with overcoming his love-shyness enough for him to marry a great and attractive wife, something love-shys almost never say about any other drug. Before it became illegal some psychotherapists reported that it greatly accelerated the therapeutic process. It has shown initial success in treating post-traumatic stress disorder anxiety in conjunction with talk therapy. I hope that researchers will obtain government approval for trials using ecstasy to overcome love-shyness.[5]

Personally conducting further research is highly recommended before using any drug or supplement, even prescribed ones. What drug or what dose works for one person may not work well for another. You may need to try various things to find what works best for you. Perhaps more importantly, seek out the proper specialist. While your primary care physician can prescribe psychiatric drugs, employ a psychiatrist's expert knowledge about these drugs and how they interact.

Using drugs that bring out negative aspects of yourself, or even noticeably change you, is not good in the romantic arena. Have some experience with any drug you do take before or during a social event, so that you know what to expect. When you are on a date, limit your drug use. A glass or two of wine with dinner is great, but don't throw back shots. You want to connect with your date and interact on the same wavelength. Therefore, as a general rule, mirror your date; if your date does not drink alcohol, then neither should you.

Street time

Since no formal love-shy therapy exists and drugs have only limited and indirect use, love-shys must seek out and develop their own therapeutic regimes. Even though no existing program may specifically focus on love-shyness, our modern, abundant, service-orientated culture makes available a number of options. Since many people have issues with intimacy and dating and place

high importance in finding a life partner, enterprising individuals and organizations produce services to help lonely souls. The trick is figuring out which offerings suit love-shys' needs.

Ironically, one organization that may benefit love-shys is Sex and Love Addicts Anonymous, SLAA, which is modeled on Alcoholics Anonymous. It seems that a sex addict uses sex to get the emotional support he desperately craves but can't obtain. Overly promiscuous people can use sex to push others away and keep their emotions at bay. Thus, the sex addict can have as much of a problem developing and maintaining healthy relationships as love-shys. More importantly, the larger SLAA chapters have a subgroup for "sexual anorexia." The SLAA defines sexual anorexia as "the compulsive avoidance of giving or receiving social, sexual and/or emotional nourishment." This definition jives with love-shyness. To quote more of the anorexia page from the SLAA UK website:

> [B]eneath the surface, anorexia is a busy addiction: it consists of not doing something, and not doing something, and not doing something. Not trusting, not committing, not surrendering... Whether our anorexia is social, sexual, or emotional, we awaken to the fact that we are not experiencing the giving and receiving of love that is so precious to human life.[6]

Unfortunately, sexual anorexics comprise only a small part of the SLAA membership, so only SLAA chapters in the largest cities have separate anorexia meetings. You can find a local group from their website, www.slaafws.org. A list of questions is read at the beginning of the meeting, and many questions relate to love-shyness. For example, feeling empty and incomplete when we are alone, seeking casual sex even though it is not the best for us and avoiding responsibility seem to be qualities that sex anorexics and love-shys share. Since SLAA is based on the Alcoholics Anonymous 12 step program, if you don't admit that you are an

addict, the program as a whole may not benefit you much. The meeting I attended helped me look into myself and realize that I use my Asperger's and my phobia as excuses, and to admit to being addicted to doing nothing. The few other love-shys who attended sexual anorexic groups claimed them worthwhile, but they had limited use for me.

A novel take on group social encounter therapy that recently started is Cuddle Party. Listening to an interview with the founder, Reid Mihalko, I got the impression that, while probably not technically love-shy, he definitely tends towards it. He may have developed Cuddle Party as a way to overcome his love-shy attributes. A Cuddle Party is a casual, non-sexual, non-alcohol and non-drug get-together where people, well, just cuddle en masse in their pajamas. Besides the emotional well-being one receives from the touch of another, this situation would obviously benefit anyone who isn't completely comfortable with human touch. With the relaxed atmosphere of no expectations, it looks like a great way to meet cool people. See www.cuddleparty.com to see if there are any events near you. A love-shy who attended one found it great therapy, but he warns that there may be a dozen guys for every woman unless the gender balance is controlled.

Give a man a fish, and he will eat for a day. Teach a man to fish, and he will eat for a lifetime. A logical tack for finding therapies that focus on making us comfortable talking to and pursuing attractive members of the opposite sex is to seek guidance and teaching from experts in this field: pickup artists, or PUAs. Some enterprising pickup artists put on seminars and workshops teaching guys how to approach women. While many of the training programs benefit men at or near the love-shy level, some are not for total beginners. If you have serious interest in a particular offering, familiarize yourself with the presenter's website and read all his books to make sure his training is right for you. Many of their pickup and seduction strategies heavily rely on gimmicks and tricks to get a girl to sleep with you right away. You might think these tricks allow you to quickly achieve a relationship with

a woman by bypassing mating ritual requirements. Instead, the idea is to learn how to speed through the requirements. However, your love-shyness and social awkwardness may prevent you from carrying out these tricks adequately.

Nevertheless, PUAs are good for teaching love-shys because they have romance and seduction down to a science. Usually lecture sessions combine with real-world tutoring where the instructor accompanies his small group of students to bars and public places for practice hitting on women. What could be better for a desperate love-shy than this kind of training with an experienced teacher who personally supervises his students? Even though we know in theory we need exactly this type of training, many of us are turned off by it. Most likely, our love-shyness influences this opinion. Do you fear success?

It may be a while before therapeutic offerings by certified practitioners can produce the same positive results as a "boot camp" with a PUA. Since no therapy is perfect, you have to choose something. Since I have not attended any PUA training nor interviewed anyone who has, I hesitate to list any specific ones. Their in-person training rather than their books is what will most benefit love-shys. Www.stylelife.com markets to virgins as well as more experienced players. You can even get an intensive one-week course by actually living with the instructor in his London apartment through one site, www.puatraining.com. Also check out www.theapproach.com and www.lovesystems.com/mystery-method. Www.howtosucceedwithwomen.com advertises a weekend "approach camp." Unfortunately, none of these offerings comes cheap. To achieve maximum benefit and get your money's worth from these classes, wait until you have implemented this book's recommendations for your life.

Even though many PUA techniques are too advanced for love-shys and you may not respect PUAs' attitude towards women, you can learn practical things from them. Master PUAs agree that when it comes to dressing to meet women, flashy and tacky trump boring and conservative. First impressions are very important, and many women notice flashy men. PUAs know that plenty of women are out there, so they never show desperation or compromise themselves for women. Like good salesmen, PUAs know when to give up and move on to the next woman so as not to waste valuable time, money and emotional investment. Long pursuits only contribute to obsessing and ignoring other possibilities. Thus, the general rule of pursuit is that you need to up the romantic ante every time the two of you meet. The PUAs believe that women run on emotions, and like to experience a range of emotions. The PUA known as Mystery recommends changing venues on a date, which at minimum makes a woman feel that she has experienced much with you.

Speaking of dates, the PUAs know that cheaper is better. You may think that a first date with someone you really like should be a special and important celebration since you haven't had a date in years. You probably want to take her to a fancy Italian restaurant and impress her. Although you may enjoy the meal, you will likely waste money. On a first date both of you may be so nervous that neither of you has much of an appetite or focuses on the food. A date doesn't have to be an expensive dinner. A date is simply a time for getting to know someone, so no reason to spend big. But don't be a cheapskate either. Instead, act like a man who spends his money wisely. Art museums and the like are places to take a date cheaply or for free. Talk to the woman beforehand and figure out her interests. Chances are she would rather do something unique and inexpensive that interests the both of you than go somewhere typical and pricey. Increase the price of dates and gifts as the romance progresses. Some people like to limit first dates to an hour or two, which allows enough time to find out if the two of you are compatible and is not too much time to spend together if you aren't.

While many PUAs participate in the seduction game for casual sex, love-shys can learn and gain from this outlook. Love-shys need experience, any experience. I don't wish to endorse casual sex as a lifestyle but more as therapy and emergency treatment.

While the vast majority of love-shys, myself included, want serious relationships, I am attracted to casual sex. Perhaps this interest is due to having sexual tension that requires immediate release. Or I may subconsciously want experience with casual relationships so as to not ruin or use a serious relationship for dating practice. But probably my biggest reason for wanting one-night stands is for bypassing standard courtship rituals.

Unfortunately, one-night stands do not bypass courtship. Instead, they condense what would be multiple dates into one evening or a couple hours, making it even harder for a love-shy to adequately satisfy all the necessary romantic steps. With normal dating, the love-shy has time in between dates to analyze the situation and plan what needs to be done on and for the next date. A one-night stand does not allow any time for analysis except perhaps when the woman goes to the bathroom. Working the casual encounter leaves little room for typical love-shy errors. A regular courtship usually allows a male love-shy more than one opportunity for making moves, whereas exhibiting any hesitation with a possible pickup may prove a show ender. Love-shys need to take it slow, but assertive and sexually uninhibited women tend to be fast and intense. Love-shys' fear and apprehension of sex condenses and intensifies. So quick casual sexual relationships are often too much for love-shys to obtain or handle. Don't kick yourself for messing up these situations.

An easy way out many of you love-shys take is coming on to women whom you don't find that attractive. You may do this out of desperation or because you realize that a woman who doesn't ring your bell from an attraction standpoint won't ring your love-shy anxiety bell as loudly either. I generally recommend going for whoever you can to gain experience. But beware of the pitfalls of going after someone to whom you aren't that attracted. Except for dealing with your anxieties, you may feel nothing emotionally between you, which can make you feel even emptier.

The person you pick up may not be your ideal partner, but she's most likely a heck of a lot better than who you are with

right now, namely no one. *I just want that special someone,* you plead. Consider this as practice. It may be better to have a light and short encounter with someone you aren't that attracted to than to develop something serious. For the inexperienced and inhibited man, casual sex can ease performance pressure. While ideally the love and non-physical intimacy between two people should ease the sexual pressure, they add their own stress of not blowing a potentially serious relationship.

If you make a positive connection with a woman at a nightclub, act mature and sophisticated. When she gets ready to leave, offer to walk her to her car. When you are at her car, get her phone number if you haven't already. Most importantly, kiss her on the lips. This sets up the relationship as a physical one. You may then ask if she wants to come back to your place. If she does indicate her readiness, go for it. If not, you have set the stage for a sexual relationship by kissing her. Once you have kissed her or any woman you date, every time you meet kiss her on the lips as a greeting, even if just picking her up from work. Do not worry about what others may think. You two are together as a couple, and kissing signifies this fact. If she does not want to kiss you for whatever reason, she will turn her head or back off. Once a certain level of intimacy has been achieved never back down from it, only escalate it over time. Once you start holding hands, do it during all the appropriate times. If you are on a date, offer her your arm to hold on to.

I believe relationships exist on a continuum rather than always having clearly defined boundaries. The typical problem is that the guy wants casual sex, but the woman wants romance. The guy gets sex by being romantic. So do not add disclaimers such as, *I'm just expecting this to be a casual hookup.* If you have sex after a first meeting or first date, a non-serious relationship is implied. A relationship formed around casual sex will have difficulty becoming serious.

Love-shys seeking casual sex must treat it as many stereotypical men do: pure fun. If you make a mistake or perform poorly, who cares? You likely won't have to see the person ever again. But do not take this as a license to be rude, disrespectful or unconcerned about safety. Act chivalrously and open doors, including car doors, for her and scoot her chair in for her when sitting down at a restaurant as you would for any date. Go after any woman who strikes your fancy and appears interested in you. Remember that in general men more than women want casual sex, so women will usually be impressed if you take the relationship slower and deeper, as long as you actually take reasonable action and pursue it. Even at a wild party, men overtly expecting to bed women right away turn off most women. Since love-shys tend to place too high a value on finding that perfect woman, going after the obviously less than perfect woman provides valuable experience and will make you realize there is no perfect woman for you, just plenty of woman who would be great for you.

Aside from programs offering specific assistance regarding love and romance, love-shys may find various types of general therapies useful. These therapies may not directly allow you to overcome your love-shyness, but they can help you deal with it. Investigate assertiveness training. With so many women in the workplace, management often supports assertiveness training as a way for women to learn to compete and deal with men. For you guys, this type of training sounds like an excellent place to meet women practicing their assertiveness along with learning important skills. Love-shys may find the logic of neuro-linguistic programming intriguing and powerful since it involves fairly simple straightforward techniques to reprogram the brain. The neuro-linguistic programming field has branched out to become quite broad; many practitioners offer various seminars, workshops, books and audio programs, so you will need to do your own search to find a teacher whose methods suit you.[8]

Some love-shys highly recommend meditation for generating internal calm and self-awareness. There are various types of meditation, yet you can start practicing by sitting in a quiet place with your eyes closed and observe the thoughts that come into your mind. Try to minimize your thoughts. Breathe slowly, deeply, quietly and regularly. You may combine meditation with visualizations and positive affirmations.

As another avenue, people offering hypnosis therapy claim it works for phobias, but likely it won't help much if you don't deal with your emotional and other issues too. Interestingly, hypnosis can be used to figure out if a physical symptom is psychosomatic. If the symptom goes away while under hypnosis, its cause is mental, not physical. It would be interesting to see how well a love-shy would do over time if programmed during a hypnotic trance with something like, *You will suavely and without hesitation go after women you find attractive.* There are many books out there on self-hypnosis, and these techniques can be quite powerful, so I do not recommend that you attempt them without some expertise.

A helpful general-purpose therapy for love-shys is cognitive behavior therapy, or CBT. Often therapists will employ this therapy with their love-shy clients. Most simply, CBT is about recognizing and eliminating negative thinking and converting it into positives. Much of the last section of Chapter 2 is based on Cognitive Behavior Therapy. Burns' (1985) *Intimate Connections* is an excellent introductory CBT guide for shy people. Eliminating negative thinking is quite important for dealing with love-shyness, although some love-shys have complained that talk therapy too heavily devoted to CBT can come across as lifeless. And eliminating negative thinking only goes so far if the thought doesn't even enter your mind that you should approach a particular woman and make a move.

To complete this chapter, the late Eric Berne claims that who we become as adults is due to scripts created during childhood that guide us through life. Since life is so open-ended and full of possibilities, our script gives us direction and purpose. Berne claims a life script is internalized by around age six. Our interpretation of our parents' commands and actions creates a script, which we live out usually for the rest of our lives. As children we automatically absorbed parental injunctions, precepts and

permissions. Berne writes, "Man is born free, but one of the first things he learns is to do as he is told, and he spends the rest of his life doing that"[7] (p. 216). Our script tells us whether we are going to succeed or fail in our life undertakings. If you are love-shy, then most likely your script calls for you to be a loser or a failure, at least regarding sex and love. If your script calls for you to fail romantically, then your subconscious will continually sabotage your attempts with women.

James and Jongeward describe how scripting develops:

> Infants…begin to pick up messages about themselves and their worth through their first experiences of being touched or being ignored by others… Children who are cuddled affectionately, smiled at, and talked to receive different messages from those who are handled with fright, hostility, or anxiety. Children who receive little touch and who experience parental indifference or hostility are discounted. They learn to feel they are not-OK and perhaps may feel like a "nothing."
>
> Children's first feelings about themselves are likely to remain the most powerful force in their life dramas, significantly influencing the psychological positions they take and the roles they play.[9] (p. 87)

While one parent can instill scripts, usually both parents are involved. When two people's scripts overlap with a place for each person in the other's script, the two people will become good friends or marry each other. Two people's scripts need to complement each other for them to pair up. Therefore, they subconsciously agree on the script to give their children. Berne observes in *What Do You Say After You Say Hello?* (1972) that "usually the parent of the opposite sex tells the child what to do, and the parent of the same sex shows him how to do it" (p. 279).

Berne writes, "All of these script types have their sexual aspects. 'Never' scripts may forbid either love or sex or both" (p. 207). Even scripts placing restrictions on sex and love can still call for the person to marry. Thus, most love-shys fail to fulfill their scripts in both their and their family's eyes. Often we love-shys have such a difficult time with our parents because our lives do not follow the script they worked so hard for us to fulfill. This tension from our parents can be especially troubling when we cannot fulfill the basic pattern of getting married and having kids, common goals for a happy life. Without evidence that they have successfully done their job of perpetuating the family along with passing on their morals and values, parents can feel like failures. They may increase their pressure on you not to do anything out of the ordinary that in their eyes would in any way lessen your chances of obtaining a wife.

A script can be thought of as an unconscious life plan or, perhaps, a "primal drama." It can take an experienced therapist versed in script analysis a while to identify a person's script. Often daydreaming brings up and then reinforces script-related thoughts and scenarios. Berne found that some people's scripts are similar to fairy tales or classic mythology, namely the ancient Greek stories based on archetypes. I believe our scripts can be guided by stories, and today most people experience stories through movies. While I doubt movies create total life scripts for us, if we see a particular movie that significantly reinforces our parental injunctions and our personal childhood experiences, we may internalize the movie. After reading Berne and rewatching a movie from my youth, I realized I had internalized this movie. Similarly, I noticed a friend's life uncannily following his favorite movie for good and bad.

Just as the hero in an action movie never questions his role, neither do we humans much question the scripts we follow throughout our whole lives. Not only are we disinclined to investigate our own scripts, but just as when filming a movie, nobody—whether directors and producers or parents and society—likes actors who

question and deviate from their given scripts. Wouldn't you like to find a more worthwhile purpose in life than what your script calls for? Wouldn't you like to live a free life and not feel like you live in a completely written movie? Follow Berne's advice and respond to the negative and unproductive voices in your head "loud and clear: 'But, mother, I'd rather do it my own way and win'" (p. 276). The general way to release yourself from your script is to give yourself permission. *I give myself complete permission to have sex with and love women. I give myself permission to succeed.* Berne claims, "One of the most important permissions is a license to stop acting stupid and start thinking" (p. 124).

The more permission you have, the less your script binds you. Repeat some of the previous and following permissions out loud and see if you feel a lead weight lifting. *I have permission to be in healthy romances. I have permission to have and enjoy meaningless and casual sex. I have permission to pursue women successfully. I have permission to have a long and happy marriage.* Berne's writing reminds me of my Landmark Education training where I was taught to release myself from my rigid programming by becoming possibility. Say, *I am the possibility of success.* When you say to yourself, *I can do anything,* what thoughts come into your mind to contradict that statement?

Berne explains a first step a person must take:

> In order to break away from such script programs, he must stop and think. But he cannot think about his programming unless he first gives up the illusion of autonomy. He must realize that he has not been up to now the free agent he likes to imagine he is, but rather the puppet of some Destiny from generations ago. Few people have the courage or the elasticity to turn around and stare down the monkey on their backs, and the older they get, the stiffer their necks become.[7] (p. 216)

I hope that you as a love-shy have gained insight into what you have to do both formally and informally to treat your love-shyness and its symptoms. All kinds of help are available to you. Little of this help may directly lead to overcoming your love-shyness completely, but explore your options. Attacking your love-shyness from many angles at once tends to produce significant breakthroughs.

Notes

1. Boeree, C. George. *Viktor Frankl.* Accessed on March 22, 2009 at http://webspace.ship.edu/cgboer/frankl.htm
2. Harris, S. R., Kemmerling, R. L. and North, M. M. (2002) "Brief virtual reality therapy for public speaking anxiety." *Cyberpsychology and Behavior 5*, 6, 543–550.
3. HITLab. *Virtual Reality Pain Reduction.* Accessed on April 30, 2008 at www.hitl.washington.edu/projects/vrpain
4. Shippen, E. and Fryer, W. (2007, first published 1998) *The Testosterone Syndrome: The Critical Factor for Energy, Health & Sexuality—Reversing The Male Menopause.* Lanham, MD: M. Evans.
5. The Norwegian University of Science and Technology (2009) *Ecstasy For Treatment Of Traumatic Anxiety.* Rockville, MD: ScienceDaily. Accessed on February 2, 2009 at www.sciencedaily.com/releases/2009/01/090108121656.htm
6. Sex and Love Addicts Anonymous (UK). *Anorexia—Sexual, Social & Emotional.* Accessed on April 30, 2008 at www.slaauk.com/anorexia-sexual-social-amp-emotional
7. Berne, E. (1976) *Beyond Games and Scripts.* New York: Grove Press.
8. Wikipedia. *Neuro-linguistic programming.* Accessed on March 22, 2009 at http://en.wikipedia.org/wiki/Neuro-linguistic_programming
9. James, M and Jongeward, D. (1971) *Born to Win.* Reading, MA: Addison-Wesley Publishing Company.

Chapter 5

For Women

Sex it up

You women finally have your own chapter. Or at least, I address women directly most of the time. Men, please do not pass over this chapter, because it functions as an integral part of this book and much applies to both sexes. Women may be wary of a man giving them relationship advice: *What's a man doing in the women's locker room?*, but a woman wrote one of my source books of dating advice for men, *Understanding Women* (Miller 2004), so certainly one sex can learn from the experience and teachings of the other. Some of you may complain, since female love-shys are so well hidden, that I should not generalize after only studying a few of them, which may be a valid concern. But up to now, no one has even tried to identify them, much less deal directly with the topic of female love-shyness.

Since I am a man, major issues can prevent you accepting what I write. Just as I hate it when my mother tells me how to act as a man, women hate hearing how to act in a feminine way from men, especially when that advice involves acting more sexually. This female sentiment is buttressed by a long history of male dominance that relegates women to the status of purely sexual objects. I cannot deny that my advice for women happens to coincide with what love-shy men like myself truly want: sensitive, assertive, intelligent, sexy women. A man cannot teach a woman how to be a woman, and attempting to teach the basics of the hidden curriculum of women's sexuality and dating comes across as from the 1950s. Also, with the broad and complex topic of human sexuality, exceptions to all blanket statements exist. In the long run, I envision this chapter functioning as the backbone of a future book written empathetically by a woman who thoroughly investigates love-shy women.

I endeavor to empower women whose shyness and love-shyness have blocked much related to romance and sexuality. Love-shyness is partially a phobia of sex, so this chapter does focus on sex. While most love-shyness involves other intimacy problems too, the physicalness of sex-related issues make them the most obvious and easiest to address. By dealing with your sexuality issues and attempting to act more sexily, your anxieties can arise for you to confront and overcome. Even if people see you as quite attractive and you have no problem attracting male attention, still consider my advice valid. Dealing with love-shyness relates more to you and your anxieties than how others perceive you.

I write with lonely single women in mind, since love-shy women without significant others are more in need of advice. Yet some mildly love-shy women who can have relationships are unable to live without a man. If you have never gone for long periods of your adult life without a relationship, you might want to step back and try to live without a man for a while. This action should make you more mature, more confident and less dependent. Watch out for "Nice Gal Syndrome" where your innate self-worth is tied to your romantic relationships and your sexual confidence. One woman claimed, "I would humiliate myself a million times over to make him happy."

Even though men bear the brunt of love-shyness since they are usually expected to make the moves, arguably women must act first. It is the woman who dresses to look attractive, and who spends significantly more time doing her hair and makeup. This preparation works to attract men, since they are visual creatures. Most women do not then stand by passively and wait for men to see them. Women hook guys with their eyes and flirt. Flirting shows that you are interested in the man for more than his knowledge of whatever subject you are talking about. Flirting shows that you are interested yet playful, which is the romantic message you should project to a man you fancy.

While it's good for both men and women to be able to flirt, it's much more of a requirement for women. Flirting may be the one normally instinctual skill that, when lacking, is a big problem for females but not nearly as serious for males. Men don't need to flirt as much as they need to recognize flirtatious behavior directed towards them and take assertive action. Since the historic human mating ritual expects women to be mostly passive, women use flirting as a subtle way to connect with potential mates. Flirting from across the room is both safe and gives a positive message to the guy. If you cannot flirt reasonably well, you will find it much harder to attract a man.

Shy women may feel that flirting is too outgoing an action for them. Eliminate this misconception and embrace the subtle nature of flirting. You can't get much less minimal than eye contact, the most basic and important form of flirting. Eye contact alone may not be enough if the man is clueless or distracted. If you combine even minimal flirting actions with eye contact, it should make a strong impression on a guy. Depending on the situation and despite your love-shy inclinations, go extreme rather than subtle. *Intimate Connections* (Burns 1985) makes this point:

> It's often better to have a smile on your face and to be a little red with embarrassment because you're acting slightly outrageously than to come across in a dull, serious

> way. If you're too sincere, people will get nervous because they simply won't know where you're coming from. When you're being blatantly flirtatious, it seems to set people at their ease. (p. 90)

Before I understood more about flirting, I would treat an initial encounter with a prospective romantic partner more like a serious job interview. Of course, knowing that you should flirt more makes sense in the privacy of your home, but actually remembering to do it and feeling comfortable doing it in a social setting are different beasts. Thus, you should practice flirting both to get comfortable doing it and to make it more automatic. Relax and bask in the subtle and ambiguous beauty of flirting. You risk nothing by doing it. It is so subtle that men do not even remember it. Recalling a couple's first meeting, the boyfriend will usually believe he initially spotted her and made the move. The woman remembers better that her eye contact and flirting preceded the man's actions.

Feeling afraid and cautious about flirting is negative thinking on your part, and these emotions need to be overcome. Do not hesitate to flirt. You are not offending anybody. You actually compliment the man with whom you flirt, indicating, *You are an attractive man, and I like being in your presence.* Everybody loves to receive compliments, so don't hold back with your flirting. What could possibly be wrong with spreading positive vibrations, unless you flirt with a man whom you know is already spoken for or you flirt with men other than your date? Think of it as a grand smile. Men love it. No one will tell you to stop flirting.

Flipping and tossing your hair. Licking your lips. Laughing. Playing with an object in an absent-minded way. Fiddling with your necklace or other jewelry. Looking at his face, especially his mouth. Giving him a coy glance. Fluttering your eyelashes. Raising your eyebrows. Adjusting your clothes or primping and preening. Leaning in towards him. Touching yourself, including your face or hair, in certain ways. Exposing your neck. Eating

foods in a sensual way. Blushing—so don't feel embarrassed if you do. Touching him. Using a sexy tone of voice. These are all simple and basic moves. Yet more options exist. Mirroring his body builds rapport. Lingering with him a little longer than would be expected for the encounter. Ideally, flirting naturally expresses your building tension and excitement. The biggest flirting actions for both sexes are eye contact and smiling, so always do both. Flirting may well induce the other person to begin mimicking your actions.

Intimate Connections offers more good flirting advice:

> At first, for practice, flirt with people who don't make you overly anxious. A lonely graduate student [advises]: "Remember to wear something that you feel sexy in. Flatter the man because it's fun and show him that you enjoy his company. People will react positively, and this will help you overcome your feelings of insecurity and self-doubt. Don't forget that you can also *touch* the other person. You might want to touch his arm and say, 'Oh, what a nice shirt you're wearing.' This can do a great deal to set people at ease and generate warm responses." (p. 91)

As a woman, you probably feel uncomfortable when a man who you don't know well touches you. However, men love it when a woman touches them no matter how well they know her. For both sexes it signals positive movement towards physical intimacy.

Pilinski (2003) stresses the importance of touch in building intimacy. "There is nothing that conveys a deeper sense of intimacy and warmth between two people as does physical touch—and between a man and a women, touch can become electric if handled correctly" (p. 167). On a first date touch is critical, but it must be done mildly, subtly and politely. Pininski continues, "When you're getting to know a woman, it's appropriate only to touch her hands, arms, shoulders and upper back areas… At first, your touch should always be fleeting" (p. 168).

Guys, brushing her hair out of her face when you are talking to her is a good bold move, but may be too much for a woman to accept on an early date. It shows you want to see her eyes and maintain a direct connection. Women, if you flinch when a date touches you, either he touched you too intimately, you aren't into him or, most likely, your love-shyness has created an aversion to touch. Love-shy women should work to overcome this aversion by practicing touching and being touched, starting with non-sexual situations.

Before actual touch happens, a potential couple "touch" each other with their eyes. Eyes are not only receptors but transmitters of information. The book *Secrets of Sexual Body Language* (1994) by Martin Lloyd-Elliot contains, in the midst of plenty of excellent photographs and descriptions of flirting behavior, a good quote by Victor Hugo from *Les Miserables*:

> The power of a glance has been so much abused in love stories that it has come to be disbelieved in. Few people dare now say that two beings have fallen in love because they have looked at each other. Yet it is in this way that love begins and in this way only. The rest is only the rest, and comes afterwards. Nothing is more real than these great shocks, which two souls give each other in exchanging this spark. (p. 60)

Most romantic communication is nonverbal, especially initially.

Lloyd-Elliot (1994) continues emphasizing the power of the eyes:

> Give any man a dreamy, five-second burst of gazing and his toes will curl, his heart will flush, and he will become putty in a woman's hands. When men try the same thing they usually blow it, because they stare. (p. 71)

As you break initial eye contact, look down to signal romantic interest. The eyes and the mouth are the most sexually interesting features of the face, which is why for millennia women have applied makeup around the eyes and lipstick on the lips. The more dilated someone's pupils, the more sexually attractive the person, and a reason why candle-lit dinners are romantic. While eye contact alone sufficiently verifies romantic interest, kick it up a notch by flirting. Using your eyes and flirting to carrying on a "conversation" with someone can progress romance without a word being uttered. Of course, before long you actually have to talk to the person.

Even though body language and eye contact are significantly more important than what is verbally spoken, you can flirt with words. Verbal flirting can take the form of a compliment, and the more outrageous the compliment, the more obvious and impactful the flirting. Innuendo, double entendres and humor are great too. How you say something is usually more important than the actual words. Men often confuse a woman's friendliness and talkativeness for sexual attraction. You men need to understand that women are often naturally friendly and sociable, and just because a woman is talking to you does not necessarily mean that she wants to go to bed with you or has any romantic interest in you. Thus, the inclusion of nonverbal flirting can help distinguish between friendliness and romantic attraction. When in doubt as to the other's true intention, use your intuition. Ask yourself if the other person's body language is inviting and open or blocking and closed.

Dancing can be considered a form of flirting. While moving on the dance floor is advertising yourself to everyone in the place, if you dance close to a guy while looking at him you are seriously flirting. If a guy doesn't respond when you dance near him, there's probably nothing else you can do to attract his interest.

Use flirting for more than attracting someone. During a date flirting indicates positive interest. Regardless of their confident exteriors, men and women are insecure creatures who need frequent reassurances about their attractiveness and innate self-worth by people they find sexually attractive. If you really like the guy, you'd better flirt with him during the date, or else he will believe you have lost interest in him. Flirting should set the tone for the date: fun, sexy and interesting.

Be wary of flirting too heavily and give your date the wrong idea that you are ready to spend the night with him. If he is truly interested in you, not only will he wait for you, but he will fantasize about you in the mean time. I would say that as long as you are not touching him much besides holding hands, then you are not leading him on too strongly no matter what other flirting you may do. If he makes a touching move, sometimes it's better for you acknowledge it, say, with a little smile than to ignore it, which may indicate to him that he needs to do something more blatant to get a reaction from you. Touch is a main language of courtship, so you need to keep ratcheting it up for the romance to proceed. Of course, go at your own comfortable speed, as long as you are actually moving forward and not stalled out.

Guys want to know what's going on in your head. Or, at minimum, they want to know how they stand with you. If you are so shy that you can't seem to say much during a date, at least smile, look him in the eyes from time to time, nod in agreement and flirt. But you have to speak up for yourself and say what you want. Don't blame him for taking you to the tractor pull if you agreed earlier to go with him. If you determine the guy is not for you, make sure you are assertive enough so he gets the picture. *I had a nice time with you this evening*, is the polite thing to say whether you liked the guy or not. Either add to it, *But, it's not going to work between us*, or, *Let's do it again sometime*. Due to my Asperger's I want a clear and truthful turn-down from a woman. Just tell me I'm not your type. Imagine my lie-hating autistic frustration after a woman at work whom I found extremely attractive turned me down with, *I don't date coworkers*, and then started dating a coworker.

Tell a date that you're shy and need to take it slower and that it takes you longer than most women to warm up to a guy. This explanation gives him the understanding he needs to help him not feel so frustrated. Remember not to talk specifically about love-shyness until the relationship is solidly underway and you feel compelled to mention it. Even if the date goes well and it seems like you talk his ear off, telling him you are shy is most likely a turn on for him. It may make him feel special, because he thinks he is the only one who sees the real you. Once you act very unshy on a date, the guy can really love it, because he thinks, rightly or wrongly, that it was him who got you to open up.

Flirting can help during a boring date. When he drones on about his master's thesis, you should start acting more sexual and suggest doing something more active such as dancing. This should make him realize that his demeanor and yours are not congruent and he needs to do something to jump on the same page as you. If your flirting does not draw his focus from himself to you, it's time for you to move on.

When someone tosses the label of "flirt" on a woman, it usually is synonymous with being called a tease. This happens either because she flirts with every man in sight, or her level of flirting does not match her interest in the person. Love-shys should err on the side of over-flirtatiousness. Except while at most workplaces, political rallies and funerals, people would rather be with a fun-loving flirt than with a somber person who treats everything in a business-like manner. Calling someone a flirt is not a seriously derogatory label. Being called a flirt should be taken as a compliment for love-shys of either gender.

Some women may think they have to dumb themselves down when they see men constantly swarming around bubble-headed bimbos. Are the men around these women even the types of men you want? Consider that the bimbo is just a better flirt than you and the situation has nothing to do with her IQ. Does she seem concerned about war in the Middle-East or women's inequality in

the workplace? Or is she out having fun leaving her personal and global worries at home? There are times to ponder and discuss weighty issues, but these times are probably not during opportunities for meeting available men. If you and a prospective romantic partner are caught up in an intellectual topic, you may forget to flirt or feel that flirting is inappropriate. Switch to a lighter subject, such as anything remotely sensual or sexual where flirting could fit right in. Ideally, flirting should complement your sophisticated qualities. An intelligent woman flirting can be extremely intoxicating to those men who crave deep conversations with a lover.

Flirting builds romantic tension. Straightforwardness defuses this tension. I see myself making this mistake when I want to act assertively and show a woman that I really like her by saying something like, *I'm really attracted to you.* My feelings and emotions come out in a serious, direct way. This is a sure way to kiss romance goodbye. You need to develop a flirting vocabulary so your romantic emotions come out through flirting rather than as words on a telegram. Words become much more important as the relationship becomes serious, as when you expect him to say, *I love you.* At the beginning the relationship is not yet serious, no matter how attracted you are to each other. Keep it light and fun, NOT *I have something important and serious to tell you; I'm falling in love with you.* Do not say this on an early date no matter how intense your feelings are for the person.

You men must give her time to make up her mind about you and develop a serious attraction to you. Being direct requires a direct answer. Hold your forthrightness until you receive positive indications from her at the proper time during the development of the relationship. Don't *tell* a woman how you feel about her so much as *show* her. Most women are very socially observant. While it may not seem logical, women will more often than not find a guy more attractive if early on he does not come right out and verbally express his affection. You do not want to disclose too much too soon. Keep your romantic partner yearning to learn more about you. Instead of directly disclosing your feelings, give her heartfelt compliments. The love-shy heart is big and lonely, so once the love-shy guy makes a little bit of perceived headway with a woman, he opens the emotional floodgates way too early. Maybe only experience can cure this inappropriate action.

Flirting can help a man out of other love-shy mistakes. If you find yourself receiving a major negative reaction after acting sexually assertive, it is either because she is not interested in you or you made the move at the wrong time. Either way, how you respond implies much about yourself. Of course, you may say something like, *I'm sorry for being so presumptuous.* But, whether you say it while flirting or whether you say it with embarrassment are worlds apart. One way shows you as an assertive yet polite high-status male, while the latter denotes you as a love-shy with bad timing who's uncomfortable with his sexuality.

And before this stage, guys, going half way with the flirting may make her think of you as creepy if you don't get up the nerve to ever talk to her. You may play peek-a-boo for a little while, but soon you need to actually speak with her. At least smile when she sees you lurking. This goes for you women too. Luckily, you don't usually have to start the conversation unless the guy is too shy to do so. But you do have to flirt. And once you start flirting do not stop until you lose interest in the person. You have made a connection, so continue it.

Flirting pierces the heart of shyness. You work to draw attention to yourself. At home in front of the mirror, develop and practice some signature flirtatious moves, perhaps starting with a smile and a flash of your eyes. Make sure your moves have an element of sexiness, because someone can perceive you raising an eyebrow as an indication of astonishment rather than sexual interest. Walk down the street and practice using your moves with everyone you find attractive. Do not put pressure on the other person or expect him or her to do anything. You are merely expressing yourself. How the other person reacts does not matter at the moment. If you can't comfortably flirt with anyone on the

street, you won't be able to do it when the time comes to flirt with that irresistible hunk. With any flirting move, you might want to use it just a few times with a man on a given evening. While slightly nervous flirting may be OK for a woman, extreme nervousness and flirting does not combine well. Channel your nervousness through flirting so you enjoy rather than fear the rush.

What happens when you notice a guy checking out your breasts or other female attributes? Are you proud and glad for the interest, or are you shameful and embarrassed? Although women find it unpleasant to be viewed in a purely sexual manner, try to reframe your reaction into something positive like, *I must be a pretty sexually attractive woman since he so blatantly stares at me.* Guys, remember it is extremely rude and off-putting to stare or even more than discreetly glance at a woman's boobs and her body. I know they are right out there in front of you, perhaps accentuated with a little cleavage, but resist the urge to look. You may think you are getting over your love-shyness and acting like a typical man, and you are. But it is still horrendous manners and a bad habit that tends to have you talking to her chest instead of her face.

Beware of sending out unintentional negative romantic signals. Crossing or folding your arms, fidgeting, keeping your mouth closed and lips pressed together, looking away to prevent any eye contact, yawning, shifting body posture, maintaining a rigid posture, covering or blocking your face with your hands, moving your head side to side signifying no, chewing gum and generally not paying attention to him are all negative indications. Body language rarely lies, and our body and face constantly broadcast our state of being. Despite your dating desperation, if you are doing one or more of these negative actions, you probably are not into him. However, your love-shyness and fears generate these same reactions, so if you think your love-shyness instead of your instincts is producing these unwanted actions, you need to change quickly to positive flirting. Luckily, a man usually won't hold it against a woman if she appears to change her mind and now finds him attractive.

Women feel they must turn down a man as gently as possible out of politeness and to minimize the damage to his ego. Negative body language is useful in this regard. Unfortunately, men often fail to pick up on the hints giving them the cold shoulder. This is too bad, because the sooner the man figures out he's not wanted the better. Guys particularly need to learn to spot rejection and negative signals quickly. If a guy fails to notice you are giving him the brush off, act assertively and tell him you just aren't interested. Don't worry that you can't make up a decent excuse quickly. It will bruise his ego less for him to walk away from you now, rather than hours later after he continued talking to you and buying you drinks while building you up in his mind.

To flirt well you must feel comfortable and sexy. Therefore, you need to wear comfortable and sexy clothes. While sexy often trumps comfort when it comes to fashion, if you can't breathe or move, you aren't sexy. Don't wear something so sexy that it makes you feel uncomfortable, as social and emotional disaster will likely result. If you have an outfit that shows more of you than you are comfortable with, first try it out around the house until you feel at ease and able to act like the outfit would have you act. Even if you only wear it out in public once, your sexy image will stick in men's heads for a long time.

I recommend reading *Exhibitionism for the Shy* (1995) by Carol Queen to help coax that vixen (or male fox) out of you. The book is not about going around in public wearing only a trench coat but about how to draw out that erotic part of yourself unselfconsciously. Even stuck alone in one's room, reading it will bring a person closer to her or his true sexuality. Queen makes many suggestions for the budding seductress or seducer such as, "If you haven't experimented with clothing to get you in a sexy mood, consider playing dress up" (p. 123). In the book her friend Rita relates how she got from her feelings of insecurity to her current erotically competent state:

> I had to let go of certain hang-ups about my body—it was really a process of shedding self-hatred and the feeling of being insecure, unpowerful, unlovable, ugly. I took slow steps. I remember dragging one of my best friends down to a lingerie shop and buying an outrageous black lace thong teddy. (p. 124)

Men are visual creatures, and you never know when you will run into that handsome man. Although overalls work well for gardening and painting, women should rarely wear them in public unless picking up a load of hay. You tomboy women don't have to go for frills and lace; just start wearing closer fitting clothes that flatter your shape and prove you are a woman. It's not so much what you have, but how you present it and how you use it. Men are often more attracted to a woman acting and dressing sexily instead of someone who may have more classical beauty but doesn't exude any hint of sexual energy. It is not about money either, because most guys can't tell and don't care whether you wear a $50 or $5000 dress. They only care how you look in it.

If you have short hair, think about letting it grow long. Fashions constantly change, but one basic rule does not; most men like long hair on women. Try it out for a few months. If you don't think the extra work taking care of it is worth the increased male interest and improved feeling of sexiness, you can always cut it. Longer hair gives you a prop for flirting and gives you an integral part of your sexy costume.

Perhaps you feel too overweight to be sexy. Don't let fashion magazines dupe you with their airbrushed and digitally manipulated images of anorexic models. Once you start obsessively comparing yourself to other people you are done for. Studies consistently show that most women underestimate how attractive they really are. Depression can further skew a woman's impression of her body in the negative direction. Chances are you are a lot hotter than you think. Read *The Beauty Myth* (2002, first published 1991) by Naomi Wolf to help you overcome your feelings of inferiority.

However, the more one approaches his or her ideal *healthy* body weight, the more people will be attracted to him or her. This statement includes anyone who is too thin. Anorexia, perhaps, may occasionally link to love-shyness, as this eating disorder usually starts at puberty. One former anorexic claims her biggest fear during puberty was of men and sex.[1] Despite what you think your mirror and scales tell you, a few pounds or so above your ideal weight is no big deal, so don't act like it's the end of the world if you can't fit into your favorite jeans.

Women and men with an aversion to sex may subconsciously make themselves unattractive to avoid dealing with sex and sexual issues. As you work to improve your appearance and men start responding sexually to you, your deep psychological issues regarding sex may surface. Work to consciously face these issues rather than fall back into your former unhealthy habits. At least start by realizing the big difference between appearing sexually attractive and actually having sex. As long as you are ashamed of your sexuality, no diet will ever work for you.

As a woman you may respond to my advice with *Fashions and the type of women men find attractive change over time.* Obviously. And the media does play a role. What does not change is that, like all animal species, humans are hardwired to find healthy people attractive. Everyone has a certain body type with a particular build and metabolism. Some people are naturally large and will never mesh with what society pictures as an ideal body. No worries. You have to use what you have got. If you exercise regularly and stay in otherwise good physical condition, no one can complain. Your attitude and how you act matter most.

Because the deck is stacked against you as a love-shy, you may have to work harder to attract the opposite sex. This is not about abandoning your feminist ideals but about living practically. This is about stepping out of your normal modes and confronting your sexuality issues. Learn to flirt even in a minimalist

way, wear outfits in which you feel sexy and make your body as attractive as reasonably possible. Relax. As long as you can get out there and play the game confidently and comfortably, men will notice your attractiveness and come to you to enjoy your admirable qualities. It is not the most attractive woman who gets the most male attention but the woman who sends out the most positive signals to men. Confidence is queen. Feeling good about yourself is attractive.

The world is your oyster

From the male love-shy and shallow male perspectives, women have it easy when it comes to forming romantic relationships. Historically, the man takes the initiative and makes the first moves and risks rejection. The man plans, calls and sets up the dates. Of course, it is not exactly true that women have it easier but, since sex automatically pops into the heads of most men when in the presence of a woman they find attractive, you normally need make no effort to trigger this response. Since you prepare yourself every day for your job by looking presentable, you might as well make the most of it. Use your newfound flirting abilities to have doors opened for you. If you have a problem morally with using flirting in a teasing manner, ask yourself if you do not flirt because of your moral or political convictions or because of your love-shyness. Practice flirting for maximum benefit. Batting your eyes at that automotive mechanic may get your car worked on sooner. Practicing in non-romantic situations provides feedback to see if your flirting and sexy attitude works. Men are naturally moved to go out of their way to help a woman they find attractive, even with a woman with whom they have no chance of having sex. I'm not suggesting necessarily taking advantage of men. Guys, this flirting advice applies to you too, even though women appear less susceptible to this type of influence.

Many people's initial reaction will be to reject outright my advice to flirt at work, rightly arguing that sexually based customs should not exist in the workplace. This is not about the workplace. This is basic instinctual male—female interaction that happens to take place at work. It could be argued that I lead women back to the 1950s. Instead, I'm trying to rescue the 1 or 2 percent of women stuck in the dark ages. Once women have understood and mastered the basics of sexuality, then they can gain the more complex and mature perspective of the subject that the modern women's movement provides.

As a woman you are in control sexually, so you need to act like it. Theoretically, if you only want casual sex, you can blatantly flirt with just about any guy and quickly find yourself in bed with him. Of course it's about finding the right man. Instinctively, a woman sizes up a man by figuring how good a father he would be with both supplying genetic material and raising offspring. Even if only for a one-night stand, this criterion still influences a woman when choosing a man. Love-shy women seem like love-shy men in that they may settle for someone not quite right for them, worrying that they can never find another. Getting a man worthy of you, rather than just any man, leads to true empowerment. Maximizing who you are and what you do allows for plenty of romantic options. At least then you won't let men walk all over you.

A significant step for obtaining a proper partner requires breaking free from your parents' programming of you and your subconscious. We often fail to see how much our parents have influenced our romantic life. Not only may we find ourselves attracted to a person similar to our opposite-sex parent, but we may put up with abuse from our mate primarily because a parent suffered the same abuse. If one asks a woman whose father physically abused her mother if she wants a husband who will beat her, of course, she will emphatically say no. But often she will go out and marry such a man, sometimes repeatedly. Thus, it is important to deal with these subconscious issues, not only to have the capability to marry, but to marry the correct person. This can only happen if you forcefully and directly deal with your issues. This may mean breaking up with a guy who is not right enough for you and leads you down the same old rotten path.

Our parents influence us more than we realize. If you happen to act wild and sexy do you think, *Oh, my Goodness. I can't believe I'm doing this. What would my parents think?* Much easier said than done, but do not let your parents continue to influence you negatively.

Can you masturbate without thinking that it's a sin? Are you programmed to believe, *Oh, that part of me down there is just for having babies?* Or, *Satisfy your man and don't concern yourself with your own pleasures?* Make sure that you can give yourself guilt-free orgasms. "[M]asturbation can simply be a physical expression of self-love and the first step in accepting yourself as a sensual, sexual creature," *Intimate Connections* proclaims (Burns 1985, p. 261). If you can't produce the big O on your own, how can you expect a man to? Buy a vibrator and find some porn geared towards women or indulge in romance novels. Notice your negative thinking like, *I could never go into an adult themed store.* While you could order online, if you have such negative feelings about these places, likely you need actually to go into an exotic boutique to face your aversion. These places cater to normal folks of both genders looking to spice up their love life.

You need to deal with your frigidity, although this complete task may prove difficult without a lover. First look inward and contemplate if Masters and Johnson's general description of females with sexual dysfunction applies to you: "For some reason, her 'permission' to function as a sexual being or her confidence in herself as a functional sexual entity has been impaired"[2] (p. 315). Love-shy women may find *The Power of Sexual Surrender* by Marie M. Robinson helpful. Even though women may discard this book because a conservative woman wrote it in 1959, what Robinson labels frigidity looks a lot like female love-shyness. For example, she claims, "Frigidity is always rooted in incomplete knowledge

gained in childhood and adolescence" (p. 17). And just as loveshy men complain about men's required assertive role, Robinson observes, "I have yet to hear a woman suffering from a frigidity problem who did not deeply resent both of these facts [that the man is the romantic initiator and the woman is the wooed]" (p. 207).

For those who have never experienced an orgasm, she advises:

> [O]rgasm cannot be sought entirely rationally. It will arrive when it will arrive, as the end process of a total change in a frigid woman's deepest psychological attitudes. It cannot be sought separately or as an end in itself. Indeed, to seek it directly, to wait upon it, to try to force it are the surest possible ways of postponing its arrival. (p. 217)

She also keenly observes that once a woman starts dealing with her issues and opening herself up to sexual pleasure and self-satisfaction, as a defense mechanism her subconscious may unleash a bunch of negative thoughts about men. Robinson blames the feminist movement for legitimizing blanket negative characterizations of men. Delete your ideas that men are brutes, animals, idiots, women haters, useless, need to be changed or any other overarching negative.

Although as a man I cannot vouch for her advice, I respect Robinson's insight because she describes my own mother in detail:

> I call her the all-mother type. She is a distinct anomaly. In the first place, she is definitely classifiable as sexually frigid... Psychologically speaking, however, she exhibits almost the perfect picture of normalcy. She is happily married, is a very giving and altruistic person, and is totally loyal and devoted to her husband. She is above all, a wonderful mother, willing and able to give the very

> best of herself to her children... There is generally little reason why the all-mother type of woman should seek to change herself in any way... [T]he matter can be a subtle one, for this type of woman...tends to be overprotective of her children or tends to have a hard time letting them go from the nest when that period in their growth has arrived. (pp. 68–69)

Most parents of love-shys are too doting, protecting and controlling of their kids. They can find it difficult to strike a proper balance between protecting them and pushing them out the door and may have their children continue living with them well into adulthood. Parents' divorce can greatly increase shame and lower self-esteem in a child even while both parents separately overindulge the child. When parents treat their adult love-shy offspring as a child, it leads to all sorts of negative feelings in the offspring like frustration and resentment. When the love-shy acts out due to these strong feelings, his or her actions only reinforce the parents' belief that the love-shy needs more parenting and control. Unfortunately, the parents are often the least understanding as they have been married for some time and forget or don't know the emotional devastation of long-time singleness. No matter how much they love you, your parents may not always work for your best interest.

If one or both of your parents physically or sexually abused you, allowed you to be abused or was an alcoholic or other drug abuser, you need to deal with this assertively. Traumatic incidents from the distant past still have tremendous influence over your current and future relationships and cause major intimacy problems. You probably can't trust anyone anymore. You need to employ serious counseling. If you believe you were abused by anyone as a child, I highly recommend you obtain a copy of Dr. Susan Forward's 1989 book *Toxic Parents.* Her book discusses how controlling and manipulative these parents can be and how it affects you. While being sexually abused as a child often makes one promiscuous as an adult, such childhood traumas often have the opposite effect on a shy child; she completely withdraws. Forward states, "[M]any adult children of alcoholics become painfully shy" (p. 75).

Gilmartin (1987) claims that emotional abuse by parents contributes to the creation of love-shyness. There is no law against abusing a child emotionally, but the resulting emotional devastation can be equally severe as from physical or sexual abuse. Worse, emotional abuse is often invisible to all concerned and can continue for a lifetime. We usually have difficulty noticing childhood abuse perpetrated by our parents, because as young children we assume our parents are godlike and we may block childhood trauma out of our mind. But our parents will continue acting like they always have, which gives us a chance as adults to pick out their destructive behaviors and attitudes towards us.

Discovering and dealing with our own romantic and sexual issues makes our parents' problems obvious to us. My family still cannot accept that I have Asperger's, even after reading a draft of this book and after I started speaking professionally about my Asperger's. Parents may not accept their child's Asperger's diagnosis for various reasons. Parents, and others, may be blind to their child's Asperger's when they see the child as high functioning in most other areas of life. Parents may harbor guilt that they caused the condition or did not do enough about it. Or parents may worry they have aspects of the genetically influenced condition and deny it in themselves. My parents view me as inheriting both of their shyness and other traits and don't need a syndrome to explain how I am. Since professionals can misdiagnose conditions like love-shyness and Asperger's, parents can be wary of unfamiliar diagnoses.

Unfortunately, people focus on the obvious problems of the stressed-out offspring rather than the successful parents who have no complaints about themselves. Since not accepting their son or daughter as he or she is is a documented trait of parents of love-shys, do not expect your parents to accept your diagnosis easily.

Do not expect them to convert to a new type of thinking, which would require them to remove a whole belief system and replace it with a more enlightened one that illuminates how poorly they treated their extra-sensitive child. Parents already prone to avoiding their sexuality issues will likely deny yours.

As you deal with these issues, your family may not stand behind you. When you consciously and actively confront your family's long-established ways of being, they may resist and use subtle means to keep things as they are. Since your family has functioned as a close-knit unit for decades with its own spoken and unspoken rules, your siblings may side with your parents, which makes you feel like it's you against the world. Your parents may become defensive and act as if your openly facing your love-shyness is an attack on them. Emphasize to them that you are dealing with these issues for your own life.

To deal with this and other kinds of rage directed at your parents, you may want to write all of your gripes and problems with your parents in a letter to them. Do *not* send this letter, especially if you have already exploded into them. Instead, read your letter out loud pretending your parents are present. Keep revising and rereading your letter out loud until the words have no emotional meaning and you have nothing else to say to them. Thus, the next time you see them you can have a pleasant social engagement without these major and stressful issues surfacing.

I foresee that one day parents will receive help from a support organization similar to Parents, Families and Friends of Lesbians and Gays (PFLAG) for family and friends (and possibly potential romantic partners) of love-shys. But mainly, parents have to accept that something is wrong with them and want to change.

Once you have reclaimed your life back from your parents, you need to do the same with society's influence on your sexuality. Women are caught in the double standard where females are supposed to be good girls and not sleep around, while society judges male promiscuity less harshly. This double standard is losing power but still exists. Give yourself permission to be your

own person and not follow societal norms. Once you have eliminated your negative outside influences, you are in a good position to judge whether any internally generated negativity regarding male advances comes from love-shyness or because you don't like the guy. As in male love-shys, active female love-shyness masquerades as lack of interest in a ready romantic partner, so be vigilant.

Luckily, men understand that love is a game in which the male usually pursues. Acting sometimes hot and sometimes distant in response to romantic advances is typical female courtship action. As long as you give your man more than occasional positive indications of your affections, he will not give up on you. Even after a female love-shy has exchanged vows with a great guy, all is not hunky-dory. Strong negative reactions to intimacy and sex can cause major marital issues. It seems that love-shys are more prone to divorce, which, like most cases, is generally due to each partner not providing what the other requires. This results in a reciprocal downward spiral. Additionally, the lack of relationship experience may lead to divorce. However, I do see female love-shys as being similar to their male counterparts in that they tend to be highly monogamous and faithful.

Marriage is not a cure for love-shyness, nor is having children a cure for intimacy problems. All sex and intimacy issues must be worked out before having kids. Just because you have sex does not mean you have overcome these issues. Successfully dealing with love-shy issues will give both you and your current or eventual partner increased satisfaction with life. If you take control and properly work for it, you can have it all: a great husband, healthy children and a joyous sex life.

Go for it

Much of this book deals with enabling shy men to overcome their passivity, grab the initiative and pursue women, because society and the human mating ritual expects this male action. Ideally, society should allow a legitimate way for passive men to succeed without compromising their innate nature. Luckily, society changes as women relentlessly pursue equality in all areas of life. Traditional male and female roles blur. Women pursue career paths that have them competing with men, while some men stay at home and take care of the kids. Based on this trend, one would expect women to begin dropping their more passive courtship role and more actively pursue men.

This scenario is happening. Women are assuming a more assertive role in initiating romance. In the United States women actually ask men out on dates. At least, that's what the studies report. While we in the older generation may not notice it, high school and college age females pursue males more assertively than similarly aged women of the past. The women's logic is simple: *Why should I have to wait around for the guy to call me when I can call him?* As a male love-shy, my main frustration with the women's movement is that it has not gone far enough. If women want equality between the sexes, then women should bear similar responsibilities in all areas of life including dating.

Society is free enough now to allow you to break from traditional roles and become whatever kind of person you innately are or want to be. Do what works for you. Walking down the marriage aisle with the person of your dreams is what ultimately matters in your, your family's and society's eyes, not who saw whom first and who initiated contact.

Recent studies find that when it comes to sexual behavior, males and females differ less than most perceive. While one may think of the male as more prone to philandering, Adrian Forsyth notes in his *A Natural History of Sex* (1993, first published 1986), "A survey of hundreds of human cultures reveals that female extramarital sex occurs in three-fourths of them and is common in more than half of them" (p. 25). Forsyth, whose fascinating reports on the sex lives of all kinds of animals puts human mating behaviors in perspective, finds examples of species where the

female is the assertive one and the male is passive. He concludes that these species:

> do more than simply dispel the notion that there is such a thing as a masculine or feminine behavior pattern inherent in the gender. They also show that the sex roles played in courtship, territoriality and aggression depend on the relative investments of time and resources made by the two sexes. It is this theory, based on the costs and benefits of investment, that makes sense of masculine and feminine behavior. (p. 69)

From a purely biological perspective, the cost to the human male for the physical act of mating is some seminal fluid. Mating costs the female the possibility of becoming pregnant for nine months and then acting as the principal caregiver to the offspring for years to come. The introduction of reliable and practical birth control has led to a decrease in human female restriction of mating possibilities, but the risks of sexually transmitted diseases and birth control failure still exist. Because women tend to be more discerning and have built-in intuition for identifying good mates, shouldn't women cut through the passive waiting games and make sure they connect with the person they want?

In the workplace, with the threat of sexual harassment accusations constantly looming, men become hesitant to show attraction to female coworkers. Thus, it becomes much easier if the woman initiates romance with a coworker. While women are commonly attracted to alpha males, men are much less concerned about the professional or social ranking of women. A woman in a position of power often makes a man feel both intimidated and turned on, which is often the complex reaction most women produce in love-shy men for similar reasons.

Given this environment I strongly suggest that shy women act more assertively in the courtship arena. Such actions give you excellent practice to expand your limited comfort zone. Forcing

you to deal with the extreme anxiety of assertive action will lesson your anxiety in other romantic situations. Another goal is significantly to increase your possibilities for obtaining a quality partner. Not only will assertive actions increase your contacts, you become more competitive in the mating game. Only selecting from men who actually approach you limits your choices. If you can't flirt well, you have to be more assertive. You don't need the level of assertiveness of a typical guy, however. Start with small acts of assertiveness such as moving to a table closer to where that single attractive guy sits. Any little thing you can do proactively to increase the possibility of connecting is good.

Instead of actually approaching strange guys, learn from the guys' playbook and have or do something that draws people to you and works as a conversation starter. Franklin Parlamis, author of *The Passive Man's Guide to Seduction* (1996), recommends playing chess in a bar to give those around you something to watch and talk about with you. People doing interesting things attract others. If you are an artist, sketching or painting in the park is cool. Show off, or at least do in public, any of your neat talents.

The classic and best "prop" is a dog, which also shows that you are responsible and could make a good parent. Dogs are great for lonely people. They give you a reason to look forward to coming home, as your dog will greet you enthusiastically no matter what kind of day you had. Stroking and grooming a pet also helps meet the lonely person's need for physical contact with another living being which they would otherwise lack in their daily lives. Dogs also provide an additional level of safety. Smooth operators might borrow a dog or start a dog walking or running service. Pets are good for those on the autism spectrum as these people often relate especially well to animals. Unfortunately, this advice is not for those of us who barely take care of our own needs. Pets can function as stress relievers, but they also create tension, especially during housebreaking and other training.

The next step on the road of female assertiveness is to approach men deliberately. You don't need to actually hit on a guy and ask for his phone number. As a woman all you have to do is go up to a guy and start a conversation about almost anything. And I mean anything. If you start talking about something totally trivial or oddball, the guy should pick up on the real reason you started talking to him. If you discuss a more serious subject that interests you, then you will find out what he thinks about it and a long conversation may ensue. If the guy doesn't respond positively, he isn't interested in you or may be a clueless love-shy who half an hour later will be banging his head against the wall wondering why he didn't react to your overtures.

Bring in your flirting. Sure, solidly flirting with a guy from a distance is positive action on your part. But, what if he doesn't respond? Did he not notice you, does he already have a girlfriend or is he not into you? What if he flirts back but still doesn't come and talk to you? Maybe he is too shy to act. Whatever the case, you will probably never know until you actually talk to him. Being assertive allows you to stop fiddling around wondering if the guy you like really likes you. When you do finally talk to him, flirt, either with body language or with your words. In fact, think about approaching a man as a form of flirting. For men too, short-circuit those crushes that cause you to daydream and fantasize about a particular woman by actually taking action to pursue that person. It will be a relief for you either way.

You might need to do more than just make first contact and actually ask him out. If you actually come on to a man, then you face the possibility of rejection. Equality means either sex opens themselves up to the sting of rejection. You don't need to take it this far unless the guy is really shy. Instead of asking a man out for a date, arrange something low key under the guise of friendship to make you appear less forward. Ask him to join you for coffee rather than dinner. Men seem to have an easier time shifting relationship gears from friendship to romance.

Assertiveness is not the sole domain of men. Obviously, testosterone plays a part in assertiveness, and women with above average amounts of testosterone are more assertive. It is hard to say

how much of a woman's timidity and passivity is cultural, how much is personal inborn genetics and how much is due to being female. If some women are naturally assertive, can all women become like this if they consciously choose to do so? Can love-shy women gain the courage to approach men? Why not? If I can overcome my passive wiring to pursue women actively, then I see no reason why women can't do the same. I consider the idea that women can actively pursue men a big secret, giving women in the know a leg up in the mating game.

Watch out for the pitfalls that can derail assertive women. More than the fear of rejection, a woman does not want to appear too forward and give a guy the wrong impression that she is easy. An assertive female is seen as more sexually available, therefore men consider her more attractive. While it is good to be viewed as attractive, you don't want to send out the wrong signals. If you approached a guy because you thought he was a bit shy and wasn't going to approach you, the guy is probably not going to be overly aggressive with you, but who knows? Once the ice is broken and he sees that you are attracted to him and that you actively sought him out, he may think it is all green lights to your bedroom.

It's up to you to provide the proper pace to show that you do not plan to take him home right away for a one-night stand, but that you are naturally, socially talking with him and are interested in the normal course of courtship. Get him into long conversations and tone down the flirting once you believe you've hooked the dude. But don't play hard to get. You've probably been using that angle your whole life. Playing hard to get ups the ante but is risky for love-shys. On the other hand if he still seems too shy to take the initiative to ask for your phone number, he may not be into you, so you giving him your phone number without him asking for it may be useless. But if he is actually shy then in a few days he might work up the courage to call you, likely after some encouragement from his buddies. If he doesn't call you and set up

a date, then he is too clueless or not interested. For either reason you should drop him from your list and move on.

Another possible negative when acting assertively is that a few men are too programmed with the traditional mating roles and do not find assertive women attractive or are intimidated by them. This is a chance you have to take. This kind of guy is probably too old fashioned for you and not a good catch. Perhaps he's a guy a love-shy woman really needs, but he is too set in his ways to accommodate any of your other love-shy issues. He may feel insecure since you are performing the courtship ritual he should be doing. If he is this insecure about how the two of you first interacted, imagine his insecurity about any number of other things.

It may raise a red flag when a woman is forward, because the man may think that you are after something and want to take advantage of him. He may worry, *If a woman this beautiful comes over and chats me up, it must be too good to be true.* Being sincere and not pushing things to strongly or too fast is often the best way to diffuse this fear. Don't act like a stalker, overly desperate or domineering. Since gender roles are going through an upheaval, many men will take it in their stride. I think today's modern man wants a sophisticated and worldly woman. However, when you approach a guy and act somewhat nervous like you have never done this before, it may set the guy at ease.

Don't think that your brains and wisdom turn off men either. Intelligence is a positive feature for anyone, although some insecure men may not want a woman whom they perceive is smarter than them. If you are into such a guy, get the man to realize the two of you complement each other, and play up his abilities, such as his practical and mechanical knowledge, perhaps by asking him for some advice. Every man vitally requires respect from and to feel needed by his woman, and responds well to someone who shows interest and knowledge in, for example, his favourite sport. In general though, if a man does not appreciate your intelligence, seek another who does.

While you may have a choice about whether to be romantically assertive or not, I predict women whose looks don't have men automatically turning their heads will find themselves increasingly left out if they remain passive. When certain women assert themselves, they raise the bar and force women in general to step up their pursuit of men. While we all dream of that perfect mate whom destiny has in store for us, the reality is that mating selection is fiercely competitive. Women who bare more skin generate more male interest. Using makeup gives you an advantage, because it makes you more attractive. However, dressing overly sexily or using too much makeup becomes a turn off if it makes you look slutty. I don't expect love-shys to hit these limits, though. As with your makeup, have your assertiveness look as natural as possible.

Perhaps the greatest problem with bypassing historic courtship procedures is determining how much the guy is really into you. If a guy actually takes the chance to make a move on you, which shows a certain amount of interest, he risks rejection. But, for naturally extroverted guys, hitting on you may be no big deal. And for really shy guys, five seconds of eye contact with you may make him consider marriage. If you do the initiating, you may need to take the relationship more slowly to assess how much the guy is into you. Give him more opportunities to prove his attraction and devotion to you, even if only having him buy you drinks and dinner. If you want a casual and short-term relationship, that's fine. Don't feel that because you initiated contact, you can't end the relationship at any time. And don't become so assertive and confident that you believe you can conjure up romance and love when no mutual feelings exist.

Never feel pressured to have sex. Never go to bed with someone because of guilt, obligation, or the belief that it will change that person. Sex is usually an expression of love, but do not use it as a shortcut to love. While you may be using sex to fill an emotional need for intimacy, the guy may be doing it much more to fulfill his physical need. My call for assertiveness and taking control of your sexuality does not imply promiscuity.

Despite overcoming your shyness, you may still find yourself not acting assertively with men. Such inaction may be due to your childhood programming to be a "good girl." The good girl may only have sex within marriage. Possible incursions around this directive happen when the female becomes swept away by the moment and the man's passion. Only then does the good girl have an excuse for unauthorized sex. *It just happened.* Acting romantically assertive can be felt by the good girl as sinful, since there is a big difference between having something done to you versus actively doing something. Likewise, you may feel obliged to wait until you are in love before taking assertive romantic action. You must release yourself from this burden of being good. You are not an independent women if you can only be sexual in male-approved circumstances. By not being required to surrender to the man, you may be more active and conscious during love-making, which may increase your pleasure and satisfaction.

Alexander Avila wrote an excellent book called *The Gift of Shyness: Embrace Your Shy Side and Find Your Soul Mate* (2002). He mentions how shyness and its accompanying traits are actually positive, even though our boisterous world places little outward emphasis on them. Dr. Avila identifies the following strengths shy people usually possess: sensitivity, a natural tendency to be a long-lasting and faithful romantic partner, excellent listening skills, an ability to self-reflect and think deeply, modesty, gentleness and mystery. If you want these characteristics in a partner consider that to gain the treasures such a man has to offer, you may have to work a little harder and sail your ship a little further to connect with him. Acting assertively enhances rather than depletes these characteristics in you.

Extrapolating on the future ramifications of female assertiveness, I see positive implications for humanity. Men will not need to be nearly so aggressive in their pursuit of women. This may lead men to produce less testosterone and become less belligerent.

If more women choose passive men, then men will retreat from stereotypical male behavior. Perhaps, society will eventually enlighten men to not disconnect from their emotions. This will produce much less destructive male behavior.

Parlamis (1996) announced this specific trend when he wrote, "May I be the first to welcome you to the era of the passive man" (p. 140). He:

> started talking to women, asking them what they thought about dating in the late 90s… They didn't like the idea of being picked up; they wanted to do their fair share of the picking… [T]hey wanted to talk to someone intelligent, someone who wasn't trying to snow them or mow them down with clever lines. (p. 11)

If we are entering the era of the passive man, can we not reasonably assume it is also the era of the assertive woman?

No matter how much more active women become in courtship situations, I don't see men ever completely losing their role as the expected initiators. Any assertive actions by women are still played out on the larger stage of men being required to make the overt moves. Perhaps I ask too much of you timid women, but any little movement on your part to connect with a man goes a long way. Whether you actually act more assertively with men, at least in your mind you now have a wider range of options. Assertiveness takes many forms. Sometimes your self-confidence is all you need to start the romance ball rolling.

Notes

1. *Independent* (2007) "Understanding anorexia: A thin excuse." September 18.
2. Masters, W. H. and Johnson, V. E. (1970) *Human Sexual Inadequacy.* New York: Little, Brown and Company.

Chapter 6

Going Pro

Work the pole

Because no love-shy specific therapy exists, love-shys need to develop and seek out their own therapy using available services. A useful therapy must employ that which induces the love-shy anxiety, namely attractive women, while in a therapeutic or somewhat controlled environment. While you may have a talk therapist whom you find attractive, the formalness of the therapy does not allow you to be open about your attraction. If you mention your feelings towards her, she may suggest you start seeing a different therapist. At minimum, she may not allow you to bring up the issue during your sessions. Standard therapy requires that there be no romantic entanglement between therapist and client.

Yet one must directly face and deal with the romantic-sexual tension. Instead of something to avoid, this tension must be a major focus of love-shy therapy. Merely discussing with a therapist issues related to this tension will not treat the underlying problem. Love-shys must get themselves in situations that induce

the anxiety in a controlled environment. Since setting up a controlled romantic situation is impractical at best, we focus on the sexual tension. Luckily, service industries are well established that cater to men's need for female contact and intimacy. Since these services usually fall under the category of entertainment, it becomes up to each individual love-shy to use these services for therapeutic purposes and not get turned off by their sleaziness nor get carried away and waste excessive money on them.

Many of you may have moral issues about employing women to help you in any intimate way. Like much of this book, this chapter offers up possible solutions to your seemingly intractable problem, and you need to choose appropriate solutions for your particular situation. This chapter also informs therapists about the direction love-shy therapy needs to take with the hope of birthing a respectable, potent and practical love-shy therapy that avoids the sleaziness and moral issues surrounding typical sexual services.

Gilmartin (1987) addresses morality concerns:

> Of course, moralists by their very nature have always been uncomfortable with all non-marital manifestations of sexuality anyway. Thus, they can be accurately deemed part of the love-shyness problem in American society, NOT of its solution! Moralists need to be advised of the fact that in order for a love-shy man to attain that ultimate goal of a lasting marriage (which they themselves so enthusiastically exalt), they must allow that love-shy man to experience whatever therapeutic regime the best empirical research points to as being best at painlessly and successfully conquering the love-shyness problem. (pp. 530–531)

Carol Queen suggests that those who speak loudest against others' sexual uninhibitedness have their own serious sexual hang-ups.

"Crusading against other people's sexual behaviors and images lets them wallow in a very safe form of sexual obsession[1] (p. 32).

Talk therapy for those with social problems is a starting point. Although therapists dealing with high-functioning mentally challenged adults will give some useful advice and encourage these people to seek out romantic partners, dating progress is glacially slow. These clients cannot be brought up to speed by only giving them basic advice such as how to dress and how to act. These people missed out on many parts of the whole string of childhood pre-sexual and adolescent sexual experiences that contribute to the sexually and romantically mature adult. If therapists require that these people be sufficiently "cured" or able to act almost totally normal before attempting to date, the only women these people will be hitting on is fellow senior citizens. We race against time. The longer before any kind of dating or sexual experiences start, the further behind they become. How are love-shys and Aspies going to learn to interact properly with the opposite sex if they don't get any practice? Critical real-world experience involving "normal" people is missing from standard therapeutic settings. Without a reliable social structure in place such experiences happen only too infrequently.

Love-shys, especially those on the autism spectrum, often have a knee-jerk reaction when touched. Skin and touch sensitivities can exacerbate an aversion to sex. If a woman's touch elicits fear rather than a positive response, it will strongly turn the woman off. Many autistics do not like the light touch often associated with eroticism, and some do not like hugging. Therefore, a first order of business is to get a massage. An experienced masseuse can give you the type of touch you prefer and help you decrease your aversion to touch, provided you explain what you like and don't like. Having a professional massage is a completely mainstream service that athletes and regular people use to keep their bodies healthy. Massages relieve stress and start to satisfy love-shys' need for touch. Although receiving a massage is strictly passive, the main thing is the contact itself.

Do not let anything keep you from employing massage therapy. If you lack money, go the cheaper route and have a half-hour rather than an hour session. Or find a masseuse just starting her career or working inexpensively out of her home. Perhaps a massage school has a local class where the public can receive inexpensive or free massages given by students. Males are often concerned they will get a male masseur. Diffuse this common issue by asking straight up for a woman. Love-shys scared of novel situations may fear not knowing what to do, especially in a situation involving taking off their clothes in a place of business. Tell the masseuse it is your first time, and she will instruct you similarly to the way a nurse would, giving you privacy and time to change.

The important things are to relax and tell her your problem areas, both sore and tight muscles and tactile issues. Take a shower before your visit, or at least don't smell from a long day of work. She will be greatly offended if you expect or imply anything sexual. Massage therapists are fairly extensively trained and licensed by the state and distance themselves from erotic masseuses. Don't get embarrassed if you have an erection or pass gas during the massage. They are experienced professionals who have seen it all before. If the former happens to pop up, suggest that it's time to roll over on your stomach. Relax and enjoy the massage. A rigid body has a hard time experiencing pleasurable sensations. Use a massage to release all tension from your body. Use this tension-free experience as a baseline for how your body should feel. Develop a habit of practicing self-massage and stretching the tight and stressful areas of your body. Like most new experiences, it takes at least a second time before you become completely comfortable and fully appreciate the massage and awaken a new feeling of touch. Don't underestimate the usefulness of massages. The price of a massage may become insignificant compared to damage caused by your untamed stress flowing out of control.

Once you appreciate the hands and touch of a woman, the next step is gaining the ability to relax in the close company of beautiful women. I suggest going to strip clubs. These visits do not constitute a major continuous therapy, rather one where going a few times may be all that a love-shy needs to obtain the required therapeutic benefits. Additional occasional visits may prove helpful as an evening out at a strip club can help to boost a lonely man's self-esteem when he is too emotionally drained to go after women. The strip club may be the best place to go when you have lost all energy to pursue women but still want their presence. Perhaps only at a strip club is an anonymous man appreciated for being a man no matter his emotional state, allowing him to scrape his ego off the ground and put himself together.

While many love-shys and those with Asperger's may find slipping dollar bills into dancers' g-strings pointless, it's all part of the game. For many love-shys, especially those with autism, the noise, flashing lights, cigarette smoke and everything else can be too much. But, if you want to act like a typical man then sometimes you have to put up with unpleasantries if at all possible. Make no mistake; this is therapy. Interacting with strippers can really magnify your subtle Aspergerian characteristics, since strippers have little patience dealing with such traits. The totally romance-free sexuality of these women can break through love-shys' naive romantic notions about sex.

Think of a strip club visit as a male rite of passage. Primitive societies often have rite-of-passage ceremonies initiating boys into manhood. Led by tribal elders, these rites have the basic structure of separation, transition, and reintegration into society. Our society has no such ceremony—a group of guys taking a man to a strip club for his first time is about as close as one comes to a socially acceptable sexual rite-of-passage ceremony.

Strip clubs get the love-shy focusing externally unlike the introspection of conventional therapy. The therapy part comes from becoming comfortable touching and being with good-looking, half-naked women while carrying on conversations with

them. I'm not talking about groping the women. Instead, when a woman sits down by you practice touching her like you would with a good date. Hold hands, put your arm over her shoulder or lightly brush her arm or leg. Each establishment and each woman have their own boundaries, but these limits are usually way more liberal than the average woman's so roll with it.

These places expand your comfort zones while giving you experience. Be courteous and proper by tipping and perhaps buying drinks for women who hang out and talk with you. You are in control, so don't get suckered out of your hard-earned cash. Savor the feeling of being wanted and needed by sexy women.

Tease is the operative word, so never expect to date a dancer, no matter how much she comes on to you. In a strip club you are a mark from whom they try to extract as much money as possible. Strippers can look you in the eye and tell you with seemingly total sincerity whatever you want to hear. Since strippers are very sexually experienced and you are very inexperienced, there is not much of a match.

Never take a real date to a strip club. All but the wildest and most sexually open women will find it a big turn off. You need to respect your date, and taking her to anything related to heavy sexuality is quite presumptuous and will likely make her uncomfortable. While walking into a strip club and having a beer may seem totally casual to the average man, it will be foreign and off-putting to most women. On a date you want to focus only on her and not on any other women.

You may think it degrading for women to work at these places, but rarely is anyone forced into the profession. By contrast, one stripper told me, "I would be going out to the bar and dancing anyway. I might as well get paid for it." Of course, she oversimplifies the situation since strippers, like any service workers gunning for tips, put on a happy face. At least in the United States, strippers are part of the standard free-market workforce and not coerced to work. Some may not like their job, but they have made a choice based on how good the money is.

An additional important therapeutic benefit of these places is the ego boost. Having a sexually tinged conversation with an attractive woman is great for boosting a man's confidence. Therapists should not underestimate how fragile love-shys' egos are. Even if the love-shy achieves financial success and excels in his field, his success does not translate well to his sexual-romantic ego. Sure, offering *good job* and other compliments during talk therapy are positive ego boosts, but they are only drops in the ocean compared with what love-shys require. These types of compliments help the love-shy man's general self-esteem but fail to address the man's romantic and sexual ego. With little sexual experience a man's ego is based on women's reactions to him. Only members of the opposite sex can build this self-esteem in him. A woman does not have to say anything specific to boost the man's self-esteem. An attractive woman conversing with the man will provide an increase to his self-esteem more than any compliment by a man could.

Pursuing women requires a great deal of confidence. Love-shy therapy must include a significant increasing of the male's ego, and in my experience this differs sharply from traditional therapeutic approaches. Love-shys require positive sexual indications from women. To obtain the important benefits of standard therapies love-shys must accept that most female therapists do not act like this. In an attempt to overcome this problem, a few studies have used what is called biased interaction. Montgomery and Haemmerlie reported in 1986 their studies where they set up shy male and female subjects to interact with members of the opposite sex.[2] The subjects did not know the true purpose of the studies. The assistants doing the interacting were given a fairly free rein with what to discuss and were basically instructed not to be negative in any way, not to discuss sex and not to make or accept any dates. Each subject had several 10- to 12-minute social interactions with different assistants. Montgomery and Haemmerlie claim that thanks to mere positive platonic interactions with the opposite sex the "subjects managed to overcome their shyness by attributing their successful outcome to themselves and their own behaviors" (p. 503). Even being told afterwards the true nature of the experiment did not diminish the outcome, and the subjects reported positive benefits six months later. Aside from possible logistic and ethical issues regarding hiding the actual objective from the clients, such short-term treatment is inexpensive, easy to administer, and appears to produce long-term benefits. Even if shy subjects are told beforehand about the bias, I suspect the treatment would still boost their self-esteem.

An effective love-shy therapy would involve positive interaction from females. Ideally, the women should be attractive, but attitude rates higher than physical beauty. The women need to put on an air of sexual approval and respect of the male clients. Little things like having the room warm enough so that the women never need to put on coats are important. Dating should be fun and not clinical, and love-shy therapy should reflect this sentiment. This type of interaction places a large burden on the woman. She has the dual roles of inducing the anxiety while supporting his ego. She must act attracted to the man while limiting their interactions to a professional level. The fact that love-shys have so few women in their lives compounds this problem because love-shys tend to demand too much and overwhelm the women. Females involved in this proposed male love-shy therapy may not have to be board-certified therapists. The characteristics of such a woman who could perform this role include being comfortable with her and men's sexuality, having few personal issues, having some psychology background or aptitude, and being willing to go beyond conventional therapeutic approaches.

I hope that, as a love-shy you understand that it takes some radical action to deal with your love-shyness successfully. It involves exploring outside of your normal, secure comfort zone. It involves interacting with attractive members of the opposite sex who will boost your desperate ego. It involves going to places that put notions of conservative sexuality to rest. It involves walking out of a club with a smile on your face.

The surrogate bandwagon

Conventional sex therapy usually focuses on prescribing specific sexual interactions for the couple to carry out later at home and so has little to offer the chronically single person who does not have a ready sex partner. I found it extremely depressing to leave a consultation with an esteemed local sex therapist with the impression that neither she nor anyone else could help me. She left me with no leads or advice and mentioned that no sex surrogates work in the state. Obviously professionals can choose theirs clients, but it seems to me that most sex therapists only deal with the sexual problems of married couples and not the problems of people unable to achieve any type of sexual relationship.

The major therapeutic regime Dr. Gilmartin (1987) recommends after practice dating is sex surrogate therapy. He claims, "Any truly comprehensive program calculated to guarantee a complete cure for intractable, chronic and severe love-shyness *must* incorporate a program facet that entails use of sexual surrogates" (p. 527). Sex surrogates are therapists who will actually have physical intimacy up to and including sexual intercourse with their clients. Real sex surrogates have gone through extensive training and are not at all the same as prostitutes.

Gilmartin explains about surrogates and their role:

> Briefly, a sexual surrogate is a young woman who has been trained in techniques of helping men to overcome various sexual problems such as premature ejaculation, impotence, and inability to please a woman. Today hundreds of sexual surrogates are employed in various sex therapy clinics throughout the United States. About 60 percent of the clientele served by these women are married; the other 40 percent are single and divorced. In the majority of instances sexual surrogates work directly under the supervision of a certified clinical psychologist or psychiatrist. (pp. 527–528)

Intellectually we may have no problems with casual sex, but when it actually comes to performing, the problems overwhelm us. By working up to and having sex with a therapist, almost all of the psychological sexual problems will present themselves and be addressed. If a person has a phobia of things sexual, then what better controlled therapeutic environment is there than a sex surrogate? Employing a sex surrogate confronts very deep love-shy issues in a controlled, caring, relaxed setting.

Most surrogates claim to use the method of sensate focus, a therapeutic technique developed by Masters and Johnson.[3] They are considered the founders of modern sex therapy and the first to suggest the use of sex surrogates (pp. 146–154). Conventional sex therapists often prescribe sensate focus exercises for married couples with sexual difficulties. During sensate focus partners focus on sensuality rather than the act of intercourse. The participants concentrate on the sensations of the present and work to tune out all distractions. Sex phobia expert Kaplan outlines the process. "[T]he partners take turns gently and leisurely caressing each other's nude body… [T]he genitals are not stimulated directly, and [there is no intercourse or orgasm]"[4] (p. 94). This action treats performance-related anxieties by having pleasure and the sharing of pleasure, not intercourse or orgasm, as the goal. Kaplan claims, "[Sensate focus] remains the best method devised to this date for the *in vivo* desensitization of simple sexual phobias" (p. 94). This method focuses on overcoming fear of touch and fear of intimacy and removes traumatic numbness. It also should help with communication during and about sex. Sensate focus exposes the person, perhaps for the first time in his life, to the full experience of sex including experiencing his and his partner's nudity, various touching, kissing and just being with a sexual partner.

Generally the surrogate will break down the sensate focus treatment into a number of stages with each phase more intense than the last. Usually each stage requires one or more sessions. Phase I forbids any genital contact. Phase II includes genital stimulation through gentle caresses and teasing without any vigorous, rhythmic stimulation leading to orgasm. Phase III usually focuses on self-stimulation to orgasm while in the partner's presence. The next step before actual intercourse consists of stimulating one's partner to orgasm manually or orally. This gradual, systematic exposure to increasing intense erotic experiences mirrors and condenses typical sexual development while growing up. One can easily perceive how this treatment would be the best thing for treating all kinds of sexual phobias.

A confused few may argue that no one needs to train for and experience sex outside of a committed relationship. While this sentiment may apply to the majority of healthy people, it does not apply to those with serious sexual handicaps and problems. All indications point to most love-shys as being ill-equipped sexually to enter marriage competently. The ability to please your spouse sexually is a standard requirement for marriage. A female partner expects action rather than confusion from her man. She expects to be seduced rather than to play the role as a teacher. She expects sexual satisfaction rather than having the situation focus solely on the love-shy. Basic telling and showing what to do is not sexy. When the basic fundamentals need to be taught or if there is a severe underlying psychological condition, a knowledgeable third person is needed. Sex surrogate therapy helps love-shys with the process of obtaining healthy marriages. The sex surrogate can give a quick and powerful boost in the one arena that love-shys need it the most, and at a critical time in their lives: now. While I'm not sure all surrogates receive training for dealing precisely with a phobia of sex, they are trained for dealing with shyness and ignorance with sex. Start saving up your money, boys.

The naïve may consider sex surrogates and prostitutes interchangeable because they both exchange sex for money. The occupations differ significantly by the goal of each service. The primary goal of the prostitute is to give pleasure, whereas the goal of the surrogate is to provide therapy. The primary focus of a prostitute is the sex itself, unlike surrogate therapy where actual sexual activities may only comprise something like 10 percent of the whole time with her. While sex surrogacy may exist in a type of legal limbo in many jurisdictions, on a practical level visiting a sex therapy clinic can eliminate the underworld and seedy elements related to prostitution to which a socially and sexually ignorant, desperate guy can easily fall victim.

Some people may worry about the clients objectifying sex, since it takes place outside of a loving relationship. Again, this therapy should be considered a prerequisite for obtaining a loving romance. Love-shys are quite romantic at heart and perhaps less likely than the general population to objectify sex. I believe the lack of exposure to actual women and actual sex is what most objectifies women and sex, since a love-shy only has exposure to substitutes like pornography. A desperate virgin is most interested in any possible sex and tends to lower his standards to include emotionless flings. He focuses on what he does not have. He may seek out sex itself rather than finding the best person with whom to have a romantic relationship. Some people may also worry about clients developing an emotional attachment to the surrogate. This is known as transference and can happen with any type of psychotherapy and even with teacher—student relationships.

During my first sexual experience, I was completely confused and clueless. My stupefaction is not surprising now that I understand about Asperger's and my phobia of romantic intimacy. My problems confused the woman. In fact, we didn't even go all the way, and it turned into a frustrating time for both of us. Here was a beautiful woman who really cared for me and was attracted to me, who knew me well and seemed quite socially and sexually experienced and capable. Yet she couldn't alter the outcome of the encounter. If I had visited a sex surrogate before that experience, I might be married to this woman today.

Many of those with an autism spectrum disorder, which can disconnect them from their sexuality in some way, are in need of surrogate therapy. The newness and everything else about an autistic's first sexual experience can overwhelm. The tactile defensiveness common with autistics can make sex unpleasant. One thinks nothing of speech and social skills tutors for autistics, so why not sexual tutors for the sexually challenged?

Yet as Gilmartin (1987) warns, sex surrogates are not a cure-all for love-shyness. They are only one aspect of a total love-shy treatment. They only focus on sexual issues. Surrogate therapy works as an adjunct to other therapies. During standard talk therapy one's love-shyness can easily cause the client to avoid discussing important sexual issues. With sex surrogacy the sexual issues become present. Remember love-shyness is more than a phobia of sex.

Although I believe that this therapy will substantially help *any* love-shy who seeks this treatment, it's not a complete love-shy solution. I do not classify sex training as an integral part of my proposed love-shy treatment but as a separate distinct therapy. One can't guarantee that surrogate therapy will sufficiently treat love-shyness. Sure, it will treat sex-related issues, which are quite important, but how much will it help you with approaching women? The treatment will give you a burst of confidence, but it is not a complete love-shy therapy.

The other bad news about sex surrogates is that there are very few and their price is fairly high, usually at least $2000 or $3000 for a series of treatment sessions. This price typically includes sessions with a separate therapist who oversees the treatment. In the United States sex surrogate clinics operate almost exclusively in New York City and major Californian cities like Los Angeles and San Francisco. London and Amsterdam are two European cities with clinics. Isolated clinics and surrogates do exist in a handful of other cities. Such treatment is not covered by health insurance plans, and travel and housing costs increase the cost further.

If you decide to employ the services of a surrogate, watch out for prostitutes advertising as surrogates. It's best if there is a clinic with a separate therapist who will oversee your surrogate treatment rather than a single woman operating out of her home.

The lone surrogate may be less expensive, and you may receive equal benefits as from a formal clinic, but be wary.

You can check out the website of the International Professional Surrogates Association at www.surrogatetherapy.org. While they do not license surrogates, they have a professional code of ethics, offer training for surrogates and generally work to make sure their vocation is as professional as possible. The American Association of Sexuality Educators, Counselors and Therapists has a website at www.aasect.org, but this organization encompasses all sex therapists. As author and sex therapist Bernie Zilbergeld writes, "The vast majority of sex therapists don't work with surrogates"[5] (p. 402). However, you might need to see a standard sex therapist for a referral to a surrogate clinic.

For those who think surrogate therapy is just about sex and fun, he claims, "Surrogate therapy is hard work for the client. The work causes his problems to surface, and then he has to learn and perfect the skills necessary to resolve or handle them" (p. 344). This treatment is not a quick roll in the hay. It is serious work you must commit to. It starts with a doctor's exam proving you have no sexually transmitted diseases. Zilbergeld also notes that the team of surrogate and therapist is especially helpful for shy people who find it easier to talk with the other person rather than bring up concerns directly, which allows the therapist to defuse emotional issues. Males surrogates exist for female clients, but they are even scarcer than female surrogates.

If there is one specific cause I wish love-shys, related professionals and the public in general to take up regarding love-shyness, it would be building a surrogate industry and legitimizing it in the public's view. Basic love-shy therapy does not inevitably require extensive training and complex procedures to implement. Nor does it necessitate changing public opinion. In contrast, sex surrogates require extensive training, a non-hostile legal environment and basic public acceptance. An industry needs to be created that offers sex surrogates for virginal and inexperienced autistic and love-shy adults. Coping with this demand will take

much more than merely opening schools for surrogates. Society's erotophobia needs dealing with on multiple levels.

Sex surrogates need to operate in every major city. If your only available doctor is a ten-hour drive away, chances are you won't go to the doctor unless you are on your deathbed. The same holds true for love-shys. Since love-shyness isn't a life-or-death situation, most love-shys will never travel far for treatment. Love-shys may be worse than the average person when summoning the gumption to take care of a medical or psychological problem. If I can drive to my nearest major city for a clinic, it greatly increases the chance that I will actually go through with the treatment. If I can have a consultation appointment beforehand, meet with the therapists and check out the place before committing, I will feel much more comfortable and apt to go along with it. Local access facilitates multiple visits. Also, eliminating travel expenses of airfare, hotel, rental car and meals puts local therapy in closer reach of underemployed love-shys. Since surrogates deal with more than love-shys, their practices can be commercially viable once accepted by the public.

Various mental health professionals may dismiss sex surrogates as a 1970s fad that never took off. We need to deal with society's erotophobia surrounding this issue. I see nothing demonstrating our society's irrational fear of sex more clearly than not allowing effective sex therapy for people so dysfunctional as not to be able to have sex their whole lives. Everything possible needs to be done to make surrogate therapy as mainstream as possible. The sex surrogate occupation requires a very special type of woman who is in short supply. Societal pressures must not dissuade these rare women from pursuing this important field. Likewise, much must be done to ensure that the people who desperately require this therapy have access to it.

The world's oldest profession

Sex surrogate therapy represents the best existing love-shy treatment, but as it is not practical yet due to limited availability and high cost, its ubiquitous bastard step-cousin, prostitution, may be a viable alternative. Prostitution exists in every city but laws governing its legality are complex and vary internationally. Before deciding whether to engage the services of a prostitute, you need to fully understand the legal implications relevant to your locale and also question how you feel morally about this industry. I do not have the authority to advise you on these issues; they require personal introspection and exploration. By disclosing my personal views on the use of prostitutes, I am in no way giving you permission or encouragement to break the law or compromise your moral values.

I see any sex that a love-shy can obtain as beneficial. Any sexual encounter will be a vast improvement over your current situation. Only you can decide if the benefits are worth the costs. Theoretically, overcoming your anxieties surrounding sex as part of a cold transaction should translate into a lower anxiety level in a loving sexual situation. I'm not saying that your sexual anxiety will decrease by visiting a prostitute, only that the increased experience will allow you to handle your anxieties better. By navigating the sex-for-money landscape you gain experience of sorts, experience that will have to substitute for actual romantic participation. Your experience should at least make you less intimidated by sexy women. Women want a man who takes control in the bedroom, and only through experience can you develop your role as an assertive male. *Practice makes perfect.*

Many love-shy men are romantic at heart, but by placing their first time having sex in so high a regard, it tends never to happen. Removing romance from sex can reduce the anticipation and expectations of their first time. Actual sexual experience brings you down to earth, and your fantasies may change. Be aware that using prostitutes carries health risks. It is important to practice safe sex to avoid contracting diseases.

One reason you might have for visiting a prostitute is to lose the virgin label. While many people find virginity a serious stigma, others believe one's virginity is a great gift. To give this gift to someone who has no emotional significance in your life can be seen as throwing away something precious you can only give once. Thus it is important not to place too much meaning with first sex.

Until you have overcome your love-shyness to a certain degree, the only way for a passive, phobic male like you to achieve sex is by directly paying for it. The older you grow the more difficult overcoming love-shyness becomes. The only available professional who can guarantee you losing your virginity belongs to the world's oldest profession. Set a goal that if you haven't had sex by a certain age, then you will apply whatever means necessary to do so. After you have satisfied that goal, think about employing a professional every time you go a certain period, like two years, without sex.

I followed that scenario. At about 30 years old I finally had a decent job but was still extremely socially and sexually frustrated. I then determined I must pay for sex. However, more than wanting to lose my virginity inspired my visit to a prostitute. I had to know if I was psychologically blocked from having sex with a prostitute as I had been blocked with my many opportunities for romantic sex. Would I run away or would my mind blank out as it had done on previous romantic and sexual encounters? As I suspected, I had few obvious psychological problems with the encounter. Was it a positive experience? I guess it was OK. I cannot say with certainty if it produced positive long-term benefits, but some months afterwards I obtained what was technically my first girlfriend.

I partially justified my first visit to a prostitute as an exploration into what I now know as love-shyness. The encounter proved that my problem related more to romantic situations than

purely sexual ones. However, since up to that time I was unable to participate in one-night stands or other forms of casual sex, it was more complex than mere romantic anxiety. I circumvented the mating game by paying for sex. Without the knowledge and ability of standard courtship behaviors when there is no "script," I could only execute a formal sexual transaction. My phobia seemingly flared up much less during the prostitute involvement. One strong reason why love-shys have little enthusiasm for "women of the night" is that it seems to these men that they need only gain courtship instructions or something similar to have regular sexual relations; that if they could just muster up enough courage, success would be right over the next hill and they won't have to deal with any of this messy sex-for-money business.

Non-virgins may look back on their first time and conclude that the experience wasn't that great or important. However, as long as you haven't done it, it remains a big deal and a required rite of passage.

The therapeutic benefit that prostitutes may produce much better than any other professional therapy is exposing love-shys' conscious and subconscious beliefs about pleasure. Until negative subconscious attitudes conspicuously surface, the love-shy has little knowledge of or impetus to deal with them. After P.B., who we met in Chapter 3, returned from an out-of-country sex vacation where he set no agenda except for his own pleasure, he reports:

> I relished the chance to hang out with confident men who had no shame or reservation about their own sexuality and who saw life as a party and an adventure rather than a painful experience to be endured. At the end I felt that my problem was not so much shyness but fear and shame about pleasure and my refusal to accept the good things in life which I was easily able to access. Using PSYCH-K, I examined my subconscious mind and found that it does not believe that I deserve to enjoy pleasure and luxuries.

> I think sex therapy fails so many love-shy guys because they visit prostitutes a few times and the experience causes an explosion of shame and anxiety, which leads these men to conclude that sex therapy doesn't work and even causes these feelings. However, the shame and anxiety are not created by the sexual experience. Rather, they are revealed by it. What we need is massive amounts of shameless pleasure and debauchery to persuade our subconscious that pleasure, joy and happiness are good and normal for us to have and to accept.

For everyone's safety do not employ streetwalkers, underage girls and women obviously drug-addicted. Instead search the internet for "erotic provider reviews." If you do arrange to meet a prostitute, dress and prepare like you would for a big date. Treat her professionally, with respect and like you would any date. Keep the financial part discreet. You have to play it by ear, but generally follow her lead regarding the cash. The important thing for you to do is relax and enjoy it. There is no need to impress her. Remove any performance anxiety. You will never see her again, and she won't care.

Remember that the prostitute is there for sex. It's all about business for them. The sooner they make you come, the sooner they finish their job. Therefore, it becomes up to you to guide the situation away from raw sex and towards therapeutic goals. Be truthful with her. Start by telling her you are a virgin or, at least, inexperienced. The biggest thing you have to do is slow things down. Talk with her. If you have an hour session, perhaps keep your clothes on for up to half an hour. Get used to touching her. If so inclined, back rubs or foot massages work as a way to begin touching each other. Who would know about sex better than a woman who does it for a living? Talk freely with her about all kinds of intimate sexual topics so that you have a conversation like you have never before had with a woman.

Don't consider going to a prostitute as accepting defeat. Instead, look at it as an educational and therapeutic tool to get you prepared to play the real game. Comparing hourly rates between various therapies, prostitutes generally charge double the price of professional talk therapists and half that of sex surrogates.

Much of what I say may apply to you virgin women out there too. Confidence and a feeling of ease regarding sex will boost your game. While women can always find willing casual sex partners, love-shy anxieties may prevent some women from following through with courtship rituals. Male prostitutes reportedly treat women better and the experience is generally more therapeutic than that which the opposite gender encounter. A professional male lover is more likely to give a woman sexual satisfaction and a worthwhile experience than some drunk guy she picks up. Also, the pure sexuality of the situation allows a woman to separate lust from love, something she may be unable to do except in artificial situations.

Whether you ever employ the services of strippers, surrogates or other sex workers, at least you know that these options exist. You may wait forever for sleazeless love-shy therapies to happen.

Notes

1. Queen, C. (2002) *Real Live Nude Girl: Chronicles of Sex-Positive Culture.* San Francisco, CA: Cleis Press.
2. Montgomery, R. L. and Haemmerlie, F. M. (1986) "Self-perception theory and the reduction of heterosexual anxiety." *Journal of Social and Clinical Psychology 4*, 4, 503–512.
3. Masters, W. H. and Johnson, V. E. (1970) *Human Sexual Inadequacy.* New York: Little, Brown and Company.
4. Kaplan, H. S. (1987) *Sexual Aversion, Sexual Phobias, and Panic Disorders.* New York: Brunner/Mazel.
5. Zilbergeld, B. (1999) *The New Male Sexuality, Revised Edition.* New York: Bantam Books.

Chapter 7

On Your Own

What?! This is it?

Reaching this last chapter after implementing various recommended actions, you may feel that nothing has changed and you are still love-shy. Do not feel shortchanged, because I titled this book a *Survival Guide* not a *Love-Shyness Elimination Guide.* This book has covered much ground, and by reading it you have too. While you may still be love-shy, much has changed. Your knowledge of your situation has increased significantly. Also, importantly, your attitude should have metamorphosed. Consider this book a starting point providing you with a plethora of helpful resources.

While perhaps most love-shys will never completely remove their condition, they can deal with it to such an extent that its effects on their lives are minimal. Even if you believe yourself cured, that doesn't mean you will never have another anxiety attack or will never run away from an attractive woman. Overcoming love-shyness relates to how you deal with your phobic attacks,

not only to reducing their number and severity. Six months from now you may find yourself not going after an obviously available person. You may think, *Has anything really changed?* Yes, much has changed even if you still don't have a girlfriend or pursue every available woman. Instead of beating yourself up, accept yourself, your mistakes and that you are doing as much as possible. One day an easier opportunity will arise with a more appropriate mate. Six months ago would you have even been in the correct physical and mental place for that opportunity or even recognized the opportunity? Although we have focused primarily on your problems, it is also important to acknowledge your accomplishments.

If you still feel little hope of achieving a cure, remember that this condition is primarily a psychological problem and not a birth defect or physical injury, so curing yourself is possible. If no treatment options currently exist for you, consider that professionals and the outside world can only help you so much. It is up to you to have a life and take charge of situations as they arise. If all the comorbid conditions are sufficiently dealt with and you improve yourself and enough areas of your life, your can manage your love-shyness. The important thing is to feel confident that you have done as much as you can to conquer it and never give up. Love-shys and those with autism frustrate easily and give up too early. If something bad happens, it reaffirms our negative expectations and past negative experiences.

Eventually you have to shift your focus away from yourself and your problems and out to the world. When you busily deal with the world's problems, your issues seem insignificant. While your problems may not exactly melt away when you concern yourself with others, at least the negativities from your issues diminish. Don't become obsessed with this whole topic of love-shyness. You end up living your label, *I am love-shy.* When you become so singly focused on finding that special someone who will make your life happy and complete, you block out other areas of your life, which increases the pressure to succeed romantically. With

romance and sex, performance pressures decrease the possibility for successful outcomes.

Eventually you have to say, *Enough is enough. The time has come for action.* Often in the grand scheme any action is the important thing, rather than making sure a particular course of action is 100 percent correct. Someone in the loan business once told me that if his company is not having a certain percentage of its loans default, then it is judging loan applications too conservatively and not writing enough loans. Likewise, if you are not making mistakes with women, then you are not interacting with them enough. If women do not reject you, then you do not hit on them enough. Even the missed opportunity of not talking to a woman means that at least you are out there and recognized the situation. Accept the fact that you will make more mistakes with women than the average male. Without making mistakes, you won't learn. Self-assuredness comes from experience.

Don't wait for your perfect mate to come along before taking action. Consider the following estimation. If one out of every ten women you approach or meet gives you her phone number, one out of three of these that you later call may go on a date with you. For every five first dates you go on, one may lead to a second date. For every five second dates, one may lead to a third date. For every three third dates, one may become a serious girlfriend. For every five serious girlfriends, one may lead to marriage. Thus, you will need to approach 11,250 women to get your wife! Of course, I roughly calculated these numbers, and with practice and experience you can improve the odds at each step. But you can't experience the higher levels until you master the lower ones. Plug your own smaller numbers into this equation, and you will still get a number in the 100s if not 1000s. That means you have to hit on a woman every day of the year if you want a wife. So you better get busy! This is not to say you must come on to every woman you see.

This estimate shows that you must accept and not fear rejection. This acceptance only happens by getting rejected often. The worse your chance of success, the more chances you need to take. The more often you play, the better your chances to win. You can get romantic and sentimental and say, *I'm just looking for that special someone.* Aren't we all? But how do you find her? How do you get her? How do you make sure she is the one? By trying many possibilities and weeding out what doesn't work you hone in on what works for you.

Rephrase what you see as failure. One woman gives this advice:

> What do you consider "failure"? Is it that you don't end up having sex with her? Is it that you don't end up married? Is it that you don't end up in a long-term relationship? Is it that you don't get a name or phone number? Is it that she doesn't speak to you? Is it that you don't have all your dreams materialize from one introduction? If you talked to her and she said a few words back, is that a failure or success? If you see her again and she smiles at you and remembers you, is that a failure or success? If you go on a date but it doesn't turn out well, is that a failure or success?

While going after every woman who crosses your path may be unrealistic, once you resign yourself from attempting any pursuit of one girl, the more apt you are to have that same mindset and not go after the next one. And the next one could be the one.

By practicing something often enough it becomes automatic. We train our brains by repeating an action over and over. Adult brains change and adapt. Our experiences and our reactions to them either reinforce our brains' wiring or create new circuits. Scientists call changes in the organization of the brain neuroplasticity. If a certain area of the brain is damaged, other areas can take over its function. You don't actually have to experience something to change your brain. Merely imagining yourself performing an action helps to program your brain.

I used a visualization technique to reprogram my brain to be less anxious. Recall that neurons communicate by releasing neurotransmitters, and the adjacent neuron will fire if it receives a sufficient amount of these molecules. Just as you need neurons to fire to move you into action, some neurons fire to make you anxious and block you from taking action. Since you have a low anxiety threshold, it is easy for these anxiety-producing neurons to fire. Consciously reprogram your brain on the molecular level by visualizing having a high anxiety threshold. I visualized a tiny me standing very small next to a very high, impossible-to-scale wall.

There is no shortcut around practicing approaching women until you feel comfortable.

Work seems a good place to start. Since love-shys socialize so little, our jobs play a big social role. We often come in daily contact with a variety of female coworkers. Since we dress up to go to work and do a good job, female coworkers can view us as competent and attractive. And we can see them in a similar light. Unfortunately the workplace brings its own set of obstacles. We usually create the wrong vibe at work, as due to our lack of female interaction, we can stare at female coworkers as if they come from another planet. Love-shys exude a certain sexual stress that turns women off. When it comes to sexual harassment it's not your intentions that matter, it's how the woman feels. She won't understand your love-shyness and may think of you as an inappropriately sexually aggressive guy.

If a coworker accuses you unjustly of sexual harassment, do not remain your normally passive self who stands stunned and speechless during traumatic incidents. By the time you find out about the complaint, you are the last to know and start on the defensive. A former Marine love-shy offers this advice:

> Go to your supervisor and immediately request or demand a meeting with the accuser and her supervisor. At this meeting declare that you are being wrongly accused,

> because if you were interested in the accuser you would have asked her out and certainly at this point that isn't going to happen. I've been accused twice of harassment and in both cases if you get your supervisor on your side you have little to worry about. It is critical that you act unjustly accused and outraged. Yes, this takes some "balls," or you're the victim once again.

If you have Asperger's syndrome, now may be the time to disclose this fact. But, it won't change the facts of the incident. Mentioning love-shyness may only prove that you have a problem that the company doesn't want to deal with. Consider consulting a lawyer, since your job and professional reputation are at stake.

Often people advise love-shys and Aspies not to get romantically involved with coworkers. However, work can greatly help shy people get to know each other. Acting romantically interested in a coworker allows to you to experience you love-shy issues and to help overcome them on a daily basis.

In general, having hard and fast rules such as never dating a coworker are unhelpful, as such rules or affirmations may be based on immature thinking or incomplete information. Here are some attitudes that you may hold and the problems with these views:

I will not engage in one-night stands or accept women's offers for them.

You don't have to seek out casual affairs, but you better grab such rare opportunities. Be thankful a sexually open and assertive woman has come your way and finds you attractive.

I offer and will accept nothing less than a serious relationship.

No relationship starts off as serious. Relationships become serious over time. Only through practice will you gain the experience to support and maintain a healthy, serious relationship. Think playful rather than serious to help keep your performance anxiety at bay.

I will not seek desperate relief for my sexual desire.

You're masochistic. Relief is one of the biggest things loveshys need. Yes, you should have standards, so don't get involved with someone who repulses you. At least masturbate every once in a while.

I want to make sure sex is a meaningful experience for my partner and myself.

Sex is just sex. The first time you have sex, you're going to fumble around and finish quickly. You have a worthwhile goal, but you have to start somewhere. Rephrase your affirmation as, *I vow to have a powerful and fulfilling sex life.*

I'll gladly treat a woman like a lady if she deserves it.

Don't make the woman prove herself or pass tests. You're suppose to prove yourself to the woman. You have enough problems meeting and dating women as it is. Treat all women with respect.

I'll never get married, because I have to make up for lost time by being with as many women as possible.

Sure, make up for lost time, but never set nevers for yourself. Cross or burn that bridge when you get to it, not before the relationship starts.

I'm waiting for the perfect person.

While you're waiting for her, spend time with less perfect people. Then when that perfect person comes around, you're ready for her.

I'm sick and tired of female passivity.

Me too, but consider it almost a physical law like gravity. While women are becoming more assertive, don't hold your breath. Most of the actually assertive ones have already latched onto cooler guys than you.

P.B., mentioned earlier, sums up the problems with these affirmations:

> It sounds uplifting to hear you renounce pre-marital sex, but there is one problem. You can only renounce what you have, not what you don't have. I have known dirt poor

> people who claimed they renounced wealth and power and total losers who never had a date who claimed they renounced loveless sex or all sexuality. It is easy to renounce what you don't have because you will not miss anything. This mode of thinking just makes you feel good about your failures. You have created an unattainable ideal. You have raised the bar so high there is no way the world could give you what you want. As a result you are not responsible for your situation.

While it can seem that you are acting assertively and being true to yourself and standing up for yourself by not behaving how the world wants you to act, you end up uselessly jousting at windmills. You may be totally true to yourself, but you'll be very lonely. Pick a better cause in which to invest your energy.

Love-shys may complain that the world and I are asking them to become someone who they are not. No one is asking you to change your essence. Shyness is not part of your essence. Instead, it blocks your essence. You were not born shy but born introverted with a low anxiety threshold. These traits made you shy. Just because you are introverted doesn't mean you can't do things like public speaking and performing. Just because you have a low anxiety threshold doesn't mean you should avoid doing things that make you anxious. Being confident and self-assured is like being happy; it's a state of mind.

Acting self-assured and confident is like dressing up and acting appropriately for the situation. You may complain that by dressing and acting in a way that isn't you, you present a false impression to women. So what? Is a woman wearing lipstick and makeup presenting a false impression, or is she enhancing her image? You could even quote Brad Blanton's 1996 book *Radical Honesty* where he quotes from *Awareness* by John Stevens. "If I calculate and put on phony behavior in order to please you, you may love my behavior, but you cannot love me…" (p. 57). True, a relationship based on lies and manipulation is bound to fail,

because you can't keep up the charade forever. And if your partner senses you withholding, then she will likely do the same and you will never experience and know each other's true selves. Instead, present the many and varied sides of yourself. Women love to discover your different positive aspects. As Blanton emphasizes, honesty and full and open communication is always the best policy, so present yourself in the best possible light.

While you may not have been born a charismatic alpha male, don't fret. It's OK being a beta or gamma, and you still can get great women. You don't have to be the life of the party and the center of attention to have women find you attractive. Confidence comes from being comfortable as you are. Trying to be someone you're not is not attractive. By being yourself, women may approach you.

The more interest a woman has in a man the more action she will take. Thus, one solution to not changing your passivity is to become a high-quality man to whom women will flock. The standard method is to become wealthy. You would be wrong to think wealth only attracts women interested in money. Possessing money, like being great looking, is something many women find attractive. Of course, since love-shys often barely make ends meet, you need to find another path. Women are drawn to musicians. Pilinski (2003) mentions throughout his book how rock stars embody women's ideal mate. Just purchasing a used guitar and learning a few songs can turn a woman into putty in your hands. It doesn't matter so much what type of music you play, just that you sound OK. Artists in general have this pull, but not quite like musicians.

Even if you can't carry a tune to save your life, develop rock star traits. The idea is not necessarily to be a musician or artist, but to excel at something and do it for an audience. While you may think it a stretch to talk or perform to thousands of people at a time, some love-shys and Aspies are drawn to broadcasting. In a radio booth you are in complete control. You usually do all the talking and follow a script, and your audience isn't physically present.

Right behind the possessions of fame and money, and generally associated with them, is success. Be outstanding at something, usually the more mainstream the better. When it comes to mating, the free market reigns. If there is a dearth of quality males, females will aggressively pursue them. Although men abound, ones with fame, money or success are in short supply. Notice that this ranking usually has nothing to do with these super alpha males' looks or the size of their genitalia.

Find and build your own creative, unique, possibly extreme path out of the love-shy jungle. Once you work hard enough and achieve success, you can float down the river out of the jungle. Generally this requires putting together and following through on a multi-year plan for a major accomplishment. And, when the end is soon in sight, your motivation and morale will greatly increase. Do it. Once a few people look your way, others follow.

Problems we like to have

Some people may feel that this book focuses too heavily on the physical issues of mating, and not enough about actual love. After all, the term is love-shy and not sex-shy. Physical intimacy is the language, while love is the meaning and the message. If you can't speak the language, then your message is irrelevant. Kissing, sex and the rest of physical intimacy are about conveying love. If you are unable to express love through the physical act of touching, how can you expect appropriately to express it verbally, emotionally or spiritually? I hope I haven't given you the idea that I promote casual sex. Many of your missed opportunities with women may seem like missed opportunities for sex, but likely they were also opportunities to start romantic relationships. Do not confuse sex with love. Sex is the icing on the cake of an intimate relationship.

You may be down on Cupid these days and think love is a myth. Romantic love exists, and, as anyone who has been in love can attest, worth the struggles to obtain it and the broken heart when it leaves. Cupid has been there for you, but your condition prevented you from receiving the gifts of his blessing. I believe a natural force exists that brings people together romantically. Yet you have to apply intellect and knowledge when choosing a mate. You have to know the kind of person you are looking for, so you fall in love with the right person. Since love-shys often suffer from both being overly romantic and intellectualizing love, they can use pointers for what to look for and what to look out for. Rather than wishful thinking, you should plan for the future and notice what clouds your selection process. Everybody wants sex and intimacy and usually marriage, but these things need to be with the right person and not based on desperation. Furthermore, love-shys need advice for when they actually have relationships.

Some male love-shys may think they should hook up with a female love-shy or at least a shy woman. This may be the easiest way, or it may be the hardest. If both of you are shy, you know generally how the other thinks and acts, and you both expect a similar rhythm to romance. Then again, if both of you are shy, neither may make the first move. Asperger's–Asperger's romances are similar, but seeking someone with an autism spectrum disorder limits you to 1 percent of the population. More importantly, if both people have this condition, a certain emotionalism or empathy is missing, and it can be like the blind leading the blind.

You need a mate who shares many of the same beliefs and interests as you. Having a partner with similar intelligence and sense of humor can help create a solid, lasting relationship. Without interests in common and participating in shared activities, it becomes difficult always to do things together. Yet at the same time, I believe opposites attract and make appropriate pairings. As a couple you are a team, and each partner's qualities, skills and attributes should make up for weaknesses in the other.

Interestingly, apparently woman can instinctively tell from the smell of a man not only his health but if his DNA complements her own. Use cologne sparingly. Pilinski (2003) writes, "It turns out that women are drawn to the natural (unperfumed) scent of any man whose MHC [major histocompatibility complex] genes turn out to be completely dissimilar to her own" (p. 40). In the spirit of Gilmartin's (1987) mention of esoteric knowledge, the website www.maximumattraction.org claims to have mapped out people's types. The website author asserts that merely by shaking hands or touching a person, you can feel the person's compatibility with you. An "electric" feel is best, and cold and clammy is worst. If you can figure out and spot your ideal partner, the overwhelming natural chemistry between the two of you will make it easier for the relationship to happen and continue.

Although the popular term these days for someone who seems sent from heaven as your ideal partner is soulmate, for me the correct term is twin flame. I used to wonder why I was unable to hook up with the woman I thought was my twin flame even though she waited years for me. With such a perfect partner more than mere love-shyness comes into play. Many of our psychological issues surface and intensify in the presence of our ideal mate. Then love-shyness greatly amplifies these negative issues, and we lose the person. Losing what seemed like our perfect mate may be the greatest love-shy distress.

Once you find someone special and develop a real romance, watch out for the relationship moving too fast. Without relationship experience, you need to take it slow. Don't underestimate the length of courtship. Moving in with each other too early seems to be a common problem with love-shys. While this set-up seems like a dream come true, it is usually the woman who wants this, often as a prelude to marriage. You may think that living together and sharing a bed every night with a woman would be heaven. Love is nature's psychotherapy after all. You should, however, be dating for some months before moving in together. I recommend cohabitation as a prelude to marriage. Courtship and dating is

about presenting yourself in the best possible light and about going out and doing fun things. When living together you see the unwashed sides of the other person.

We tend to look at a romantic partner not as he or she is but as we envision our ideal mate. The sad story of one love-shy man is telling. The guy participated in a church group with more women than men. A woman actively pursued him, which made the man happy. Her actions appeared OK because of the lopsided gender ratio of the group—and it was a church group after all. They quickly married, and she proceeded to dominate him and make his life hell. He was too timid, too overwhelmed and too desperate for a woman's company to annul the marriage. They divorced after less than two years, and she tried to take half of everything he owned. He claims the experience further traumatized him, and neither had remarried 20 years later. The way to marry a healthy woman is to be a healthy man yourself and to progress the relationship normally. Just as some men will say anything to get into a women's pants, some women will do whatever they need to hook a man. It takes experience to know when a romantic partner is just going through the motions.

If you date a divorcee, pay special attention to see if she has a pattern of unsuccessful relationships with men, or if she is over-compensating from her last man by being with you. This is subtle and hard to figure out, but try to perform some amateur psychology and not purely go by what she says.

Once you finally have a relationship you may still be quite desperate. Many people, even the most romantic and freedom-loving love-shys, tend to bring jealousy and possessiveness into their relationships. Your possessiveness starts making unreasonable demands on the other person. This leads to bitterness, aggression, alienation and anger, and you start on the path to the dark side. You may think you are acting out of love, but it turns into ownership and manipulation. You know your relationship has serious problems when there are lies and broken commitments. If you are making ultimatums and demands, it is not love. The less desperate you act, the better off you are.

Glover (2000) observes, "Nice Guys are often attracted to people and situations that need fixing" (p. 9). Seeking to help someone as part of the romance process seems honorable but is not good thinking. It makes us go for people with problems, and turn romantic motivations into duties. This is a quite negative style when we are the ones who really need the help. Never go into a relationship thinking of the other person as a project or someone to fix. Acting like a psychiatrist is condescending and never sexy. What you see is what you get, so accept your partner as he or she is.

As with dating, maintaining a relationship or a marriage requires skills and experience. Just because you got her into bed or you two are a couple or you got married does not mean you can rest on your laurels. Some basic relationship advice: listen and empathize. Remember that loving her and making the relationship work for the long haul are more important than winning an argument. Sometimes it is best to keep your mouth shut. Focus on solving problems rather than winning arguments. When in an argument with your lover (or anyone), work towards peaceful conflict resolution. Learn to say "I" and not "you" and avoid the word "but." The highest goal of conflict resolution is to come away with a better understanding of each other. Don't feel you have to live up to some masculine stereotype. Admit when you are wrong. Don't feel that you need to dominate. An intimate relationship requires making sacrifices, compromises and commitments and putting in work.

Miller (2004) offers men this advice when their woman tries starting an argument or a fight:

> When this happens, just sit there and let her go off. Don't block her out—listen to what she's saying because it's very important for her. Don't taunt her and don't start screaming back… [S]he might be PMSing. But if you ask her, "Is

> it that time of the month?" understand this will infuriate her even more…
>
> Something really must be bothering her. Do your best to get it out of her and let her talk about it. If this doesn't work, I wouldn't recommend standing there and taking her crap for very long. Nobody deserves to be treated like this. Take a stand and tell her you're not going to put up with this… If you don't stand up to her right then and there, you're facing a lifetime of being whipped.
>
> Most times when women do this, they simply want to know that you'll stand up for yourself. If you don't respect yourself enough to do it, then why should she respect you? Stand up to her and let her know this isn't cool with you. Never disrespect her or, God forbid, hit her. Just let her know that she's just driving you crazy and you're not going to take it. (pp. 187–189)

Basically, love is caring, intimacy and attachment. In a romantic relationship keep up compliments and appreciations. Be assertive about your own needs and wants, but don't spring them on her. Keep in touch with each other. You may find it interrupting and a chore, but it is better than the alternative of being all alone. Don't lock your love away like some prized possession. Stay attractive. Maintain honesty. Watch out for becoming a romance or sex "addict" and not really caring about the other person. Watch out if you are compromising your own needs, values and ethics for the sake of her or the relationship.

…And they got married and lived happily ever after. Yeah, right. Do not let society, parents, social groups or your potential spouse determine what's best for you. Do not be forced into marriage. While jitters before a wedding are common, if you have serious reservations or even have to ask yourself if it is the right thing to do, then it may be better to back out now, even with the reception hall booked and the invitations sent out. *If you have to ask yourself if you are in love, then you aren't.* A successful marriage requires

more than just both of you being in love. Don't settle. It's better to be single than trapped in a failing marriage or go through a divorce. Does it feel right? Is there desperation involved? Is it in both of your best interests?

Relationships take work. You have to find ways to sustain the relationship over time. Keep things fresh and exciting by doing and trying new things. Take responsibility for the relationship. Enjoy it, of course, but remember another love-shy hurdle and another problem await you over the next hill. As an inexperienced love-shy, you are already at above average risk for divorce. Worse, when people marry later in life for the first time, they have higher expectations, and the stakes are greater. Do not take anything for granted. Do not think, *Now that I am married I can dive into a busy career.* It takes a lot of work, and perhaps luck, not to become part of the scary statistic of half of all marriages ending in divorce. You will both change and grow over the years, and the relationship will evolve and mature. You need more than compatibility and commitment to each other to make the marriage last.

One very important factor for maintaining a marriage is having a healthy sex life. Having an ongoing sexual relationship requires regular—but not tightly scheduled—sex, romantic or erotic talk and affectionate and erotic touching. However, one or both of you may have a below average libido. Even after doing everything recommended in this book to eliminate all the mental roadblocks to unleashing your sexuality, you may still have a lower than average drive. If both of you have similar drives, that's great. Otherwise, unless one has hormone replacement therapy as discussed in Chapter 4, problems may arise. Don't fret too soon as you or your partner's body may rise to the challenge. But, now that you actually have a lover, you can go to a sex therapist. Don't live with problems, address them. Often love-shys and their partners will have significant sexual issues to attend to. It is best to communicate and not hide these issues. Variety and breaking out of routines are good.

Marriage will not end your love-shyness. People often marry someone with about the same level of romantic skills as themselves. For love-shys this may increase the chance that their offspring will become love-shy. If you do not overcome it, you could pass it on to your kids. If you choose to reproduce, alleviate possible negatives for your offspring by doing such things as having other positive role models available who are free and secure in their sexuality. Likely, you want to make up for lost time and not rush into having children right away. This is an excellent idea, so practice effective birth control. Use these childfree years to become completely secure in your and your spouse's sexuality.

I propose that for people in general, the ability to obtain and maintain healthy relationships is proportional to one's mental health and psychological stability. A good relationship should help you recognize psychological issues and deal with them. Life is about increasing and improving your consciousness. Love-shys are especially vulnerable to separation, rejection and criticism from a love-interest. It's about accepting yourself first. To be an intimate companion you must talk and listen, which requires more than having functioning mouth and ears. You must open up about yourself. That's what intimacy is. You need to relate to each other on significant levels. If you talk or are in any way distracted when your significant other tries to tell you something new, interesting or important, she will find you useless as a confidant and a friend. Likewise, you must find topics about yourself to talk about.

Usually a love-shy's first girlfriend will dump him. Not being romantic enough, being socially awkward and generally clueless about how to treat and be with a woman can easily lead the woman to dump the love-shy guy. Usually the guy is so desperate that he will not break things off. If you do get dumped take it like a man. Don't beg, bargain or whine. No matter how much you thought the two of you were meant to be together for eternity, it's over. Chalk it up as another learning experience. While women can be loath to give specifics about why they ended a

relationship, you might make the experience less emotional and more informative if you ask her to give you pointers about what you did wrong.

Perhaps a significant sign of maturity is when the love-shy does the dumping. When the relationship has run its course, you should recognize this time and not let desperation blind you. Break up directly and honestly. Love-shys can have almost as hard a time ending a relationship as starting one. Do not break up by complete avoidance, cheating or repulsive behavior. Also, the *Let's take a little break from each other for a while* will confuse and disillusion the love-shy. Either it's on or it's off. Aspies especially can't take this kind of gray. I used never to know how to end any relationships. To end a long male friendship, I would just stop visiting him and never answer his phone calls or emails. This would leave him totally confused and frustrated. Even at work I would get fired rather than quit, passive-aggressively waiting for the other person to act.

Glover (2000) observes how Nice Guys can be "bad enders":

> Nice Guys have difficulty getting the love they want because they spend too much time trying to make bad relationships work... Even when Nice Guys do try to end a relationship, they are not very good at it. They frequently do it too late and in indirect, blaming, or deceitful ways. They typically have to do it several times before it sticks. (p. 118)

Miller (2004) advises:

> You don't want to be in a relationship with this girl anymore and continuing on with it is pointless and destructive. And, if you don't like her but keep on dating her, that's like, a bad thing to do. It's like you're lying to her. Be a man and break it off before it goes any further.

> As with asking a chick out, there is no easy way to break up. For all you know, she wants to break up with you. But don't be an ass and wait around for her to start hating your guts. Don't be a jerk and stop returning her calls or avoiding her. Make a clean break. Give her a call, tell her you don't want to see her anymore and expect a major ass chewing. Take it like a man and allow her to yell and scream for a good five minutes. Let her call you a slime ball and then be on your way. Tell her it was nice knowing her and you hope there is no hard feelings and then hang up and move on with your life. Believe me, this is the easiest way to go about it. Don't ever play mind games or any of that. Do it like a man. (pp. 182–183)

Also, don't break up by leaving a message or by texting.

Experience gets you figuring out what you like and what works and what does not work in a romantic partner. Engage in as many romantic relationships as possible to bring out your issues. One piece of advice floating around is that you should quickly get in and out of three relationships right off the bat, since a love-shy's first relationships are likely doomed. I don't recommend breaking off relationships for no good reason, but the underlying theme rings true. You want to marry whom you feel is the most incredible person in the world, not the first person with whom you didn't make any serious romantic mistakes. Judging from the divorced men who remain love-shy, being active and competitive in the dating world may be the best treatment for love-shyness.

Wrap it up

I hope you have received at least a fraction of the therapeutic benefits from reading this book as I did from writing it. Notice the positive aspects of love-shyness. One benefit may be relief from the stress of having kids. You have more disposable income and no diapers to change. You may eventually have children, but better late than too early. Think of all the people who had to drop out of school and missed many things because they became parents. While love-shyness creates its own stresses, it produces fewer gray hairs than raising children. Many people your age are envious of you and your freedoms.

More importantly, unlike most people who coast through life—not that they don't work hard to accomplish their goals—you are forced to confront your life programming and have real impetus to overcome it. Attractive people who never face a major life crisis rarely seek out more and deeper meaning and understanding of their lives. As Socrates stated, "An unexamined life is not worth living." People for whom everything comes easy have no desire to see how society, their parents and their childhood programmed them. Yet everyone has psychological garbage in his or her head that needs addressing and removing. If you were merely shy, you would not delve into all this knowledge. By overcoming your programming you break out of what life handed you, and become a much better person for it. The majority of people who have loser or negative life scripts never consider fighting them. Investigating love-shyness has brought us through issues that many people have to some degree but have no pressing need to address them. Thus, once you have solid relationship experience under your belt, you will go far and may stand a better chance than the average bloke to have a successful marriage. Many guys grow up with built-in confidence. Love-shys have to develop it on our own. Former slave Booker T. Washington sums it up: "Success is to be measured not so much by the position that one has reached in life as by the obstacles which he has overcome"[1] (p.39).

There is a certain love-shy charm. Women are attracted to kind, intelligent, honest and nonviolent men who listen well. Women find it refreshing to be with a guy who seems to care about them, who isn't pressuring them into sex and who is quite

innocent. Parlamis (1996) writes, "Women have always been—and will always be—attracted to the qualities of the passive man" (pp. 13–14). Shyness and Asperger's are not necessarily negative things.

Thank you for reading this book, especially those of you who dislike the spiritual and non-scientific aspects. One reason for expressing spirituality in this book is to show that one can be spiritual and sex-positive at the same time. Have you become an atheist in part due to resentment over religion helping cause your love-shyness? Are you so depressed that you can't see why a loving God would create this life situation for you? Once you fully understand your situation, then you can see how you were placed in your life to maximize your spiritual and psychological growth. One atheist love-shy in Canada envied my spirituality, because I have something to live for and something to place my faith in. Even as an atheist, you can place faith in yourself and give yourself goals to give your life meaning. At least, understand that one's belief systems create one's reality. Thus, the less your belief systems limit you, the more possibilities you allow into your life and the more the universe rewards you.

Love-shyness is relatively unknown, and this fact in and of itself creates problems and frustration. Thus, as part of one's therapy, I urge love-shys to originate and support love-shy causes. Online groups are fine but do not substitute for in-person interactions. You don't need to be a therapist to start a support group. Organizing such a group is a good way to get out, do things and meet people. Plan meetings in restaurants and bars. Post fliers in your local college campus. If you don't advocate for love-shy causes, who will besides me?

Join almost any kind of men's group. Dr. Glover (2000) claims, "[Participating in a men's group] is the most effective tool I know for facilitating the recovery process" (p. 16) and "connecting with men is essential for reclaiming masculinity" (p. 97). In men's groups men set aside their armor and interact with other men in an emotional and safe way. These groups will show a man

that masculinity means more than things like aggression and homophobia, and the groups help remove the guilt laid upon men by feminism. Being able to express your emotions and problems in such a group relieves you of the requirement of a girlfriend for an emotional connection. Thus, you become less needy for female companionship. These groups are part of the larger trend of what is known as the Men's Movement.

The Men's Movement has popularized groups that use rituals to connect their members with the healthy part of masculinity that modern culture buries. These ritual groups, which generally have a non-denominational spiritual leaning, help men get in touch with themselves and their situations by providing mythology and archetypes that each man can relate to on a personal level. While I do not want to dissuade anyone from participating in such a group, a standard men's discussion group is probably more appropriate for dealing with love-shy issues. A ritual group will likely provide less direct and complete answers to questions about dealing with women than a men's support group would. Investigate men's groups because these men who are evolving past the old, stereotypical ways of being a man represent the future. These men are our allies in the fight for a more enlightened society even if they don't know about or understand love-shyness.

Ideally, science in general will eventually accept love-shyness and make it an official diagnosis. A major reason why people do not accept love-shyness is that no one corroborated Gilmartin's (1987) study. No scientist or researcher seemed to think that we or our condition were important and interesting enough to study. Or, perhaps, no one could obtain grant money for such a project for similar reasons. Thus, love-shys had to do it by themselves. Individual love-shys created websites and online groups. One can obtain the source of most of the love-shys' quotes in this book by searching the archives at health.groups.yahoo.com/group/love-shy_drgilmartin. How many of us claiming to be love-shy must there be before scientists take notice?

There are over 2400 members of the "loveshy_drgilmartin" group. While not all members are love-shy, the vast majority of them are or know someone who is. The title of the group leaves little confusion as to what the group is for, and its members agree they fit Gilmartin's description. Likewise, over 4500 users registered for the love-shy.com forum. Most of these users are not currently active as these online forums provide only limited help and support. These membership numbers result from these forums operating for approximately five years. An important aspect of these numbers is that many members only found these discussion groups and the concept of love-shyness by doing an internet search of their symptoms or from links on Wikipedia or other webpages. Do not these thousands of people crying out for help prove the existence of this syndrome? Isn't this enough corroborating evidence?

Unless you look for love-shyness you won't find it. General shyness hides love-shyness. Autism spectrum disorders hide love-shyness. The subtle nature of romantic encounters camouflages it. Institutions and individuals supposedly responsible for treating it dismiss the condition. Institutions unable to accept that teaching and perpetuating negative views on sex and sexuality produce serious psychological issues deny the condition. Parents and family members unwilling to accept that anything is seriously wrong shut out the diagnosis.

This may be the only dating book that mentions suicide. If our condition becomes generally known, the number of love-shy suicides should decrease. These desperate people would understand that the cause of their lifetime of romantic problems is a syndrome and not their own failings. Yet, I don't know how much science can speed up the process of adopting and providing treatments in order to prevent suicides. The standard scientific method requires more studies just to prove the existence of love-shyness. Then those studies require publishing in peer-reviewed journals. Pilot therapies need to be tried and their results proven to work. Years must pass before a researcher can confidently conclude that a significant number of his subjects from a given love-shy treatment have girlfriends and marriages. One can't walk out of a clinic and correctly say, *I feel really good. I must be cured.*

Only when we as a society address our collective and individual unacknowledged sexual neuroses, can we deal with sexual issues without the influence of a dank cloud of confusion. If love-shyness just needs to be known to help lift serious cases of depression and prevent suicides, one can work around science and go straight to the public. I would love to see love-shyness listed in the *DSM* as a subtype of specific phobia anxiety disorder, but I won't hold my breath waiting for it to happen. I don't expect government agencies or health insurance to fund love-shy treatments.

Neither am I optimistic that governments will pass laws making it illegal to fire someone due to love-shyness or will provide financial assistance for chronically underemployed love-shys. Ultimately, as with other conditions, governments can't legislate acceptance of love-shyness. Unlike requiring businesses to have ramps for people in wheelchairs, governments cannot mandate that people like and date those who are love-shy. The best way for governments to participate in solutions is through funding treatments and unambiguously legalizing sex surrogate therapy. I foresee love-shy treatment centers developing from private practices rather than from large institutions. Any treatment must be as inexpensive as possible for love-shys to afford. Love-shys are quite desperate, which means a large demand and the possibility of unscrupulous people preying on them. The sooner respectable treatment centers operate, the less love-shys will fall victim to scams and lackluster treatments. Love-shy victims of bad or inappropriate treatments are at increased risk of suicide.

While you may disagree with my map of the love-shy jungle or my view of reality, at least you should accept that love-shyness exists, that there are humans who for one reason or another lack the ability to mate. That's the frustrating thing. It doesn't take much logic to accept that a percentage of the population cannot obtain partners, yet almost nothing is done on a professional level to help these people.

Each society produces it own neuroses, and neurotics are driven to maintain the status quo. It is important to root out and prevent these mass psychological issues, even if the immediate solution seems to cause more problems than it solves. While love-shyness may be due in part to individual parents and situations, the same can be said for any infectious diseases as only one person infects another. Yet epidemics are only successfully contained and eradicated through public policies specifically designed to combat them. While some people may think something that non-fatally affects only 1 or 2 percent of the population is not a serious societal issue, many conditions such as autism and Asperger's fit this description. We need to support research into and publicity about love-shyness.

Will you non-love-shys and you with neuro-typically wired brains do your part? The love-shy community has been unable to create viable treatments on its own. Although our community is quite small, spread out and not cohesive, what is most lacking is non-shy, average people organizing and supporting us. We could use women volunteers going on practice dates with love-shys.

One love-shy calculated how much love-shyness costs society by having its sufferers continually underemployed. Surely, the cost of government-sponsored research and treatment would be repaid through the extra income taxes that recovered love-shys would pay from their lifetime of increased income. Such calculations do not include the emotional toll love-shyness takes, much less the suicides. Kids today have it easier. I wasn't diagnosed with Asperger's until my late 30s and now most cases are diagnosed during the elementary school years. There is hope for tomorrow's children.

Søren Kierkegaard said, "To defraud oneself of love is the most terrible, is an eternal loss, for which there is no compensation either in time or in eternity"[2] (pp. 5–6). For a society to do nothing about love-shyness is to cheat us love-shys out of being

able to marry and raise a family. So, on both a personal level and public level, don't give up. Many love-shys report becoming so numb and feeling so hopeless that they don't even want a girlfriend anymore. Love-shys who buy life-sized female dolls have given up with actual women.

You star in the movie of your life. You are also the director, the writer and the wardrobe and the set person. If you cannot envision yourself as the star, if you continually see yourself as only a supporting or background character, then you have a real problem. Everyone, even those with physical or mental hardships, deserves a full and productive life. Obtaining a life partner is part of that complete life. You deserve it. As the wilderness experts advise, the most important aspect in a survival situation is keeping up morale.

If you have just read this book straight through without implementing any of the suggestions, then you must make a commitment to yourself to overcome your condition. Merely buying a new wardrobe and becoming generally less shy will not allow you to overcome your problem. You have to decide whether you are going to lick this thing or whether you will never marry nor have girlfriends. Either answer is correct. If you choose to live with the inability to mate and you accept your situation, that is fine. Many asexuals live happy lives without the severe stresses of partner relationships and raising children. Some people find ignoring their sexual desires liberating and spiritually rewarding. Yet few people find self-pleasuring or purchasing sex good enough for them. Mating is more than physical release and perpetuating the species. Having a partner to confide in and accompany and assist you through life is quite wonderful. The only wrong answer is to apply yourself half-heartedly with your solution attempts.

Reread this book: perhaps not right away, but eventually. Once you get on drier land, even if not out of the wilds, you can study this book more thoroughly. While not on pavement yet, you will have a more relaxed perspective and have a better ability to digest the material. As you progress you will see yourself being able to do things that on initial reading you thought impossible. Your life may be suited to reading or implementing the chapters in a different order. Read this book at least three times to make it stick. Beware of overconfidence when you believe your love-shyness is completely cured. If you think you know all about love-shyness, then you're probably headed for a sizeable fall. Don't take everything I say as absolute truths. Observe for yourself. Once you have mastered the black and white concepts and strategies from this book, then you can move past them and rely on instinct. A high-school English teacher explained her tough grammar-grading policy by saying, "You have to learn the rules before you can successfully break them."

Late one dark night I heard God proclaim to me, "Your mission on earth is to be happy." Once you are dealing with mostly happy circumstances, you will be very happy. And it will show. *So, this is what it's like as a normal person. Life should be easy now.* There's nothing for me to do except enjoy life! I have finished the book and started professionally speaking about love-shyness and Asperger's. There is no doubt life will come to me now. When you are happy, let people know about it.

I leave you with a quote from Dr. Glover (2000):

> In nature, the alpha male and the bull moose don't sit around trying to figure out what will make the girls like them. They are just themselves: fierce, strong, competitive, and sexually proud. Because they are what they are and do what they do, prospective mates are attracted to them.
>
> As in nature, the greatest aphrodisiac is self-confidence. As recovering Nice Guys become comfortable just being themselves, they begin to look more attractive. Self-respect, courage, and integrity look good on a man. As recovering Nice Guys chart their own path and put themselves first, people respond. (p. 152)

Notes

1. Washington, B.T. (1919) *Up From Slavery: An Autobiography.* New York: Doubleday, Page & Company.
2. Kierkegaard, S., Hong, H. V. and Hong, E. H. (eds and trans.) (1995) *Works of Love.* Princeton, NJ: Princeton University Press.

Appendix A

Dealing With Shy Children

Dr. Gilmartin and I have little doubt that one becomes afflicted with love-shyness during childhood. Many influences and experiences from childhood produce lasting effects well into adulthood. As a good parent or service provider, obviously, you want to minimize negatives and ensure positives in your children. However, judging from our current knowledge of love-shyness, for the most part parents cannot consciously prevent love-shyness in their children. A child intuitively picks up on his or her parents' natural actions and reactions to sexual situations and subjects. You can't fake it. Changing your deep-seated sexual attitudes is not easily accomplished especially when you already have children. Likewise, your negative parenting patterns internalized from your own parents are difficult to alter.

Yet you can act to prevent love-shyness. Start by minimizing the problems caused by your child's shyness. If possible, focus on them before your child starts school. Here are recommendations for helping shy preschoolers from Carducci's *Shyness: A Bold New Approach* (1999). This advice seems excellent for dealing with children on the autism spectrum or with other disabilities as well.

> *Be mindful of the slow warm-up period.* Your shy child will most likely react negatively to new experiences, so don't force her into noisy or chaotic environments. Rather, ease her into situations that you believe she may reject, and take it one step at a time. Explain and be patient.
>
> *Set an example for your child.* If you back away from social commitments, your child will sense your anxiety. By your actions, show him that others are friendly and can be trusted. Entertain in your home, and maintain friendships with extended family and friends. Involve your child in your errands, socializing, and community events.
>
> *Don't overprotect your child.* Don't let her feel that she can't do something because she is "shy." Make sure that she has opportunities to interact with other children.
>
> *Communicate with your child.* Tell him about your own experiences, and let him learn from your mistakes. Explain the benefits of friendship, help him understand his feelings, prepare him for upcoming events, and together choose appropriate activities for his temperament.
>
> *Prepare your child.* Give her advance notice if your family routines are about to change. Help her anticipate what to expect. Talk about upcoming events—from car pools to birthday parties—so she won't feel surprised.
>
> *Prepare others.* If it takes a few extra minutes for your child to get used to other adults, explain to them that he is sensitive and requires a little more time to warm up. Ask for their patience in gaining his trust. (p. 187)

Carducci also mentions positive benefits of daycare, which may seem counterintuitive to stay-at-home mothers:

> It places them in a group of peers with whom they can interact, acquire social skills and expand their comfort zone. They learn to negotiate, solve problems, share, cooperate,

> and play in groups—skills that don't come naturally to shy, only-childs. (p. 197)

It also gives mom some time for herself. Doting mothers may want to put their child in a class rather than daycare, but preschoolers will have structured classes to look forward to for many years to come. Unstructured and semi-structured play allows for more social interaction and for developing social skills for when there is no script or plan.

Start from a position of acceptance. Inborn temperament is neither good nor bad. Allow your child to go at his or her pace. Remind your child of past successes and give positive affirmations. Understand that your child is extra sensitive and serious situations like divorce or bullying may wreak exceptional havoc and require extraordinary intervention. Shyness is not disastrous, and eventually your child can overcome it. Many children are shy and many more act shy when viewed through adult eyes, while only 1 percent or so of children develop love-shyness.

Determine if your child is at risk of developing love-shyness. What does your child have going against him besides shyness? Having an autism spectrum disorder places the child in a much higher risk category, but even being physically smaller may cause problems. Does your son seem not interested in rough-and-tumble play like other boys? Being a younger sibling may represent a higher risk factor. Examine yourself and your spouse for the chance that one or both of you may be love-shy. One clue is to recall how you and your spouse met and start dating. Was your romance normal in that the man pursued the woman and no third party was required to jumpstart things? How social and romantic would you label yourself and your spouse?

Don't panic if you suspect your child is at high risk or has already contracted love-shyness. At least, you have labeled the condition in your child, something completely missing from all previous generations of love-shys. Be thankful you have caught it early, which is important for dealing with any illness or condition.

The most critical thing to understand is that this is not a passing phase your child will outgrow. Not only do you have to accept the diagnosis, but you have to accept various forms of therapeutic assistance for your child. Ensure your children have good same-sex adult role models and can witness proper examples of romantic behavior in person.

If your child has Asperger's syndrome, you already have your hands full. The addition of shyness makes things more problematic. Shyness exacerbates autism spectrum issues. While getting as much socialization as possible may seem good for all children, youngsters with Asperger's can have a much lower need and tolerance for socialization. Thus, it becomes difficult to know when to push a shy child into socializing and when to hold back a child with Asperger's when he reaches his "socializing limit" for the day. A shy child may need only a nudge to join and enjoy Little League or Cub Scouts, while a young Aspie may find such activities torturous. I feel it more important in a given situation to deal with Asperger's issues than shyness issues to prevent Asperger's meltdowns.

No matter a child's mental age or social maturity, physical development usually progresses normally even if one is cognitively removed from his or her sexuality. Thus, it is extra important to have frank and open sex and sex-related talks with love-shy or Aspie children. These kids need direct, to the point discussions regarding sex. Even if your child is behind with his development of puberty, do not delay a "birds and bees" talk. At minimum, knowledge of sexuality becomes important for the child to understand his peers and why they begin to act as they do. If your child does not want to discuss it or acts like he or she knows it all, do not breathe a sigh of relief and back down from your responsibility.

Don't think in terms of a single sex talk, rather a series of talks that evolve as the child matures. There is no period in life when one's sexuality is completely latent, so it is never too early to have some basic sex talk. Karin Melberg Schwier and

Dave Hingsburger in their excellent book *Sexuality: Your Sons and Daughters with Intellectual Disabilities* (2000) explain that you need not talk about the actual act of sex to have an early discussion of sex issues and that sex education covers a range of important topics. "Most of the educational [sex] curricula that have been developed for people with intellectual disabilities would more appropriately be called relationship training because they teach primarily about relationships and safety"[1] (p. 37). Schwier and Hingsburger, who focus on children with Down syndrome, agree with other experts on childhood sexuality that for preschool and elementary school children many issues other than sex itself are substantial. Knowing the proper names of one's body parts, comprehending the difference between public and private activities and understanding personal boundaries and whom to trust are important for any child's development. Understanding the value of friendships and how to make and keep them may be most important. Also significant is boosting your child's self-esteem about him or herself and about his or her actions and abilities. Shy children and ones with disabilities especially need all the positive encouragement they can receive.

By the time your child hits puberty, he or she requires long sex talks. Love-shyness and other conditions aside, Ince (2005) cites from one study that "researchers concluded that many parents greatly underestimate the amount of sexual information their children need" (p. 160). Don't expect a sex education class to prepare your youngster for having sex or for getting along in the world. Just because your parent had a ten-minute talk with you and handed you a couple of books, don't accept that this is sufficient. Carol Queen makes no bones about it: "More kids are abused by the lack of sex information than inappropriate touch"[2] (p. 8). "[W]hy do I hear no outcry about the abuse that lies at the heart of sexual silence, of inculcated shame?" (p. xv). How can you expect your children to take good care of something that you implicitly tell them to ignore? For children with Asperger's, confusion about their sexuality represents an extra burden they should not carry.

Honesty and disseminating straight to the point facts are the best policy. I recommend Drs. Richardson and Schuster's 2003 book *Everything You Never Wanted Your Kids to Know About Sex (But Were Afraid They'd Ask)* as a great general purpose book on talking and dealing with your children about all sexual subjects. I even suggest this book to some adult love-shys, since it conveys much knowledge about anatomy, birth control, sexually transmitted diseases and stages of childhood sexual development that love-shys might have missed. They suggest when your child is younger, "The loving way you name and touch your child's body can teach him that all of his parts are good, that physical closeness is both safe and wonderful, and that he is lovable" (p. 47). If your child goes through an Oedipal stage and acts romantically towards his or her opposite-sex parent, Richardson and Schuster advise:

> Receive it with the innocence in which it's been offered. Accept your child's adoration as the precious gift of a generous soul. Avoid translating his attentions into adult terms, calling him a Romeo or a lady-killer. But admire his courtliness as you would any of his efforts to win your praise and attention. Treasure his offerings of love.
>
> When your boy hugs you and tells you he wants to marry you, hug him back and tell him you love him, too. But also tell him that he can't marry you because you're his mother. "Someday you may find someone else wonderful to marry," you might say. (p. 88)

Do not worry that feeling and acting uncomfortable talking to your child about sex leads to love-shyness. Every parent feels uneasy doing this. It is parents' sexual actions and reactions that their child picks up on years before rather than during a sex talk at puberty that most affects children's sexual programming.

Also important is not attaching shame and guilt to sex and sex play. If you are religious and do not wish your child to have sex until marriage, convey that. It is probably better to explain it in practical rather than moral terms by discussing the problems of disease, pregnancy, emotional immaturity and lack of respect for the institution of marriage. Attaching shame and sin to sex only seems to create larger problems down the line. I firmly believe that there is no sin or immorality with masturbation or birth control. Do not talk like you grew up in the 1950s or in a monastery and haven't noticed how our society has matured sexually in the past half century. If so, your child may find you quite out of touch and disrespect all that you say about sex and may not come to you for help when sexuality or other touchy problems arise.

Sex therapist Dr. Jack Morin offers this advice:

> Whether we realize it or not, all of us who are close to kids are sex educators, a responsibility that involves so much more than disseminating facts… What matters most…are the everyday messages we give our kids about their worth, the value of their bodies, and the importance of their sexuality. These messages are communicated most powerfully through touch and direct observation. There is no better sex education, for instance, than observing an obviously affectionate bond between one's mother and father. (p. 318)
>
> As crucial as it is that adults create a nurturing environment for children's sexual development, it's just as important that we avoid meddling in their sensual and sexual experimentation unless we have reason to believe they might be hurt emotionally or physically. Children have a right to sexual privacy. The process of building their eroticism belongs totally to them. Kids don't want to be asked about sex play with age-mates or themselves. If these activities are happened upon, however, we can

> reassure them they're normal and that they needn't fear punishment.[3] (p. 319)

Parents are children's first and primary sex educators. The best teacher of your child is you. The best way to teach your child is by example. When you show that you are not scared of any social situation and are comfortable with your sexuality and your romantic-sexual relationship with your spouse, this is what your child picks up on and learns to emulate. Even if he or she has passed elementary school age, adult role models mean much to the child. Fathers and other male elders need to spend more time with sons. So often in our society boys spend almost all of their time with female daycare workers, female teachers and mothers. Their peers become their only same-sex role models. I postulate that the lack of male role models tends to have boys interpret masculine behavior as that which is not feminine behavior. Thus, boys learn to behave the opposite of compassionate, emotional and social.

Once your offspring becomes an adult, let go of the reins. You can do almost nothing to help or teach him romantically except give him emotional support and respect. Your adult offspring must do it on his own. Why do you think any more of the same will benefit him? You have protected your child long and well enough, now let him or her free.

Notes

1. Schwier, K. M. and Hingsburger, D. (2000) *Sexuality: Your Sons and Daughters with Intellectual Disabilities.* Baltimore, MD: Paul H. Brookes Publishing Co.
2. Queen, C. (2002) *Real Live Nude Girl: Chronicles of Sex-Positive Culture.* San Francisco, CA: Cleis Press.
3. Morin, J. (1995) *The Erotic Mind: Unlocking the Inner Sources of Sexual Passion and Fulfillment.* New York: HarperCollins.

Appendix B

How to Present this Book to a Love-Shy

One important use for this book is to give it to someone whom you believe is love-shy. Love-shyness is an extremely embarrassing condition and an awkward subject to bring up. When a man is with his male friends he feels he must act confident and brave and not show serious weakness by discussing this topic. While love-shyness is a significant problem, it never gets talked about, much less directly dealt with. Rarely will love-shy afflicted people overcome their condition without first understanding it. *Do not expect anyone to overcome his or her love-shyness without both an acceptance of the diagnosis and the will to change.* These are the prerequisites. Reading this book does not guarantee anyone will overcome his or her predicament.

Unfortunately, most people concerned about someone with love-shyness tend to ignore the condition with the hope that it will clear up on its own. The love-shy's peers may try to smooth over the person's social mistakes, set up social opportunities or offer basic dating pointers. But they fail to deal directly with the love-shyness. This inaction results because most people have

never heard about the condition, never met anyone else with it and have no idea what to do about it. As with most serious psychological and medical conditions, doing nothing is a bad idea and makes the condition worse. Often a healthy person can identify the specific problem of love-shyness better than the love-shy himself. Until love-shyness becomes an officially recognized condition with developed and available treatments, the single most important thing a concerned person can do for a love-shy is to give him or her this book. Since professional psychologists and therapists have never heard of the condition nor understand nor appreciate it, this book is the love-shys' only reliable, comprehensive and up-to-date source of information and guidance.

If you don't know the person well and base your love-shy diagnosis on only a few brief encounters, if possible, get to know him or her a little better first. Ideally, you will have known the person in question for some time and have interacted with him or her on an informal basis. Although usually shy, many love-shys appear normal or above average in all other aspects of their life and naturally try to hide their virginity and inability to date.

What sets off red flags to the person's love-shyness is observing the individual interact with someone to whom he or she is really attracted. While desperately wanting a romantic partner, the love-shy has such a phobia of romance that he is usually unable to control his anxiety sufficiently in the presence of the object of his affection. This influence often leads to alternating hot and cold interactions since the love-shy fails to act at critical moments. The love-shy may seem romantically retarded, since they lack an understanding of the normally instinctual human dating and mating process. A love interest obsession that they never pursue properly is common. Even if a romantic situation is set up for them, they usually fall short and cannot be expected to make the first move. Love-shy females are harder to spot than the males and may exhibit subtler symptoms such as having a hard time keeping up a conversation with an attractive man.

Do not confuse love-shyness with homosexuality. Distinguishing between a gay man and a male love-shy should be easy. Homosexuals are often social with many friends, while love-shys are generally shy with few friends. Homosexuals can be touchy-feely, while love-shys are rarely so. A love-shy male may flinch when touched by an attractive woman, unlike a homosexual. Love-shys are more likely to avoid sexual topics than homosexuals.

Unlike when prescribing strong medicine, a misdiagnosis of love-shyness will likely oniy result in feeling insulted or misunderstood on the person's part and a waste of a few dollars for this book and slight embarrassment on yours. Therefore, if in doubt, give it to him or her. Your intuition is probably correct. This book still has plenty of good dating advice for those way behind their peers romantically. Even if not shy, if the person is past college age and still a virgin not by choice, definitely give this book to him or her. If you still hesitate, post a message on an internet love-shy forum, and the online support community will make suggestions.

Since you're already diagnosing the person and since many love-shys were born with Asperger's syndrome before it became known, briefly familiarize yourself with this form of autism. If you know the person fairly well, you may notice if he has general social awareness issues. Suggesting to the person that he or she has a well-documented condition accepted by the mental health community may be the easier first step, and one that he or she may more readily accept. However, Asperger's can be more difficult to diagnose because by the time he or she reaches adulthood, the person usually can get along passably in the world. School age is where the signs of Asperger's are most obvious, and you probably don't know much about the relevant aspects of the person's childhood. While some characteristics of love-shyness and Asperger's are similar, love-shyness pertains to a phobia of love.

If you are romantically attracted to a probable love-shy, you have a great opportunity to evaluate the person's reactions to you.

But you are in a difficult position, because discussing romantic problems with the object of your affection tends to deflate the balloon of romance. Plus, it's hard to fully engage a person who has a phobic reaction to you. Even though you may interact normally with the person in non-romantic situations, such as at work or with a large group of friends, getting the person alone may trigger the anxiety reactions. This is where handing him or her this book comes in.

If, for example, you find a man at church quite attractive but who seems to run from you, consider confronting the problem directly. If the love-shy man can't even accept your invitation for coffee after the service, reply to his declining the invitation with, *Why not? Do you have a girlfriend or something?* Chances are his answer and accompanying body language will tell you much. If possible, get to know him better casually and give him this book. Do not take his rejection of you personally, as his love-shyness has overwhelmed him. Remember, the greater his attraction to you, the more severe his phobic reaction. Some believe an assertive woman is precisely what a love-shy man needs. By making his love-shyness flare up, you help make him aware of his problem. Forcing him into a corner may make him see his love-shyness. If his love-shyness drives him permanently out of the church, he might realize he has a major problem. Another school of thought is to approach him in as non-threatening and unromantic way as possible. This may confuse him if he has already begun thinking about you romantically, but it may provide an opportunity to talk with him alone and to give him this book. You women who are too shy to approach men may want to read the "*Go For It*" section of Chapter 5.

Do not worry that you are the wrong type of person for the love-shy. If you make him nervous and he acts increasingly strangely around you, then he is sufficiently attracted to you. He may now avoid you as much as possible. Do not concern yourself about what you could have done differently, since likely there was no better way. This is his problem and has little to do with

you or your actions. I urge you both to pursue him romantically in the long term and help him with his love-shyness in the short term. Even if the love-shy actively pursues the suggestions in this book, having a successful romantic relationship with him will still be a long shot. Don't wait for him forever. Likely, it will be his first serious romance, and he may make fundamental errors. Therefore, I recommend not investing all your romantic hopes in him. If a third mutual close friend, instead of you with the romantic interest, can give him this book, I recommend getting this person discreetly involved.

If the love-shy has a romantic interest in you, and you are friends but not romantically interested in him, things can get difficult. The love-shy will want more from you than you can give and may not settle for anything less. Rather than seeing you as a valuable and caring friend, each interaction with you may remind him of his inability to have you or any woman as a girlfriend. This frustration may be so great that he may harbor great animosity towards you and would rather not see you at all. Your caring and friendship may ironically make him depressed. *Here is a person who cares for me and wants to be my friend, so why won't she go out with me?* Perhaps the love-shy thinks an opportunity for romance with you exists, and maybe there once was. You have moved on, but he has not and may become obsessed with you. Before getting a restraining order or getting him fired, give him this book. As he reads this book, his negativity towards you may well fall away. Do not take anything he does personally.

If you are a friend or relative of the proposed love-shy, you have it the easiest. You need only find the right time and place to give him this book, which can happen perfectly casually. *I was browsing at the bookstore when I came across this book I think would really help you.* Or, *Hey, I found this book that deals with chronically single people that you might find interesting.* Or, *I saw this book on Oprah* (I can dream, can't I?), *and it seems to fit you.* These are good, simple lines to introduce it and may be about all that you have to say. Usually even better is wrapping it up and giving it as a birthday

or holiday present. If it is given as a gift, then the person is more apt to cherish it and not reject it out of hand. However, if the love-shy will be opening his presents at a big party or during Christmas with the extended family, you probably will want to give it to him personally or insist he open it in a more private setting. The potential embarrassment could do more harm than good if he perceives your present as the equivalent to something titled *How To Get Rid of Your Genital Warts.* Privacy is the operative word. The fewer people who know about the book, the more relaxed the recipient will feel.

However, if opening of presents takes place at a small intimate family gathering, after the opening of this present, you may want to start a discussion about it as other family members may have the same problem. I tend to detest the drug addiction intervention type approach, where members of the addict's close family and friends come together to compel him to admit his problem and seek treatment, as the implications that it's the love-shy's fault will put the love-shy on the severe defensive. Yet, like a drug addict, the person has to acknowledge the problem and want to change. There is only so much anyone else can do. Accept that you have done all that you can and leave the rest up to him or her. You might want to check in with him in a month or so, to see if he has read it to open up a space for conversation. Do not expect any quick change in the person. Such changes are usually measured in seasons or years.

Please give this book to the love-shy in person rather than placing it anonymously on his or her desk. The recipient will wonder who did this and why and may wonder how many of his officemates know about it. Any apprehension regarding the book may be enough for the person to discount it. What may seem to you as a trivial amount of trepidation on his part may be enough for him to dismiss any help regarding this extremely touchy subject. Do not underestimate the phobic reaction the recipient may have to anything regarding his or her sexuality. Inconspicuously wrapping up this book helps minimize possible embarrassment.

If you expect a romantic relationship with a male love-shy who has accepted this book, do not say anything directly about the book ever again unless he brings it up. Give him time to process and deal with the information. If you don't feel comfortable talking about the subject when he brings it up, don't feel you must. During the early stages of the romance, I worry that the love-shy man will try to use a discussion about love-shyness to circumvent standard romantic procedures by removing any possible romantic tension and by looking for you to work around his romantic inabilities. If after a month or two, he hasn't said anything to you about it nor has he asked you out, you might want to ask him, *Would you want me to go shopping with you and help pick out some new clothes sometime?* By his reaction you should be able to gage if he's still clueless or if he is picking up on the material, which includes an assignment to update his wardrobe.

If you're a man romantically interested in a female love-shy, you may be tempted to forgo giving her this book and take your chances trying to seduce her. This tack is not recommended. Give her the book and don't mention it again. If she is actually love-shy, then your romantic relationship will be much better in almost all aspects if she consciously works to overcome her love-shyness. If she doesn't think she is love-shy, then the book should provide impetus for her to prove she isn't love-shy by acting more sexy and intimately. Either way, wait until you see changes in her. Best is if she actually flirts with you. Then ask her for a date. Of course, the love-shy will still have problems, but, hopefully, love will prevail.

Although, viewed objectively, anyone should want help with a debilitating and frustrating condition, presenting an unsolicited diagnosis, especially one as shameful as love-shyness, can be met with resistance. I classify possible love-shys into three groups. The first group composes the love-shys who realize something is wrong with them but cannot figure out what it is and what to do about it. Usually these people want and try for relationships but are for the most part hopelessly unsuccessful. They are most likely to receive this book positively and quickly read it cover to cover. I call this group the "headbangers," because they bang their heads on the wall in frustration wondering what is wrong. This group is the largest and most visible.

The members of the second and third groups will not readily accept your diagnosis. The second group is the "head-in-sand" group who deny or don't care about love-shyness. The third group consists of the "true loners" who are asexuals and do not care about romantic partners. Distinguishing between these two groups is difficult, especially given the lack of research in this area. Perhaps there is a bit of overlap between groups. It is not up to us to judge them. Do not argue much with them to try to convince them that your diagnosis is correct. Have them read this book so they can make up their own minds.

The head-in-sands may be unaware or unconcerned that they have a problem and have settled into thinking, *This is just the way I am.* Or, *I choose not to date.* These statements may be an affirmation from their subconscious love-shyness. In this second group I also place more social people who may date, yet seemingly never successfully, and who don't think they have a problem and probably think, *I am just always unlucky at love.* They may have a more mild case.

The true loners don't seem to want to marry or even get laid. They seem perfectly happy as asexual. It is not up to you to convince them that they would be happier in a relationship. Who knows how love-shyness, hormone levels and other conditions have affected their sexuality? Obviously, they are exposed to the world and its sex-obsessed media. Their choice is not wrong. Their road is smoother and flatter than the mountain paths one must traverse to enter and succeed in the dating world. Luckily, we live in a time when all different sexualities are more or less accepted. The best we can do for these people is to accept them as they are, while at the same time offer them information and a chance to break free.

It may be hard to tell exactly which type of love-shy a person is. It doesn't matter. Give him or her this book anyway. Most are desperate for this information, and others will at least find this book intriguing, even though they may put it last in their queue of books to read. These categories are not exact, and I mention them mainly so you won't find yourself overly disappointed if your present is scorned or not enthusiastically accepted and acted upon. Even if the person can really use this book, he or she may heap loads of negativity on you, the person doing the most to help him or her. Love-shys usually have many related psychological issues and often lash out in frustration at those closest to them. By delving into their own love-shyness, many issues will come up, and often they may not want to deal with them. Try not to become discouraged. Eventually they may come around. The important thing is for you to do your part and give them this book as soon as possible with no strings attached.

Useful Resources

Books

Attwood, T. (2006) *The Complete Guide to Asperger's Syndrome.* London: Jessica Kingsley Publishers.

Avila, A. (2002) *The Gift of Shyness: Embrace Your Shy Side and Find Your Soul Mate.* New York: Fireside.

Berne, E. (1972) *What Do You Say After You Say Hello?* New York: Bantam Books.

Blanton, B. (1996) *Radical Honesty.* New York: Dell Publishing.

Bradshaw, J. (2005, first published 1988) *Healing the Shame That Binds You.* Deerfield Beach, FL: Health Communications.

Burns, D. D. (1985) *Intimate Connections.* New York: William Morrow.

Carducci, B. J. (1999) *Shyness: A Bold New Approach.* New York: HarperCollins.

Crenshaw, T. L. (1996) *The Alchemy of Love and Lust: How Our Sex Hormones Influence Our Relationships.* New York: Pocket Books.

Emmons, H. (2006) *The Chemistry of Joy.* New York: Fireside.

Forsyth, A. (1993, first published 1986) *A Natural History of Sex: The Ecology and Evolution of Mating Behavior.* Shelburne, VT: Chapters Publishers.

Forward, S. (1989) *Toxic Parents.* New York: Bantam Books.

Gilmartin, B. G. (1987) *Shyness and Love: Causes, Consequences, and Treatment.* Lanham, MD: University Press of America.

Glover, R. (2000) *No More Mr. Nice Guy.* Philadelphia, PA: Running Press.

Ince, J. (2005) *The Politics of Lust.* Amherst, NY: Prometheus.

Lloyd-Elliot, M. (1994) *Secrets of Sexual Body Language.* Berkeley, CA: Ulysses Press.

Lowndes, L. (1996) *How to Make Anyone Fall in Love With You.* New York: McGraw-Hill.

Miller, R. (2004) *Understanding Women: The Definitive Guide to Meeting, Dating, and Dumping, if Necessary.* Los Angeles, CA: New Tradition Books.

Parlamis, F. (1996) *The Passive Man's Guide to Seduction.* Tenafly, NJ: Symphony Press.

Pilinski, M. (2003) *Without Embarrassment: The Social Coward's Totally Fearless Seduction System.* Victoria, Canada: Kipling Kat (Trafford).

Queen, C. (1995) *Exhibitionism for the Shy.* San Francisco, CA: Down There Press.

Ratey, J. J. and Johnson, C. (1997) *Shadow Syndromes.* New York: Pantheon Books.

Richardson, J. and Schuster, M. A. (2004) *Everything You Never Wanted Your Kids to Know About Sex (But Were Afraid They'd Ask).* New York: Three Rivers Press.

Robinson, M. M. (1959) *The Power of Sexual Surrender.* New York: Doubleday.

Sarito, M. D. (ed.) (1994) *Osho Zen Tarot.* New York: St. Martin's Press.

Wolf, N. (2002, first published 1991) *The Beauty Myth.* New York: HarperCollins.

Wygant, D. (2005) *Always Talk to Strangers.* New York: Penguin Group.

Movies

Rain Man (1988) Director: Barry Levinson. Starring: Dustin Hoffman, Tom Cruise.

The Secret (2006) Director: Drew Heriot.

Internet

Listed in order of appearance in the text. All sites valid as of June 1, 2008.

www.wrongplanet.net

www.loveshyproject.com

www.worldcat.org

www.love-shy.com

incel.myonlineplace.org/forum

health.groups.yahoo.com/group/loveshy_women

www.meetup.com

www.matchmaker.com

www.eharmony.com

www.plentyoffish.com

www.vrphobia.com

www.slaafws.org

www.cuddleparty.com

www.stylelife.com

www.puatraining.com

www.theapproach.com
www.lovesystems.com/mystery-method
www.howtosucceedwithwomen.com
www.surrogatetherapy.org
www.aasect.org
www.maximumattraction.org
health.groups.yahoo.com/group/loveshy_drgilmartin

Index